LANGUAGE
and POETRY

The Charles Eliot Norton Lectures

1957—1958

LANGUAGE
and POETRY

Some Poets of Spain

Jorge Guillén

Harvard University Press
Cambridge, Massachusetts
1961

Typography by Burton J. Jones

Manufactured in the U.S.A. by Colonial Press, Clinton, Massachusetts

Library of Congress Catalog Card Number 60–15889

PREFACE

Let us not take as our point of departure "poetry," an indefinable term. Let us say "poem," as we would say "picture," "statue." All of these have one quality that immediately reassures us: they are objects, and objects that exist here and now, before our hands, our ears, our eyes. In reality, all is spirit, though inseparable from its body. And therefore a poem is language. We could not accept this statement in reverse. If aesthetic value is inherent in all language, language is not always organized as a poem. What does the artist do to transform the words of everyday conversation into a material as suitable and genuine to him as are metal or marble to the sculptor?

"Words are of no use," is the conclusion of those whose inner life is so rich and complex that they judge it to be ineffable: the experience of mysticism (San Juan de la Cruz) or the dreams of a visionary (Bécquer). Others see in language a marvelous means of expression. Many writers belong to this tradition, perhaps a majority of them. (One example in Spain in recent times is Gabriel Miró.) Verse is more and more elaborated, and will rise like a mountain peak above prose. Some there will be who will marshal their phrases at the least possible distance from a prosaic level. (Of these is Gonzalo de Berceo.) The one who reaches the highest peak is Góngora, the supreme incarnation of "poetic language."

Would it not perhaps be more fitting to aspire to "the language of the poem," effective only in its context, a sum of virtues irreducible to a special vocabulary? Since words are much more than just words, and the brief duration of their sound can encompass the world, language will imply

v

form and meaning, the whole wide universe that poetry both represents and is.

These chapters, in their original and briefer form, were the Charles Eliot Norton lectures on poetry delivered at Harvard University in the winter of 1957–1958. None of the adventures of exile has been more unforeseen or more extraordinary for me than that of finding myself occupying this chair of poetry. *Un coup de dés jamais n'abolira le hasard,* but this *coup de dés* seems almost magical. The lucky winner, always astonished — it is his professional duty! — thanks Harvard University for the great and undeserved honor of holding for a year the Charles Eliot Norton Professorship. The life of any man can on occasion be very fortunate.

I am deeply indebted to my son-in-law, Professor Stephen Gilman, of Harvard University, for preparing the English version of the lectures given at that time. The present text has been modified and, in some of the six chapters, considerably augmented. The translation of the final version was made by Miss Ruth Whittredge of Tufts University.

J. G.

CONTENTS

CONTENTS

FOREWORD

The Charles Eliot Norton Professorship at Harvard was founded on the theory that any poet worthy of the name would have a poetics somewhere at the back of his mind or at the edges of his attention which, given the leisure, he might like to put into words. It was for that reason that the Norton Professor was asked to do nothing but reside in Cambridge for an academic year and give six public lectures. And it was probably for that reason too that so many distinguished poets (in the broad sense of that term assumed by the foundation) have accepted the chair — Stravinsky, Frost, Ben Shahn, Eliot, Hindemith, Wilder, Cummings, Copland, and the rest. Not all of them, it is true, have produced the hoped-for document — the unique account of an art which only a unique artist, writing candidly and truthfully about his own experience of its practice, can present. Some, however, have: Ben Shahn, for example, and Cummings among the most recent incumbents. And one, Jorge Guillén, has done even more. He has produced in this volume a reflection on the art he practices which throws light, not only on himself, but on his own European generation and on the literature of that country in which he can no longer live but which he still embellishes.

This is one of Guillén's rare works in prose but by no means the first nor even the first on its subject. Once in 1936 and twice in 1943 he published critiques of the poetry of other Spanish writers, Luis de León, Bécquer, and San Juan de la Cruz. The first was published in Madrid and the other two, such is the state of the high literature of Spain under Franco, in New York and Bogotá. All three, like the lectures which follow, were impersonal: only a reader who knew what

Bécquer had meant to Guillén would understand what Guillén's comments on Bécquer meant in their turn. But the three nevertheless laid the foundations for a poetics. The difference between them and the present book is in the wholeness. These lectures too are impersonal in tone and their ostensible subjects are the poems of other men, but the figure they bound and identify is neither Bécquer nor St. John of the Cross but Jorge Guillén. We see in the images of other poets what this poet is.

And what he is is well worth seeing. One of the prices we pay for our general ignorance of Spanish in this country is our ignorance, because he writes in Spanish, of one of the great spirits of our time. Guillén's *Cántico* which included seventy-five poems when it was first published in Madrid in 1928 has now grown, in its 1950 Buenos Aires edition, to three hundred and thirty-four, but it is closed to most of us by the fact that the one poetic quality which will not come over in translation is the quality in which these poems particularly excel — the taste and feel and cadence of the words as words — the mastery of the tongue. J. B. Trend's translation of the first eight words of *Snow* is very fine —

> The white lies over the green
> And sings.

but these eight words are not even remotely like —

> Lo blanco está sobre lo verde
> Y canta.

The loss is grave with any poet. With Guillén it is close to tragic because Guillén is a poet our time needs — both for what he is and for what he is not. We still live, in the United States and in those countries of Europe from which the wind blows hither, in that immense negation of the Nineteenth Century to which, in Casalduero's words, Guillén

has shouted back in *Cántico* his ardent "Yes." A man, if he
is to stand erect in our Atlantic world, must dig his heels
into the absurdity of his Existence: must find his dignity in
the postured dignity of Revolt. Guillén detests posture in
literature as in life. And, as for existence, the joy of joys to
him is the soul beneath the skin — the skin alive and the
soul under it.

Archibald MacLeish
Conway, Massachusetts

1

PROSAIC LANGUAGE

Berceo

Prosaic Language

Berceo

I

THE first author in the history of Spanish poetry known to us by name, Gonzalo de Berceo, is generally considered to be an excellent poet in spite of his prosaicness. In reality, poetry and prose here are inseparable terms. No Spanish writer sheds more light than Berceo on the problem of prosaic language in metric form.

Berceo never uses the word "poetry." Neither does he refer to himself as a "poet." He calls himself a "versifier":

> Gonzalo li dixeron al versificador,
> Que en su portaleyo fizo esta labor.   (S.O. 184)
>
> *Gonzalo is the name they gave the versifier*
> *Who, in his portico, did this work entire.*

Versifying is a kind of noble craft, and Berceo presents himself as a good craftsman. We are reminded of what he says of Saint Millán: "God's faithful workman" (S.M. 294). The term could not be more exact. A "workman" in the service of religion. And loyalty to God presupposes also an artist's conscience. To be sure, this fine word "artist," which has come down to us with such airs of presumption, would have surprised Berceo, always so humble. "Humble" is the adjective that describes him best, and humility, true humility, consti-

3

tutes the key to his work. This does not prevent our "versifier," dedicated to narrating the lives of others and lauding his gods, from revealing himself as a poet, between the lines. The image of the medieval clerk, of the first half of the thirteenth century — a clerk, not a monk, attached to the Monastery of San Millán de la Cogolla, and also connected with the nearby Monastery of Santo Domingo de Silos — acquires individuality in the light of certain autobiographical verses. The place is La Rioja, part of Castile, a region of vineyards and wines. It was probably in the Monastery of San Millán that the "portico" where he wrote was located.

When, as an old man, he begins his last poetic undertaking,

> Quiero en mi vegez, maguer so ya cansado,
> De esta sancta Virgen romanzar su dictado,   (S.O. 2)
>
> *I wish, in my old age, although I now am weary,*
> *Of this holy virgin to translate the story,*

he tries not to delay, making the most of the daylight.

> Los días son no grandes, anocheçerá privado.
> Escribir en tiniebra es un mester pesado.   (S.O. 10)
>
> *The days are not long, and night is falling fast.*
> *To write among the shadows is not an easy task.*

The figure of the clerk stands out thus in the double twilight of the day and of old age. Berceo, as Américo Castro observes, "incorporates into his poetry-writing his own act of writing poetry," just as "Velazquez included in 'The Maids in Waiting' (*Las Meninas*) his easel, his palette, and the act of painting." These brief hints have been sufficient to suggest to the modern imagination a medieval miniature, of a Berceo typifying his times. More than once Azorín has called up his image: "From the little window of his cell one can see the landscape . . ."

The clerk from La Rioja, however, does not appear to him-

4

self in this way; he is not a theme of his own poetry. Although his tales of saints and sinners and his praises of Christ and the Virgin comprise a world of enormous scope, there is no place in it for the person of Berceo, or, if so, only as a witness, not as a protagonist (as Chaucer is, for instance, in *The House of Fame*, where the Eagle calls him by name: Geoffrey). But all the elements of his world are linked together with such coherence that the "versifier," always in his own place, also stands forth linked to the whole, which is always harmonious. Not having perceived this whole, historians deficient in historic sense and poets deficient in poetic sense — in the eighteenth, nineteenth, and even the twentieth centuries — have considered Berceo's work formless and halting, when it bespeaks only harmony, the absolute harmony of earth and heaven, of man and God. And all of this is due to the exact language through which this harmony is revealed.

II

Berceo, the versifier, adheres to a completely new art form: the *cuaderna vía*. However varied the subjects of his poems may be, all of them are fitted into these fourteen-syllable lines arranged in groups of four, with each four-line stanza carrying the same rhyme four times. This is obviously a very strict pattern.

> El Viernes en la noche fasta la madrugada
> Sofrí grant amargura, noche negra e pesada,
> Clamando: fijo, fijo, ¿dó es vuestra posada?
> Nunca cuydé veer la luz del alvorada. (D.V. 161)

> *On Friday all night through until the hour of morn*
> *In black and bitter night I suffered all forlorn,*
> *Crying, "Son, my Son, whither have you gone?"*
> *I never thought to see again the light of dawn.*

5

Thus the Mother laments after the Crucifixion, and her anguish moves us without mitigating its violence, in accord with a slow, monotonous, grave rhythm. Berceo's stanzas establish his vision of the world on a foundation of firmness and security, and the rhythm helps to transmit what the words are saying. In this way, the obvious order of the *cuaderna vía* reflects step by step the continuous order of the Creation under the gaze of Christ and the Blessed Virgin. In contrast to the metric irregularity of the epic poems, the new poetic manner was arising under the sign of discipline. And the poet devoted himself with determination to maintaining the implacable regularity of the same strophic scheme. Meaning and rhythm come to be combined subtly:

> Como suelen las nuevas por el mundo correr. (S.D. 8)
> *As news customarily runs through the world.*

News glides with obvious swiftness on the wings of this verse. Spanish poetry is inaugurated, then, as a work of art, not as something childishly naïve. We ourselves would be naïve if we considered an artist "primitive" who wrote in the thirteenth century, the century of such imposing structures as the *summa* and the cathedral. Only if looked at through the perspective of "progress" do figures appear primitive when they are the product of periods of great maturity. Not even the bison of Altamira nor the deer of Lascaux are the work of primitives. Those marvelous silhouettes painted on the rock walls of the caves postulate an art that is the result of heaven knows how many efforts, made in historical succession, not in progressive development. It is now commonly accepted that art does not follow any line of progress. Today's poetry — *The Waste Land* — does not represent an advance over that of the thirteenth century — the *Roman de la Rose*, or the miracles related by Berceo, or by the King of Castile, Alfonso the Wise.

6

III

Using the exacting form of the *cuaderna vía*, the literary novelty of the time, Berceo relates anew (for a written tradition in Latin already existed) miracles and exemplary actions: the culmination of a much-cultivated religiosity. Berceo is the believer par excellence. No doubt, no criticism, no ironical vacillation, no cloud of ambiguity, interpose themselves between his faith and the world: visible or invisible, life on earth and the life beyond are intertwined in the unity of a single block, the Creation. This Creation cannot be broken into little isolated pieces. Everything interlocks and everything remains joined under the supreme powers, Christ and Our Lady. Of course, good and evil battle each other for the Creation, and the Devil breaks in with his rebelliousness. The works of Berceo naturally shelter more sinners than saints. And, if the saints attain exceptional heights, it is the sinners who hold the center of the stage. The concept of a world submitted to essential harmony does not exclude drama: it demands it. To the faith of Berceo everything appears to be enveloped within a single uninterrupted reality, which goes from men to Seraphim, from the air filled with the song of birds to Heaven with the songs of the blessed. No mysterious nebulosity separates the one from the other, for high or low, all are one: the work of God. As one reads Berceo one is never astonished at the supernatural. In the last analysis, nothing is supernatural; all is organically divine. The poet, never perplexed, suffers with men when they suffer, or shares the tribulations of Christ and of His Mother. But he never suffers deep-rooted anguish. He is kept from it by his way of living in God's Creation.

It is a way of living that is absolute but familiar. Berceo believes as he breathes, and this religious respiration will be identified with his poetic inspiration. In this way Berceo in-

7

carnates the model of Spaniards as seen by Américo Castro: living "through" belief, "they felt that they existed *inside* religion." The preposition *inside* is most illuminating. All of Berceo's poetry appears illumined, if we look at it this way, as the manifestation of a belief in which the believer finds himself. A belief which is converted by this metaphor of place into something material. But matter arises again spiritualized. For Berceo, there is nothing closer to normal action than its miraculous interruption. In a word, things are what they are. From this fullness of being is derived the substantive force of vision and language that makes Berceo's poetry a compact, robust, well-balanced world. Chaucer's poetry is very different from Berceo's, but one could apply to the Spaniard what Hazlitt says of the English poet: "His words point as an index to the objects, like the eye or finger . . . he was obliged to inspect things for himself, to look narrowly and almost to handle the object, as in the obscurity of morning we partly see and partly grope our way; so that his descriptions have a sort of tangible character belonging to them, and produce the effect of sculpture on the mind." Miracles do not break in in order to throw things out of order, but rather to restore them to their own being. Two blind men who

> Vivien en grant miseria de todo bien menguados,
> *Lived in great distress, deprived of all well-being,*

regained their sight thanks to Saint Millán.

> La forma destorpada tornó toda complida. (S.M. 323–330)
> *The form that was distorted became completely whole.*

And, after the "great fright" produced in them by the light, "they recovered the memory of it" — they recovered their habitual harmony. This is a miracle congruent with one's own being — so different from the mythological metamorphoses of

8

an Ovid, with their passionate or capricious intervention of the gods and their punitive transformations (Daphne turned into a laurel tree, Anaxarate into stone); although divine glorification was also possible in them, as when Caesar ascended to the heavens:

> In sidus vertere novum, stellamque comantem.

To the humble eyes of Berceo, beings on occasion show their plenitude by negative contrast:

> Más blancas que las nieves que no son coçeadas. (S.O. 30)
>
> *Whiter than the snows that have not yet been trampled.*

The poet wishes to extol the whiteness of the three doves that the three holy virgins, Agatha, Olalia, and Cecilia, held "upraised in their hands." But how could such celestial, perfect, unreal whiteness be imagined except in relation to something terrestrial, imperfect, real? The whiteness of snows that have not been walked on, but even more, that have not been, in Berceo's word, *coçeadas*, trampled by the hoofs of animals. The implicit contrast between the two conditions of the snow gives a visible sheen to the intact whiteness of the doves. This contrast is not always necessary:

> Mucho eran más blancas que las nieves recientes. (S.M. 437)
>
> *Whiter far were they than the new-fallen snows.*

Those who were whiter were the two "fair and shining persons," Saint James and Saint Millán, who descended from Heaven on two white horses to do battle against the Moslems. The commonplace simile of snow is renewed with pristine freshness by means of the epithet: *new-fallen*. This word indicates not an essence but the condition the snows are in. When they are newly fallen, they enjoy the integrity of their

9

being; then they are snows that are really snows, recently invested with their full being. This is a vision of reality as reality, but it is a vision that "invents," that is to say, that discovers and uncovers beings in the deep, calm affirmation of themselves. The *neiges d'antan* that Villon asked about are found here, marvelously preserved since the thirteenth century in this line of Berceo's: snows of yesteryear and this year, snows infused with the human soul that contemplated them through this verse about the year 1234, snows that to us are both real and spiritual, snows that, by a miracle, are living. This poetic miracle began with the intuition of the snow as an image, quite apart from the scene as a whole, the great battle of Simancas, near Valladolid, in 939, in which the army of the Caliph of Cordoba Abd-al-Rahman III suffered a great defeat at the hands of the Christian warriors of the North. Here historical fact, epic tradition, and saintly biography unite in the eyes of our clerk-*jongleur*. But the decisive actors, for him, are not the historical leaders, King Ramiro II of Leon and Count Fernán González of Castile (the epic hero), but the warriors Saint James and Saint Millán. On two very white horses "they descend through the air with great speed"; and everything — riders, horses, arms — gleams. Because it is so ideal, we might not be able to conceive that extraordinary whiteness, a whiteness that would dazzle us. But we open our eyes wider, illuminated, before the immediate revelation: this ordinary whiteness, the real one, and therefore amazing:

"Whiter far were they than the new-fallen snows."

IV

The world of Berceo arouses in us what Rafael Lapesa has aptly called a "sensation of immediacy." However far the beyond may stretch — and at times it is Heaven itself — this beyond is always near at hand, and the marvelous thing

10

that is so evident is situated right beside us, tangible, for us to share. Saint Oria looks about her in Heaven — where she is visiting, and we with her — and, seeing some "great crowds," asks: "These people, what are they?" To this conversational question she receives the reply:

> Todos éstos son mártires, unas nobles personas. (S.O. 81)
>
> *These people all are martyrs, fine and noble persons.*

This gathering is just like a religious procession in any city in Castile. "These people, what are they?" They are human beings, and they are here close by, within the grandiose limits of Paradise, which is always both terrestrial and celestial. The immediately present, no less attractive than the absent, does not require small spaces nor tiny objects. The modern reader, delighted with the concrete comparisons so abundant in this poetry, enjoys picking out figures, animals, fruits, objects.

> La cabeza colgada, triste, mano en massiella.   (D.V. 34)
>
> *With hanging head, bereft, her hand upon her cheek.*

This is the Holy Mother beneath the Cross. From the Bestiary we remember the serpents:

> Como tienen las bocas abiertas las serpientes.   (S. 66)
>
> *Like the serpents holding their mouths open wide.*

This is in "the burning fires of Hell," among the signs predicting the Last Judgment. Here is another picture:

> El lino cabel fuego malo es de guardar.   (S.D. 51)
>
> *Flax beside the fire is difficult to keep.*

It is true that our poet, with his skill in fitting images into the fourteen-syllable Alexandrine, favors this tendency to the "still-life," which Azorín carries to such exquisite extremes.

11

"On a walnut slab, smooth and bare, a glass of good wine . . .
And one nut, just one nut, perhaps a dried-up one, and three
parsnips . . . The still-life is attractive. No better ones were
painted by Lucas Menéndez." Possibly. But the person who
does not paint still-life pictures is Berceo, and the objects —
perhaps not described, only mentioned — form part of an
abundance in which all is real life, unified and in movement.
Berceo's poetry holds to the requisite of great poetry: everything is related to everything else. Adventures of sinners —
or miracles; the holy adventures of Saint Dominic, Saint
Millán, Saint Oria, Saint Laurence; the life and passion of
Christ, the life and death of His Mother, the Judgment Day,
Heaven, the Christian liturgy. The poet leads us along all
these paths without ever leaving the same place: Creation.
When one travels through it as it were on foot, it does not
seem enormous. Berceo, never an exile, always feels at home:
in his home, God's house. If we must sharpen our eyes and
our ears, we must keep our feet on the ground. On this point
Berceo shows an awareness not in the least naïve.

> Qui a mí escuchare e creerme quisiere
> Nunqua taie la cima do los piedes touiere.   (D.V. 204)
>
> *He who would hear and believe what I tell without deceit,*
> *Let him never cut the ground from under his feet.*

This advice — religious, moral, literary — should be taken
generally by anyone who would understand this Christian,
Castilian world and its representation in poetry. Devils, men,
angels, and divinities meet face to face, attract and repel each
other: they coexist. The Spanish words *convivir, convivencia*
can be applied exactly to Berceo's narrations. Universal coexistence! A cleric who is devoted to the Virgin but fond
of "secular vices" dies, and is refused burial in consecrated
ground. But the Virgin, ever merciful, orders that he be buried

12

in the cemetery. And when the order is about to be carried out, the miracle is discovered.

> Yssíeli por boca una fermosa flor
> De muy grand fermosura, de muy fresca color,
>
> *For from his mouth came forth a fair and lovely flower,*
> *Of beauty very great, of very fresh color,*

and also:

> Trobáronli la lengua tan fresca e tan sana
> Qual parece de dentro la fermosa mazana.
> Non la tenié más fresca a la merediana
> Quando sedié fablando en media la quintana. (M. 112–113)
>
> *They found his tongue to be as fresh and sound withal*
> *As is a lovely apple within, before it fall.*
> *He did not have it fresher at noon, as I recall,*
> *When he would stand and talk beside the garden wall.*

The cleric's mouth, sinning and devout, brings forth a flower. This would be in itself a worthy conclusion for his life and death: beauty in the form of a flower. But the miracle includes both his mouth and his tongue. A tongue like an apple, and, above all, a tongue like itself in its fullest functioning. And *mazana* (*manzana*, "apple") rhymes with *merediana* (*mediodía*, "noon") and *quintana* (*quinta*, "country estate"). The cleric reappears talking at a particular hour, noon, in a particular place, the garden of the country estate, with what Alfonso Reyes has called in another context the "energy of normality," which, moreover, captivates us with the prestige of prodigy.

Everything is natural, prodigiously natural, even in that Heaven visited by Saint Oria during a pause in her earthly existence. With his usual insight Menéndez y Pelayo points out the poetic value of these heavenly visions, and even goes so far as to mention the name of Dante. (Dante was born at about the time that Berceo died. The date of Dante's birth is

1265; the date of Berceo's death is not known, but the obscure clerk wrote his last work, the *Life of Saint Oria*, about the year 1265.) Berceo speaks of the ineffability of "such great visions":

> Non las podrién contar palabras nin sermones. (S.O. 24)
> *They could not be retold in word nor yet in speech.*

This is the common phrase for any experience of revelation. And yet there are moments that are very human, very close to everyday life, in absolute contrast to the sublime ordering of the *Paradiso*. Oria wants to know about her teacher, Urraca, who must surely be somewhere about. Indeed, Urraca is already among the blessed. And, as if they were still living in a little village in Castile, the holy virgins shout: "Urraca!"

> Clamáronla por nombre las otras companneras.
> *They called for her by name, all her companions there.*

Fortunately Urraca hears them right away.

> Respondiólis Urraca a las voces primeras.
> *Urraca answered them at the first cries so clear.*

Urraca recognizes the voice, but she does not manage to see her disciple, because crowds of people get in the way.

> La az era muy luenga, eso la embargaba,
> Que non podía verla, ca en cabo estaba.   (S.O. 70–76)
> *The line was very long, it kept her from her friend,*
> *So that she could not see her, for she was at the end.*

And Urraca is lost to us in the multitude, as if carried away along the village streets by the press of the fiesta. As Professor Guerrieri-Crocetti says so well: "Thus his saints, his virgins, his martyrs, the supernatural figures of his world become contemporary and present-day: they live like his poor people, speak the language of the country and of the region, they are

14

close to him, because they become men of his time and of his land." Yes, eternity and present immediacy are identified, and so discreetly that Berceo's world disguises and almost conceals its greatness. That is how Guerrieri-Crocetti can call it *piccolo mondo antico;* but there was no need to borrow, even with ironical tenderness, the title of a novel by the modern writer Fogazzaro. To Berceo no reality is "little" when it is seen in sacred perspective. This poet is what he is — and with admirable originality — because he accepts and makes his own, poetically, this vision of the Christian soul in the thirteenth century in Castile; for him earth will always be divine, and heaven earthly. This is the vision which the critic just quoted often refers to as *grossolana* — common, or coarse — thus lessening the essential poetic stature of Berceo, who, he says as a final reproach, is not "sublime." Sublimity would imply an eloquence incompatible with the very delicate humility on which this highly coherent poetry is based.

V

This general humanization — or, if one prefers, this general divinization — does not preclude, but rather includes, a hierarchical ordering of things in their excellence or deficiency. A paralytic woman, wishing to be cured, is taken before the tomb of Saint Dominic.

> Levaron la enferma al sepulcro glorioso,
> De qui manaua tanto myraclo preçioso:
> Punsiéronla delante al Padre prodigioso,
> Yaçié ella ganyendo como gato sarnoso.   (S.D. 586)

> *They carried the sick woman to the glorious tomb,*
> *From which so many a precious miracle had sprung:*
> *Before the prodigious Father they placed her on a mat,*
> *And there she lay a-whining like a mangy cat.*

15

The hierarchical distribution is made by means of the four adjectives found, in the Spanish, at the rhyme. Up above is Father Saint Dominic, who is *prodigioso*. And his miracle, which is *preçioso*. And his tomb, *glorioso*. Down below, the paralytic woman, compared to a cat that is *sarnoso* — mangy. It behooves a good reader to listen to this poetic harmony. It exists without a doubt, and without discordance: that is the point. There is no opposition of beauty and ugliness, because these categories are not presupposed here. The mangy cat appears as a repulsive animal, but not in negative function as an element of the poem. The cat in itself is neither poetic nor unpoetic: these are distinctions which apply only to the components of poetry once it has been composed, of materials taken from real life, all of which are suitable for elevating into a composition. What matters are the poetic values within the composition, not real values, such as the sumptuosity of rich robes or the wretchedness of rags. Let us cast aside any pretension to good taste. To understand Berceo and the class of poets to which he belongs, it would be in poor taste to possess good taste. In their view, poetry has not been betrothed to beauty.

And who are these poets? To find them we must go back to Holy Scripture, the pattern of Christian tradition, so different from the Graeco-Latin tradition. Job cries out that he is consumed "as a rotten thing . . . as a garment that is motheaten." This is the man that Jehovah puts to the test. Jehovah says to Job: "Behold now Behemoth, which I made with thee: he eateth grass as an ox." Behemoth, the hippopotamus, a grotesque pachyderm from our point of view, is presented here in all his dignity: as a work of God, and thus exposed to danger. Between Jehovah and his servant — this time it is the Psalmist — there rises a constant clamor: "I waited patiently for the Lord; and he inclined unto me, and heard my cry. He brought

16

me up also out of an horrible pit, out of the miry clay; and he set my feet upon a rock, and established my goings. And he hath put a new song in my mouth, even praise unto our God." From the tormented "cry" we mount to the "new song" on a ladder of ascending and moving images: pit, miry clay, rock, and on the rock the "goings" of the feet, and the final jubilation bursting from the mouth. The psalm unites the noble with the abject without giving a thought to possible differences in style. The classical tradition was wholly antagonistic to such mixtures. The late Professor Auerbach, who has elucidated the matter very clearly, writes: "In antiquity, the elevated and sublime style was called *sermo gravis* or *sublimis*; the low style, *sermo remissus* or *humilis*; and both were to be kept strictly separate." To be sure, Greek and Latin rhetoric admitted, in addition to simple style (*unum subtile*) and elevated style (*alternum grande atque robustum*), a third style called by some "intermediate," by others "florid" (*tertium alii medium ex duobus, alii, floridum*). This is the classification as it is remembered by Quintilian. Later on, these distinctions cease, and in relations of the Incarnation and Passion of Christ, as Auerbach explains, "both the *sublimitas* and the *humilitas* acquire unbelievable reality and are completely blended." Thus we come to the tomb of Saint Dominic, and our good taste will not be scandalized if we find a paralytic woman whining there like a mangy cat.

This spiritual unification leads to unification of language.

> Non quiso otra suegra sy non la gloriosa,
> Que fúe más bella que nin lilio nin rosa.　　　(S.O. 28)
>
> *No mother-in-law she wished but the Queen of Glory,*
> *Lovelier than the lily, than the rose more lovely.*

Berceo is referring to Saint Cecilia. There was nothing more beautiful then, nor is there now, than the lily and the rose.

This very real beauty of flowers and words contributes to the establishing of a major harmony, which also admits the inclusion of the word "mother-in-law." It is very difficult for the modern reader not to smile at this "mother-in-law," which represents for so many a character with comic connotations. Our sensibility, degraded by literature and manners — mediocre literature and bad manners — reacts in the opposite way from that of Berceo's pure soul. Without this foundation of purity his poetry would collapse; it is poetry that can be viewed only through a crystal, a very transparent crystal. This body, crystal, and this condition, transparency, are the exquisite culmination of elaboration, which is never formless nor rudimentary. "Purity" does not always coincide with "naïveté." It has been customary to belittle our clerk from La Rioja with the concept of naïveté, giving him a childish appearance with the foreshortening of primitive art. As Professor Kittredge pointedly observed in connection with Chaucer: "That the simplicity results from lack of skill is, I fancy, a proposition that nobody will maintain, though it has often been taken for granted (may I say naïvely?) by critics." Berceo was indeed a pure soul, possessed of that simplicity praised by Saint Francis, his contemporary and kindred spirit: "I salute thee, Queen Wisdom; the Lord save thee and thy sister, pure and holy Simplicity." Berceo is not a saint, a hero of virtue; he is only a crystalline soul. The *poverello* of Assisi, in his praises of the universe, exalts the sun, the moon, the stars, wind, water, "brother fire," "mother earth": his is a song in praise of a great spectacle. Berceo does not aspire to such grandiose effusions. The symbolic center of his world could be simply bread.

Mientre el pan duraba non cansaba la mano.   (S.D. 47)

As long as the bread would last, his hand would never tire.

18

Bread, in the hand of a Christian. Even the kingdom of the Son is the place

> Do se ceban los ángeles del buen candial trigo. (M. 137)
> *Where they fatten the angels on good fine wheat.*

The poet himself emphasizes the universal significance of bread:

> Todo el comer nombramos quando el pan decimos,
> Quando el pan ementamos, todo lo ál complimos.
>
> (E.S.M. 259)
>
> *All the foods there are we name when we say bread;*
> *When we mention bread, all the rest is said.*

Among the compliments directed to the Virgin, none is more unexpected than this verse, so justly famous:

> Reïna de los cielos, Madre del pan de trigo.   (M. 659)
> *Holy Queen of Heaven, Mother of wheat bread.*

Here, condensed into one line, is the "message" of Berceo. He ascends to this great verse by spontaneous impulse. "Mother of wheat bread!" It is the same bread that is found in the Psalm glorifying God's Creation, translated into Spanish by Fray Luis de León as *Y el pan da valentía*: "bread which strengtheneth man's heart." Bread provides the courageous repose, the equanimity with which the poet faces the world and its sinners, Christ and His Mother: Mother of bread, and of good bread, wheat bread, an emblem of substance that is truly substantial. This emblem is not in the least crude or rustic, but it is far removed, for instance, from the image with which Rutebeuf — whose muse was not at all fragile — enriches *Lis IX Joies Nostre Dame*, where he calls the Virgin

> Lune sans lueur transitoire!
> *Moon without transitory gleam!*

19

The beauty of this line, so precious as to be almost *précieux*, brings us back by contrast to our poet, an exquisite writer bred in another clime.

VI

The strong simplicity of Berceo — a simplicity of the second degree, produced by Christian Europe — is irreconcilable with ironical ambiguity, and there is a deep chasm between Berceo and Juan Ruiz, the Archpriest of Hita, the crowning figure of the Spanish Middle Ages. The admirable Archpriest would have adorned with a thousand malicious insinuations a tale such as that of the drunken monk, number twenty of Berceo's *Miracles of Our Lady*. When the monk is so far gone that "he could no longer stand on his feet," the Devil appears to him in the shape of a fiery bull, pawing the ground and threatening him with its horns. At this point the Virgin takes pity on her devoted follower, and places herself between him and the "bedeviled thing," waving "the skirt of her mantle." The Devil does not concede defeat and reappears in the shape of a dog, with wide-open, ferocious eyes. No sooner does Our Lady appear than the animal runs for safety. The monk is already staggering up the last step of his church when the Enemy attacks him disguised as a lion. Mary appears once more, and strikes the beast with a stick, rebuking him the while in angry, almost wrathful tone: *Don falso alevoso . . . Don falso traidor . . .* "Sir false betrayer . . . Sir false deceiver . . ." From this danger too the Virgin delivers her faithful follower, and in addition she takes him by the hand and puts him to bed.

> Cubriólo con la manta e con el sobrelecho,
> Pusol so la cabeza el cabezal derecho.   (M. 482)

> *She covered him with the blanket, and over it the spread,*
> *And then she placed the pillow straight beneath his head.*

20

The story ends with the repentant monk's return to the paths of righteousness. The slightest levity, the slightest hesitation, the slightest equivocation would have destroyed the poetic value of this tale, which, when read correctly, overcomes all discordances — Devil, bull, dog, lion, drunkard, vice, mercy, repentance — beneath the sublimity of the Virgin, and of the poet-believer.

It is very easy to make modern jokes about an innocently archaic style, and a skeptical, which is to say a "rationalistic," caricature will always be well received by the many readers who, thanks to Voltaire, are more intelligent as they read *La Pucelle* than was Joan of Arc herself:

> Je ne suis né pour célébrer les saints:
> Ma voix est faible, et même un peu profane.
>
> *I was not born to celebrate the saints:*
> *My voice is weak, and even a bit profane.*

Ordinary reality, which, as reflected in Berceo's intuition and feeling, is poetic, becomes vulgar when it loses its divine reason for being, the *je ne sais quoi* of the creative act. Only a small amount of malice is needed to convert poetic "grace" into burlesque wit, parody. Don Tomás Antonio Sánchez, the worthy first editor of Berceo, composed reverently and even tenderly a little poem *In Praise of don Gonzalo de Berceo*, a clever *pastiche* which he gave out, without too much thought of deceiving the experts, as a work of the thirteenth century. In it we are told that Berceo learned Latin in the Monastery of San Millán, whose monks taught him sound doctrine,

> Mucho más provechosa que caldo de gallina.
> *More beneficial far than even chicken broth.*

This broth immediately reveals its apocryphal character. It is a completely modern broth, even though the word may be

21

ancient, a broth imbibed no doubt by Don Tomás Antonio
Sánchez and by today's reader as well. The realness of the
broth is of no importance; what matters are the words that
designate it. The eighteenth-century editor realized they were
vulgar. He says so himself, in a note: "Such comparisons as
this, now considered extremely low, were very common in
Don Gonzalo's times, and even later." If our worthy scholar
had on this occasion supplemented historical knowledge with
literary intelligence, he would not have considered these "extremely low comparisons" vulgar because they were tolerated
by a taste less refined than the eighteenth century's. The components of a comparison are poetic to a poet who feels them
intuitively and transforms them. Without Berceo, the best
bread in the world would not taste of poetry; and this broth
could either be part of a poetic vision or serve as a mere
parody. The latter is what Don Tomás Antonio Sánchez used
it for. And the sound doctrine learned in a monastery by the
sound youth in question was far more beneficial than any
chicken broth which poetically is vulgar, ridiculous, and ugly.

Since neither Berceo the poet nor Berceo the believer has
denied communication between beauty and ugliness, poetry is
not defined as beauty, nor does it reject the non-beautiful because of its prosaicness: this is a later criterion, set by humanistic poets like Garcilaso. To call Berceo's language prosaic is
anachronistic, unless "prosaic" is divested of its negative connotations, and "prose" is made to embrace essential unity of
expression corresponding to essential unity of concept. In
this light we intuitively perceive continuous total reality
through a continuous, and therefore plain, language: the language of Everyman addressed to Everyman, which is to say
to those listeners who in the villages of La Rioja stop to hear
the clerk, who is also a *jongleur*, recite his poem. The pious
clerk fulfills his duty as a believer. The *jongleur* completes his

22

work with irreproachable coherence. In this dawn of Castilian poetry, language is held to its most basic level, common to the commonalty of its public, and faithful to its poetic essence. An enlightened essence when it is called by the right name. Direct mention of things is prevalent, with no need for adornment or transformation, because reality felt in this way is in itself marvelous.

> Derramáronse todos como una neblina,   (M. 278)
> *Fleeing one and all, they scattered like a mist,*

says Berceo of a band of devils. The flight is fantastic enough in itself; the modifier "like a mist" is exceptional.

> Las palabras son pocas, mas de seso cargadas.
> (E.S.M. 254)
> *The words are few, but full of sense.*

Seso, "brain," here obviously means "sense"; filled with brain, with sense, with exact form. Such a style as this cannot avoid having its ups and downs, and in its "downs" of least felicitous intuition and expression, relative "prosaicness" may appear, as it may in any author. For instance:

> Una mugier que era natural de Palençia.
> (S.D. 557)
> *A woman who was a native of Palencia.*

But this line should not be isolated. Obviously it would be inadmissible in any other type of poetry. We must leave it in its context, where this woman from Palencia is surrounded by the atmosphere of her miracle. Another example:

> Colgava delant ella un buen aventadero
> En el seglar lenguage dízenli moscadero.   (M. 321)
>
> *Before her hung a fine whisk someone had brought her.*
> *In secular language they call it a fly-swatter.*

23

Aventadero (whisk), *moscadero* (fly-swatter) are words of the secular language "as opposed to Latin, the language of the clergy," as Solalinde points out in the notes to his edition. Berceo's poems are written — naturally — in *román paladino* (S.D. 2), "plain Romance," "the plain Romance tongue," *en romanz que la pueda saber toda la gent* (M.L. 1), "in Romance so that everyone may know it." The distinction being made here is not between one language that is secret and poetic and another that is popular and prosaic, but between a written language, Latin, and another that is used orally as the means of communication between neighbors, the Romance tongue, Spanish: the hospitable Romance tongue, growing rapidly, and whose popular character must not be oversimplified. María Rosa Lida de Malkiel calls Berceo "the most copious Latinizer the Castilian language has known." But "he does not impress us as a Latinizer" because "he does not Latinize the syntax," only the vocabulary, "profusely." But to write in "plain Romance" does not mean to write vulgarly. This secular or lay language is the living language, that is to say, the prosaic-poetic language, the language of the poem. With it Berceo embraces a world indivisible from its heaven. This vision of Christian fraternity, of universal coexistence, is translated for our blessed versifier into the embrace that the modern *poète maudit* was to glimpse at the last moment: *Moi! moi qui me suis dit mage ou ange . . . je suis rendu au sol*, Rimbaud exclaims in his final *Adieu*. "I, I who called myself a magician or an angel . . . have come back to the earth." Before him he found *la réalité rugueuse à étreindre,* "rugged reality to embrace." Rugged reality, "prosaic" language that is not at all prosaic: this is the poetry of Berceo.

2

POETIC LANGUAGE
Góngora

Poetic Language

Góngora

Berceo has shown us how poetry can crystallize in direct expression. Yet not even this expression is limited to its simplest meaning. Consider his admirable compliment to Our Lady:

> Reïna de los cielos, Madre del pan de trigo.
> *Queen of Heaven, Mother of wheat bread.*

It was not literal reasoning that formulated that phrase, "Mother of wheat bread." It could perhaps have an allegorical meaning: Mother of Christ, who in the Eucharist is bread. But the image does not move us as a theological idea. This eulogy is enriched by human implications, of which we are more or less aware. Something — something essential — remains unsaid. Simple poetry is never really simple. The most artless song cannot be entirely artless if it is to be thoroughly enjoyed.

Indirect expression has been elaborated more and more over the years until it has come to form a language within ordinary speech: poetic language. Among all the modern poets of the Western world, Góngora is without a doubt the most brilliant exponent of this tendency, and the most extreme. Berceo used the words "bread" and "wheat." Góngora, in a poem to the Holy Sacrament, writes:

¡El Verbo eterno hecho grano
para la humana hormiga!   (239)

The Word eternal changed to grain
for the human ant!

The Word is the Sacrament, which is bread, or rather — referring to its origin — wheat, grain: and this grain is to man what a real grain of wheat is to the ant. The direct names — bread, wheat, man — have not been used poetically. They do not appear at all; they are only alluded to. Góngora seeks a way of expression as full of allusion as possible. This willful complexity can twist itself into extraordinary labyrinths. Labyrinths that are difficult, but not obscure, through which, if we may borrow an image from the poet, Ariadne will show the way. Góngora has written very difficult poems — some of the most difficult in European literature, yet so coherently woven that they permit very precise analysis. At the present time, Góngora's writings are the most clearly and completely explained in Spanish poetry: a task of difficulty and merit, but one that could be accomplished precisely because of their very complexity. How, on the other hand, is one to take apart simple poetry — simple to a certain extent — if it contains no artifice capable of being taken apart? Let us begin this study of Góngora by paying a due tribute of admiration to contemporary criticism in general, and to Dámaso Alonso in particular — one of the finest critics of our time in any language. The Góngora known before Dámaso Alonso is not the one known since his masterly studies. And what greater praise can one bestow on a great scholar and critic than to recognize how completely the light has been changed in which the writer thus restored is viewed? If, in the following pages, historians and commentators are mentioned frequently, but only in passing, it was inevitable that at the outset we should place side by side the names of the Cordovan poet of genius and the one who has done so much to illuminate his fame: Don Luis de Góngora and Dámaso Alonso. (Their readers and friends were wont to say, and still say: Don Luis, Dámaso.)

II

For Góngora, *poetry, in all its rigor, is a language constructed like an enigmatic object*. It is surprising enough that a literary work should permit an attempt at close definition. Here we have the words "rigor," "language," "construction," "object," and "enigma." The "object" will have to do with theme, conception, method, and style; the "enigma," with allusion and metaphor. Analysis will show how an "object of enigma" is resolved into an "object of language." Let there be no fear of Sibylline confusions. Góngora demands clarity of those who would read him attentively.

"Poetry, in all its rigor": that is to say, when it is most rigorously poetic. For Góngora's poetry permits various degrees of poetic rigor, existing simultaneously. The poet is always the same, with the same soul and the same taste. But sometimes he abandons himself to his mocking demon and cultivates satiric poetry or festive verses; at other times he gives himself over to his Muse and composes poetry consecrated to Beauty. "From the very first year in which we have any information about his literary production," says Dámaso Alonso, "until 1626, the year before his death, when he wrote his last poems, we find this parallelism uninterrupted: on the one hand, the poems in which all is beauty in the world, all is virtue, opulence, splendor; on the other, the most scurrilous kind of wit, the most pitiless mockery, and the most violent lashing out at all the wretchedness of life. Apart from both of these, there is a series of compositions, the most characteristic of which is the *Fábula de Píramo y Tisbe* (*Fable of Pyramus and Thisbe*), in which he cuts across the two planes, the absolute and the

29

incidental, mythology and the picaresque, magnificence and malodorousness." There are, then, two distinct genres: the lyric and the comic. In one he sings:

> No son todos ruiseñores
> los que cantan entre las flores. (350)
>
> *Not everything's a nightingale*
> *that sings among the flowers.*

In the other he "gossips":

> Si algunas damas bizarras,
> (no las quiero decir viejas). (294)
>
> *If certain gallant ladies*
> *(I would not call them old).*

The noble limitations imposed on their inspiration by the earlier poets, Garcilaso de la Vega, Fray Luis de León, San Juan de la Cruz, Herrera, have been succeeded — not only in Góngora but also in Lope de Vega and Quevedo — by this broad integration of many kinds of poetry, high and low, serious and light. And within the two genres, Góngora's writings are subjected to different degrees of rigor, according to the amount of pressure applied. It is not in any way possible to ascribe the purer style to the major poetry, and the less pure to the minor poetry. It would be equally incorrect to imagine a chronological sequence proceeding from the simplest verses through the more difficult to the final hermetic poems. To quote Dámaso Alonso once more: "If the poet wrote, between 1580 and 1626, one series of compositions that are down to earth and another of poems elevated in tone and concept, and if the poems of the first group are as easy or difficult at the beginning of the period as at the end, and those of the second group are as difficult or easy at the end of the period as at the beginning, is this not sufficient reason for us to cast aside the

30

belief in a transversal division (into two periods) and to substitute for it a longitudinal one that would permit two ways of writing to exist concurrently in the writer and to accompany him all through his poetic life? A chronological division does not exist; the most one could concede is a gradation, although it would be more accurate to say that the most characteristic, and most censured, poems — the *Soledades* (*Solitudes*), *Polifemo* (*Polyphemus*), *Panegírico al Duque de Lerma* (*Panegyric to the Duke of Lerma*) — emerge from all the others, from the first as well as the last, like foam on a common sea." The thing most characteristic of Góngora is this simultaneous presence in his poetry of the grave and the gay (in subject-matter and tone) and of the plain and the startling (in language and style). These deliberate gradations give breadth and depth to Góngora's work, and make it almost comparable to that of Picasso, although in the latter chronological development is of more consequence.

Poetry, then, is established first of all as "a language." This concept of poetry is antipodal to that of a San Juan de la Cruz. The mystic takes his intimate experience as his point of departure, and, not being able to transmit his experience, he turns to words as a final inadequate recourse. Góngora represents the highest exaltation of the opposite type of poet: for him language — along with the treasure of his own intuitions — is itself the marvelous goal. All his energy will be concentrated on exploiting the inexhaustible mine of words. Their potential expressive power lies waiting there for anyone who can utter them; then these words, like a magic incantation pronounced in a rite, will bring about no less an effect than the creation of a world. Any poetic undertaking must, as its first task, establish its language: its very being.

Poetry, according to the fundamental conviction of humanism, which Góngora puts into practice more fully than any

31

other writer, possesses its own characteristic language. The particular content of poetry calls for a particular form. Hence the necessity for a "poetic language," distinct from ordinary language. Those humanists and poets did not see — they refused to see — that ordinary language, always an aesthetic phenomenon, can be elevated into poetry simply by using its words poetically. The question is not one of vocabulary but of manner. Neither Góngora nor his fellow spirits took this attitude. Herrera, the Sevillian poet, explains their position: "For, as Tully says, poets speak in another language, nor does a poet treat of the same things as an orator, nor follow the same laws and observances . . . and for all these and other reasons Aristotle calls them the tyrants of diction, for poetry is extremely abundant and exuberant, and rich in all things, free, and with only its own right and jurisdiction, subject to no other." Góngora uses the designation "heroic language," and adds "that it must be different from prose, and worthy of persons capable of understanding it" (896). It was he who, in Spain, boldly proclaimed himself the great tyrant, sultan, dictator of diction, and just as boldly put into practise the kind of writing legitimized by the humanistic tradition.

His first task was to restore to the Castilian language its noble character. Castilian is Latin that has come down in the world. The corrupt Romance tongue must be Latinized, by replacing the words of conversation with learned ones, and by rearranging the order of words in the sentence according to the curve of the Latin hyperbaton. Góngora considered that "one must inevitably honor the fact that our language, by my efforts, has reached the perfection and elevation of Latin" (896). In the *Polyphemus* he writes of a shipwrecked sailor: *Marino joven* (622). Today *joven* is the everyday word for "young." Yet an annotator of the seventeenth century, Andrés Cuesta, in an unpublished commentary, felt called upon to explain: "He calls him *joven* because he was very *mozo.*" *Joven* belonged to the vocabulary taken directly from Latin books. ("A semi-cultured descendant of the Latin *juvens,*" Corominas notes.) *Mozo* was the word then in daily use. *Marino joven,* the poet says: he had preferred the learned *joven* to the familiar *mozo.* In these lexicographical matters Góngora showed excellent judgment. As Dámaso Alonso has pointed out, he limited himself to "giving currency to a series of words the greater number of which were already in use in literature and had been accepted in the vocabularies of the time . . . Only a few, really a very small minority, could be considered rare." Some of the words "had appeared sporadically . . . since the literary beginnings of the Middle Ages; others appeared at the end of the Middle Ages (cultivated forms of the fifteenth century); still others, in the efforts at ennobling the Castilian tongue that mark the course of the sixteenth century. If it had not been for Góngora, would the language have eliminated them once more? . . . There can be no doubt that the extraordinary diffusion and duration of Góngora's influence, lasting as it did well into the eighteenth century, was of primary importance in fixing in literature (from which they passed into the spoken language) an important segment of the words that make up our language today." The Spanish language digested that "dialect," though not the syntax that accompanied it, and thereby ended its existence as a dialect. Such a phrase as *marino joven* lost its unfamiliar ring, and *joven,* which had once required a commentary from a linguist, came to be a common word, and even a vulgar one.

III

Poetry, then, as language: "constructed language." If all inspiration finds its solution in construction — and art is al-

33

ways this — what is typical of Góngora is the abundance and
the subtlety of the relationships fixing his phrases and stanzas.
Never has any poet been more of an architect. Never has anyone shown a more implacable will in raising an edifice of words.
The impulse implicit in any art, making it what it is, has
reached its fulfillment in the major works of Góngora:

> simétrica urna de oro,   (382)
> *symmetrical golden urn,*

as the last line of his *décima* to Villamediana proclaims.

For our Cordovan poet, a great verbal genius, perhaps the
greatest in the Spanish language (with only Quevedo as a
possible rival), a phrase is poetic only when it erects with a
maximum of tension the picture it aims to articulate. The un-
natural break in phrasing of the hyperbaton constitutes a violent wrench, which is a form of tension. This tension takes on
value as expression. Each word, by virtue of its "place" —
the points resting on it and the points on which it rests —
produces an effect that is both structural and expressive, and
fulfills its obligation to symmetry. This is what gives the stanza
its weight, its majestic and, as Góngora would say, "ponderous"
carriage. The "dissonant number of clams" will be a

> Marino, si agradable no, instrumento.   (629)
> *Marine, if agreeable not, instrument.*

This line is divided with perfect symmetry. "If not agreeable"
would be the normal way of expressing it. The word "not,"
placed after "agreeable" to balance the "if" — thus forming
the center of the three-part line — achieves place value: "If
agreeable not." A value as on a space on a monument. Although poetry is a successive art, like music — "words in time,"
Antonio Machado later said — Góngora's verse invariably suggests a metaphor of space, and on the space is inscribed an

34

entity that remains before the eyes even as it is slipping word by word past the ear. This place value always exists in language. Thanks to the abuse supposed by the hyperbaton, Góngora emphasizes — to the advantage, often, of art and of poetry — the value of position.

Over this imaginary space, or, if one prefers its material equivalent, over the space of the page, pass a constant stream of symmetries requiring simultaneous vision.

> Paces no al sueño, treguas sí al reposo. (627)
> *Peace not to sleep, armistice yes to repose.*

In this line, when it is read with the eyes, "peace" corresponds to "armistice," "sleep" to "repose," "not" to "yes," "to" to "to." These words correspond progressively. But there is also a correspondence between the beginning and the end: "peace — repose," "not — to," "to — yes," "sleep — armistice." In short:

> Peace — not to sleep — armistice — yes to repose.

The place value of the words is thus intensified; and lines, stanzas, and poems are erected like buildings. Góngora constructs furiously, or rather, with loving patience. Symmetry demands this cult-like love. Consider Stanza XLIX of the *Polyphemus:*

> Pastor soy, mas tan rico de ganados,
> que los valles impido más vacíos,
> los cerros desparezco levantados,
> y los caudales seco de los ríos:
> no los que de sus ubres desatados
> o derivados de los ojos míos,
> leche corren y lágrimas; que iguales
> en número a mis bienes son mis males. (629)
>
> *A shepherd I, but one so rich in flocks*
> *the valleys I impede most unencumbered,*

35

the hills I cause to disappear upraised,
and the abundance wither of the streams:
not those that, from their udders down-released,
or pouring freely from these eyes of mine,
with milk flow and with tears; for tantamount
in number to my blessings are my ills.

It would be very difficult to enumerate all the words and phrases in this stanza that correspond to one another. With the possible exception of the sixth line, everything is keyed to the number three. "A shepherd I — but one so rich — in flocks" "the valleys — I impede — most unencumbered," "the hills — I cause to disappear — upraised," "and the abundance — wither — of the streams:" "not those that — from their udders — down-released," . . . "with milk flow — and with tears — for tantamount" "in number — to my blessings — are my ills." The second, third, and fourth lines contain a noun at the beginning and a verb in the middle. The ideas are drawn by parallels: "udders — eyes," "released — pouring," "milk — tears," "blessings — ills." The parallelism is antithetical in this last instance, as it was previously between nouns and verbs: "valleys — I impede," "hills — I cause to disappear," "abundance — wither." Everything goes by pairs, equivalent or contradictory. And the duality of the logic is combined with a rhythm of odd numbers: the tripartite lines.

This freedom in the invention of the phrase permits the accumulation of symmetries, but it also breaks the spontaneous continuity of the words with a sinuously discursive design, especially in the jungle of *silvas* of the *Solitudes*. Throughout Góngora's texts, but even more in the major poems, short phrases are almost nonexistent. What is sought is a robust framework of syntax. Or, in other words, copious punctuation and a wealth of prepositions, conjunctions, ablative absolutes, clauses within clauses, restrictive particles — "though,"

36

"while" — delaying the progress of the sentence by means of undulations and meanderings. The cursive design thus breaks the straight line of the sentence. These long phrases within the stanza produce an effect comparable to the effect of the gifts on Galatea.

> este de cortesía no pequeño
> indicio la dejó — aunque estaba helada —
> más discursiva y menos alterada.   (625)
>
> *this then of courtesy by no means slight*
> *token left her — though she was icy cold —*
> *more meditative and less disconcerted.*

The token of courtesy (a line with *enjambement*) — for there is courtesy in the care employed by the architect-writer — left her (the nymph) or it (the poem), although both were apparently icy cold, more meditative or discursive and less disconcerted. (The poem is less disconcerted by confused unpoetic perturbations.)

The profusion of asides determines, then, subtle combinations of rhythms and silences. The period proceeds either slowly or rapidly between pauses, many pauses, both mental and musical. The hyperbaton gives the sentence a diversity of levels and distances.

> A las que esta montaña engendra Harpías.   (631)
> *To those engendered by this mountain Harpies.*

That is to say:

> engendered by this mountain
> To those   Harpies.

One level: the two ends of the verse in a single straight line. Another more elevated line for the intermediate words, which are joined together and equidistant, forming a summit in relation to the level ground of the extremities.

37

Language submits to the will to construct, which little by little not only builds but also creates a work of poetry. And the poetry unfolds with an ease and fluidity of the second degree. The ear becomes attuned to these harmonies that are indeed harmonies, in accord with a new naturalness. This naturalness is relative and exceptional, and cannot prevail and be incorporated into the future language, which is receptive only to additions to the vocabulary, and is definitely hostile to the artifices of syntax. But Góngora, and only he, did succeed in deriving artistic and poetic advantage from this laborious struggle. Opposition to normal order — or, what amounts to the same thing, to the usual order — does not always result in an aesthetic advantage.

> De los nudos, con esto, más süaves
> los dulces dos amantes desatados.　　　　　　　　(632)
>
> *From intricate embrace, at this, most sweet*
> *the gentle pair of lovers disentwined.*

That is the way these lines read in almost all editions. But Professor Oreste Macrí is right in considering the text of the Chacón manuscript more canonical and more characteristic of Góngora:

> De los nudos, que honestos más süaves.
>
> *From intricate embrace, than chaste more sweet.*

Acis and Galatea disentwine themselves from an embrace (or, literally, untie themselves from a knot) more sweet — or sensual — than chaste. These words are superior to the abstract and prosaic "at this." On the other hand, the inversion "than chaste more sweet" does not produce a result superior to "more sweet than chaste." Perhaps for this reason the Millés conclude that Pellicer's "at this" is "much more likely" than the reading of the Chacón manuscript (1186). More likely? Less beautiful, less characteristic of Góngora.

38

In general, Góngora the architect joins forces very well with Góngora the poet: construction and creation. Of what? Of an "object." This idea of an object throws considerable light on Góngora's creation and construction.

IV

THEME. Góngora, we know, is an enthusiast for the material world, and his whole soul is concentrated in his five senses, in a propensity toward all that sets up a resistance to be joyously conquered. The sonnet addressed to "Illustrious and Most Beautiful María" (*Ilustre y hermosísima María*) sums up the poet's outlook:

> Goza, goza el color, la luz, el oro.   (451)
> *Exult, exult in color, light, and gold.*

To him gold is condensed light, light changed into something more palpable, with more of the attributes of an object. Prodigious Nature lies in the depths of his vision. But the vision is packed full of things: sumptuous, magnificent, splendid things under the noonday sun. Everything else, everything that is not an object, will be cast aside — or accepted in its material aspects only. The funeral sonnets have very little to say about death or the person who has died; what bulks large in them is the sepulcher or the tomb. Grief is only funereal gravity, a rite, and the verse too takes on monumental seriousness, and even rivals the tomb in solidity. In a sonnet on the death of Cardinal Bernardo de Sandoval y Rojas, the deceased does not appear until the eleventh line:

> a las heróicas ya cenizas santas.
> *to the heroic now and holy ashes.*

What is most important is the tomb, situated in "the chapel of Our Lady of the Cibory, in the Cathedral of Toledo."

39

Esta que admiras fábrica, esta prima
pompa de la escultura, oh caminante,
en pórfidos rebeldes al diamante,
en metales mordidos de la lima,

tierra sella, que tierra nunca oprima;
si ignoras cuya, el pie enfrena ignorante,
y esta inscripción consulta que elegante
informa bronces, mármoles anima. (508)

This you admire fabric, this supreme
magnificence of sculpture, oh passer-by,
of porphyry rebellious to the diamond,
of metals deeply bitten by the file,

an earth secures, that may earth ne'er oppress;
if whose you know not, stay your ignorant foot
and this inscription scan, which, elegant,
informs the bronze, the marble animates.

Here matter is presented at its hardest: porphyry, metal, bronze, marble; more vigorous than the diamond, rebellious to the force of aggression, docile only to the hand of the artist. Architecture and sculpture, "fabric" and "supreme magnificence": weightiness of objectivity in theme and in conception.

CONCEPTION. For Góngora the object par excellence is the solid one, surrendering itself to fate in all the tranquillity of its stillness. The quietness of things, quietly expressed, predominates over transitions of movement. In several passages Góngora uses the word *pisar*, "to tread"; but he applies it to expressions of light:

los bueyes a su albergue reducía,
pisando la dudosa luz del día. (621)

the oxen to their shelter led he home,
treading upon the doubtful light of day.

This light, when trodden upon, seems even more hard. Again we find:

40

> entre espinas crepúsculos pisando. (635)
> *among the briars treading on the dusk.*

It is a real pleasure to step on the twilight as if it were the ground. A boat glides over the water,

> cristal pisando azul con pies veloces. (664)
> *on crystal treading blue with nimble feet.*

There is a celestial treading:

> en campo azul estrellas pisan de oro. (508)
> *in azure field they tread on stars of gold.*

Even the abstract is trodden upon as if it were completely material:

> De la tranquilidad pisas contento
> la arena enjuta . . . (507)
> *For of tranquillity you tread, content,*
> *the sandy shore . . .*

The abstract can tread in its turn:

> el noble pensamiento . . . pisa el viento!
> *noble thought . . . treads upon the wind!*

This luminosity that is so corporeal is conspicuous in the great hall of a palace built by "hard lights":

> émulo su esplendor de el firmamento,
> si piedras no lucientes, luces duras
> construyeron salón . . .
>
> *its splendor emulous of firmament,*
> *if stones refulgent not, hard lights it was*
> *constructed hall . . .*

Hard lights! It is impossible to carry this objectivizing energy any farther than this. It is an energy that tends to "quantify" and not just to qualify. Góngora takes pleasure in the vision

41

of quantity, in which for him lies the excellence of the object.
When the Cyclops begs Galatea to accept him, he does it in
these words:

> Polifemo te llama, no te escondas,
> que tanto esposo admira la ribera,
> cual otro no vió Febo más robusto . . .   (630)

> *'Tis Polyphemus calls you, do not hide,*
> *for so much spouse astonishes the shore,*
> *nor other e'er saw Phoebus more robust . . .*

"So much spouse." Polyphemus is indeed a quantitative hero,
and his poetry is a poetry of magnitudes. Not "such a spouse,"
which would indicate a remarkable type of husband. "So much
spouse." He swells his volume with the substance of his tightly
packed reality. Phoebus has not seen another "more robust."
The Cyclops is applauded as if he were a superhuman athlete
in a stadium, or a stellar attraction at a county fair.

> En pie, sombra capaz es mi persona
> de innumerables cabras el verano.   (630)

> *and when erect, my person copious shade*
> *provides to countless goats in summertime.*

"When I am standing," Salcedo Coronel translates almost
literally, "my person makes a capacious shade for innumerable
goats against the heat of Summer." The Cyclops makes himself gigantic by singing his own praises deliriously before the
gaze of Galatea, and the great Polyphemic projection stretches
forth: a shadow. The "formless Goatherd" is a colossal Shadow
of Summer, stretching perhaps to the horizon, face to face with
the Sun. A shadowy spot giving shelter to other shadowy spots,
the masses of goats. At that crucial moment, before immense
space, only the most exaggerated of hyperboles would serve.
And Polyphemus touches the sky with his hands:

42

> y en los cielos, desde esta roca puedo
> escribir mis desdichas con el dedo.   (630)
>
> *and on the heavens, from this rock, can I*
> *all my misfortunes with my finger write.*

Nevertheless, as Pellicer observes reasonably, "In legal agreements, if the condition was set of *touching the sky with one's finger*, they were not valid." Nothing could be more legitimate in a "legal agreement." The *Fable of Polyphemus* aspires to being a creation.

METHOD. Meanwhile, it is the intelligence, along with the senses, that weaves a web of relationships among the objects. Relationships of a very rational character among sensible objects: this is the essence of Góngora's poetry. Galatea was sleeping by a fountain. "Came Acis," who drank the water of the fountain and looked at Galatea. Or, expressed in poetic imagery, Acis

> su boca dió — y sus ojos, cuanto pudo,
> al sonoro cristal — al cristal mudo.   (624)
>
> *his mouth gave — and his eyes, as best he could,*
> *to the sounding crystal — to the crystal mute.*

There are two crystals: one sonorous, the water; and the other mute, Galatea. The sonorous crystal does not flow any more than the mute: the nymph is equivalent in her whiteness to the water, which is also white because of its crystalline transparency. An equilibrium of plastic values is set up between the two bodies. No "impression" originated this metaphor. The affinities between the water, Galatea's skin, and crystal, real affinities, were discovered by the eyes and the reason — or rather, by the eyes of the reason. (A similar picture is described in the rondelet *De un monte en los senos, donde* [In the Bosom of a Mountain, where]. Clori falls asleep, and "Cupid Narcissus"

43

cuando más está pendiente
[no sobre el cristal corriente]
sobre el dormido cristal . . .   (325)

when he most suspended is
[not above the flowing crystal]
over the crystal sleeping there . . .)

According to Antonio Vilanova, the source of the scene in the
Polyphemus is a sonnet by Marino, *Descrive gli atti di una*
ninfa sopra il Po, in his *Rime* of 1603. And Vilanova adds:
"What is completely original in Góngora is the beautiful
metaphor 'mute crystal' with which he describes the motionless body of Galatea sleeping beside the sonorous crystal of
the brook."

In this way the images bring together objects that are far
removed from one another. The intelligence embraces more
than do impressions and emotions, which are more reduced,
more personal in scope. Frequently the metaphor consists in
creating an imaginary entity made up of two very heterogeneous things:

cuando velera paloma,
alado si no bajel . . .   (195)

when swift-sailing dove,
winged if not ship . . .

In reality all that exists is a ship, which is sailing as if it were
flying: a dove with sails instead of wings. Or, by inevitable
symmetry, the ship, having given her sails to the dove, would
appear to have wings. These fictitious crossings produce a sort
of metaphoric monster, barely suggesting a vision. What we
do find is an interplay of relationships — dove, ship, wings,
sails — which, as soon as they appear — "when swift-sailing
dove" — are made to disappear and are replaced — "winged
if not ship" — as if in a sleight-of-hand trick. Delicacy of the
senses functions along with delicacy of the intelligence. The

44

abstract and the concrete live side by side or fused together, each one counterbalancing the other.

v

Not even movement, however violent it may be, gives Góngora pause. Consider this wrestling match between two village youths:

> Abrazáronse, pues, los dos, y luego
> — humo anhelando el que no suda fuego —
> de recíprocos nudos impedidos
> cual duros olmos de implicantes vides,
> yedra el uno es tenaz del otro muro.
> Mañosos, al fin hijos de la tierra,
> cuando fuertes no Alcides,
> procuran derribarse y, derribados,
> cual pinos se levantan arraigados
> en los profundos senos de la sierra.   (659–660)

E. M. Wilson, the heroic and felicitous translator of the *Solitudes*, interprets the passage thus:

> *The one embraced the other next, and then*
> *— One panted smoke, the other fiery glowed —*
> *The double knot thwarting their joint intent,*
> *(Like the tough elms with clinging vines around)*
> *One, ivy, hung upon the other, wall.*
> *A dexterous Antaeus either bent*
> *If no strong Hercules; contrived to fall,*
> *And fallen, like the rugged pine to rise*
> *Deep rooted in the bosom of the Earth.*

Here is the prose rendering of Dámaso Alonso: "The two embrace each other; and, each imprisoning the other, they make so violent an effort to throw each other that the one who is not sweating liquid fire seems at least to be belching burning smoke. While each thus holds his opponent, they resemble an elm tree embraced by a climbing vine, and ivy tenaciously

45

clinging to the wall the other presents. If they are not Hercules himself, they seem at least to be the cunning Antaeus, the giant son of earth, who when he fought with Hercules acquired new strength each time he touched the ground, so that whenever he fell and appeared to be vanquished, he rose again with renewed vigor: in the same way the two wrestlers try to throw one another, and if they fall, they rise again like pines having their roots in the deepest bowels of the earth."

Only one metaphor indicates change: the one about smoke and fire. Of the wrestling match itself, nothing remains but two motionless positions. We see the two athletes stopped in mid-movement: first, when their holds so neutralize each other that they seem to be a vine on an elm tree in the form of a "knot." They are already "thwarted." But the poet is not satisfied with this reduction of two exertions to stability of a vegetable nature, and he continues: "One, ivy, hung upon the other, wall." Ivy, wall: the solidification is complete. The second time, the two youths are lying on the ground. "Fallen," they do not stir. As soon as they arise, they could be called "pine trees," pines that are "rooted," "deep-rooted in the bosom of the Earth." The action has almost been made to disappear by sleight of hand. Two verbs indicate it rapidly: "contrived to fall." Góngora conceives a whole conjugation of activity thus: knot, elms, clinging vines, ivy, wall, pine, deep-rooted, bosom of the Earth. Thus, Góngora wrestles with movement until he imprisons it in substantial masses of repose.

No one could be more different from Góngora than the great Francisco de Aldana, from precisely this point of view. Aldana takes pleasure in highly tumultuous images describing sports and fights. Here is a boxing match in his *Fábula de Faetonte (Fable of Phaethon)*:

46

Otro, en sí mismo reducido todo,
trabaja de tener lejos el pecho
a su contrario, y va mil vueltas dando
por ver si puede así desatinarlo.
Agora trueca el pie, y agora dobla
una rodilla, y firme está en la otra;
afloja, aprieta, deja, toma, vuelve,
prueba, finge, rodea, mueve y sacude,
ciñe, gime, reposa, tienta, impide,
se cierra, se dilata, se detiene,
se encoge, se suspende, se apresura,
agora se defiende, ora acomete,
agora muestra el lado, ora la cara,
se determina, y se arrepiente luego,
hasta que al fin, sudado y polvoriento,
o por suerte o virtud del que más pudo,
en tierra el adversario ve tendido.

Another, centered wholly on himself,
striving to keep his chest beyond the reach
of his opponent, circles round and round
to see if he can disconcert him thus.
At times he shifts his feet, and then he bends
one knee, while holding firmly on the other;
relaxes, tenses, gives and takes, returns,
tries out, pretends, surrounds, moves in and hits,
seizes, moans, takes breath, incites, evades,
covers himself, outstretches, checks himself,
crouches, holds his footing, swiftly moves,
sometimes defends himself, sometimes attacks,
now shows his side and then again his face,
makes up his mind, and changes it forthwith,
until at last, covered with sweat and dust,
whether by luck or virtue of being more able,
he sees his rival stretched upon the ground.

The fight is very clearly broken down into many separate actions, none of which runs into the next. The victory is to the verb. This dynamic vision is characteristic of the noted Captain, who was so direct in his contact with life and its turmoil that his unrhymed hendecasyllables tend toward prose; the tone is raised, however, by the great accumulation of verbs, one after the other, with nothing in between. This ostentation is perhaps unprecedented: there are five lines — from *afloja, aprieta,* "relaxes, tenses," to *se apresura,* "swiftly moves" — packed with verbs, and nothing but verbs: twenty-one of them. It is a highly original style, though it is not the best of the poet who was capable of composing the admirable *Epistle to Arias Montano.*

Of course the world of Góngora is not completely lacking in movement. In a recent study Professor Marcilly points out pertinently a number of dynamic passages, passages of crisis, uncertainty, and confusion. Sometimes a striking evocation — as, for instance, in the Moorish ballads — bursts in with an impetuosity that cannot be held back:

> Levantando blanca espuma
> galeras de Barbarroja . . .   (128)
>
> *Spraying milky foam,*
> *Barbarossa's galleys . . .*

The African campaign gives animation to the *Panegyric to the Duke of Lerma,* and in two of its lines referring to Algiers, everything — verbs, nouns, adjectives — contributes to the picture of crimson-colored undulation:

> Imiten nuestras flámulas tus olas,
> tremolando purpúreas en tu muro.   (699)
>
> *May our flame-like banners imitate your waves,*
> *billowing crimson-purple on your walls.*

When the poet's imagination confronts a cataclysm, more dreamed than observed, as if it appeared threateningly among

48

the very phantoms of night, actions are multiplied and unleashed:

> Cosas, Celalba mía, he visto extrañas:
> casarse nubes, desbocarse vientos,
> altas torres besar sus fundamentos,
> y vomitar la tierra sus entrañas. (463)

> *Things, my Celalba, have I seen most strange:*
> *marriage of clouds, running away of winds,*
> *high-reaching towers kissing their supports,*
> *and earth vomiting forth her very bowels.*

But the Góngora that is most characteristic is not the Góngora of "things" so "strange." It is significant, as Marcilly himself has pointed out, that "this desire to seize movement . . . leads Góngora to describe its curve at the very moment that marks its end." And he gives as an example the love-duet of Acis and Galatea, accompanied by the duet, equally amorous, of two doves:

> reclinados, al mirto más lozano
> una y otra lasciva, si ligera,
> paloma se caló . . . (627–628)

> *as they reclined, to the most luxuriant myrtle*
> *a pair, lascivious, if light of wing,*
> *of doves swooped down . . .*

The flight of the doves appears "at the precise moment that the pair of birds alights: *se caló*, and the poet succeeds here in defining movement by stopping it, that is to say, by the negation of it." ("*Calarse* means to drop," Cuesta notes. And he offers as evidence Garcilaso's verse: "To the bottom of the river dropping down" — *Al fondo se dejó calar del río* — so keenly analyzed by Francisco García Lorca.) In a similar scene from the *Orlando furioso*, quoted by Dámaso Alonso, there is nothing analogous to what Marcilly found in the *Polyphemus:*

49

ma baci, che imitavan le colombe
davan segno or di gire or di far alto.

their kisses, imitative of the doves,
at times would move, at times would come to rest.

There is less movement in the passage from Marino which
Antonio Vilanova proposes as a definite source of Góngora.
It is from the *Rime Boscherecce,* 1602:

Duo della Dea piú bella augei lascivi
Sovra un mirto gemean frondoso e spesso,
E de' lor baci al mormorar sommesso
Respondean l'aure innamorate, e i rivi.

Of the fairest Goddess two lascivious birds
upon a myrtle thick and verdant moan,
and to the gentle murmur of their kisses
the enamored breezes and the streams respond.

The expression of movement cannot be avoided, and Góngora does not avoid it. The bird of prey, swooping down on
the kite's nest, will, in her downward plunge, be a "feathered
bolt" of lightning. But before that she is arrested hovering
over her prey, and in that "snapshot" of her flight she is seen
as a motionless crown:

corona inmóvil, mientras no desciende
— rayo con plumas — al milano pollo
que la eminencia abriga de un escollo.   (626)

immobile crown, till she at last descends
— a feathered bolt — upon the fledgling kite
protected by an overhanging cliff.

The bird is likened to Galatea, who is *librada en un pie toda,*
"poised upon one foot wholly," and thus suspended in restrained impulse over Acis as he pretends to sleep. The pre-
vailing element of vision in this incident is immobility: sus-
pension and latent concentration of movement — which will

50

presently take place. The simile of the bird of prey is then introduced as an immobile crown. Thus it befits a Galatea leaning over a youth who is pretending to sleep. The solid world of Góngora takes shelter in robust quietness. Or, if it moves, its unstable aspect is allied to a metaphor of stability: the girls from the highlands dance with agility, even though their legs — white, "of crystal" — rise with the sveltness and vigor of pillars, and their feet support them with the gravity of the base of a column:

> Ellas, cuyo movimiento
> honestamente levanta
> el cristal de la columna
> sobre la pequeña basa.   (149)
>
> *The highland girls, whose movements*
> *decorously upraise*
> *the crystal of their columns*
> *on the tiny base.*

A world in repose, or in a repose indicating change, like the gypsy girls of Valladolid:

> En Valladolid
> no hay gitana bella
> que no haga mudanzas
> estándose queda.   (151)
>
> *In Valladolid*
> *there's no gypsy girl*
> *who's not constantly dancing*
> *while standing quite still.*

VI

STYLE. But the object dominates everything, and to the objectivity of theme, conception, and method corresponds the most suitable style, one of resplendently sumptuous materiality. Images and metaphors are drawn primarily from the con-

51

crete world. In Góngora's poetry there will always be many more things, or ideas of things, than abstract ideas. To be sure, images and metaphors, as if they were the very language of this poetry, are not adornments but the material of which the poetry is made, its "marble." Let us not consider as decorative elements that are really constructive.

To a greater extent than any of his contemporaries in Spain, and perhaps in Europe, Góngora confers on his poetry qualities of painting, of sculpture; perhaps architecture is the art he aspires to emulate. It would be unusual to find any colorless verse in his poetry.

> Salió Cloris de su albergue,
> dorando el mar con su luz,
> por señas que a tanto oro
> holgó el mar de ser azul. (199)
>
> *Chloris from her shelter came,*
> *the ocean gilding with her light,*
> *as signal that, with so much gold,*
> *the sea rejoiced at being blue.*

Blue in all its immediate presence, an intact and radiant blue, strengthened by the contrast with gold, light, that golden color of the sea derived from the blond Chloris. All of this is obvious. More subtly, in some passages color acquires unity of gamut, diffused throughout the stanza.

> Donde espumoso el mar sicilïano
> el pie argenta de plata al Lilibeo
> bóveda o de las fraguas de Vulcano
> o tumba de los huesos de Tifeo,
> pálidas señas cenizoso un llano. (620)
>
> *Where effervescent the Sicilian sea*
> *the argent foot of Lilybaeum silvers,*
> *whether a domed vault to Vulcan's forge*
> *or tomb to hold Typhoeus' monstrous bones,*
> *an ashen plain its pallid signal gives.*

No very sharp contrast relates these tones of gray, that range from silver to ash: "argent," "silvers," "tomb" for the "bones," "an ashen plain," "pallid signal." A similar unity is found in another stanza of the *Polyphemus*:

> La Ninfa, pues, la sonorosa plata
> bullir sintió del arroyuelo apenas,
> cuando — a los verdes márgenes ingrata —
> segur se hizo de sus azucenas.
> Huyera, mas tan frío se desata
> un temor perezoso por sus venas,
> que a la precisa fuga, al presto vuelo,
> grillos de nieve fué, plumas de hielo.　　　　(625)

> *The sleeping Nymph the sonorous silver then*
> *had scarcely splashing of the brooklet heard*
> *when — to the verdant shores ungrateful — swift*
> *her lily limbs she sought to make secure.*
> *She would have fled, but that so coldly moved*
> *a lazy-coursing fear throughout her veins*
> *that to the urgent flight, the ready wing,*
> *fetters of snow it was, feathers of ice.*

(We must not forget this variant given by Pellicer, preferred rightly and with taste by Alfonso Reyes: *segur se hizo* . . . Perhaps Góngora changed *segur* to *seguir* when *la segur de los celos* appeared a few stanzas later.) The range of cold tones here associates the material with the spiritual: "silver," "lily," "coldly," "lazy-coursing fear," "snow," "feathers," "ice." All this is white, next to a vibrant green: "the verdant shores." It is curious to note that an abstract epithet can take on concrete value and even acquire what is almost a coloring: *Neutra el agua dudaba*, "Neutral, the water wondered." Pellicer comments: "The water was undecided (that is, *neutral*) as to which it should believe to be sky and which a Cyclops: whether it should consider Polyphemus a human sky because it saw him with a sun in his forehead, or whether it should

consider the sky a celestial Cyclops because it had one eye."
Beyond this explanation lies a visibly fluctuating water, a
water that is truly of the sea. (Some readers might perceive
— excessively — some atmospheric vagueness.)

The feeling of sculpture is also present in Góngora's work.
Polyphemus is a statue: his black wavy hair is tossed by a
stormy wind; his beard is a torrent furrowed by "the fingers of
his hand." We are reminded of one of the Donatellos of the
Museum of the Cathedral in Florence, or a Michelangelo.
Or, without seeking so far afield, one of the Berruguetes in
Valladolid. As for the similarity to architecture, it lies more
in the manner of composition than in the suggestion of monuments. Every verse, every phrase, every stanza is an architec-
tonic composition. References to buildings are also numerous.
In the funeral sonnets there is more of the tumulus or sepulcher than of death or the deceased. Even the death of Acis, at
the end of the *Polyphemus*, is conceived thus. The Cyclops
has hurled a rock down upon the lover. What terrible, final act
will take place now? For the youth, the rock

> Urna es mucha, pirámide no poca. (632)
> *Of urn is much, of pyramid not a little.*

Acis has died; and is he already entombed? We have previously
followed the flight of the lovers, the anger of the monster, the
tension of his arms; then the rock is wrenched free and hurled
downward. Finally it stops. The poet invites us to imagine only
the shape of the rock, metamorphosed into a funeral device:
an urn, a pyramid. An urn: the body is to be found, if not
within, beneath it. Of urn it is much, but not all. Better yet
an eminence in the manner of a burial pyramid. Of pyramid
not a little. The death is occurring before our eyes, and it
seems to us already to have occurred. The solemn tone of the

54

phrase already suggests a funeral oration — one so concise that it is condensed into an inscription. *Urna*: the *u* sound, whose sonority is fully supported by the *r* and the *n*, holds a strategic position as the first accent in the line. *Pirámide*: the proparoxytone glides down a smooth incline: *Urna es mucha, pirámide no poca.*

Góngora is a passionate admirer of the beauty of the world, or he describes the world turned into beauty:

> Idolo bello, a quien humilde adoro.   (442)
>
> *A beauteous idol, that I humbly worship.*

So absorbing is the cult of Beauty that one does not see the worshipper: she alone triumphs. Everything glorifies the object. Of the subject himself we know only what the glorified object tells us. There is no introspection, no echo of personal passions. Góngora never exclaims pathetically: "I!" The absence of the historical person, complete where his great poetry is concerned, has no exception other than an occasional personal appearance in some of the lyric verse, in the youthful love poetry, and especially in the burlesque poetry. Mockingly, or half-mockingly, the author of *Hermana Marica* (*Sister Marica*) talks about himself, with an admirable emotion of childhood; and again in the little *romance, Hanme dicho, hermanas . . .* (*They Have Told Me, Sisters . . .* 44–46, 87–93). In his major poems, Góngora does not follow the example of the Spanish Petrarchists who, in imitation of Garcilaso, pause to contemplate their state, their inmost being. In a statement to the Bishop of Cordoba the then young prebendary excused himself thus: "and if my poetry has not been as spiritual as it should have been" (1214). Quite so. Góngora's poetry is far removed from "spiritual poetry." Objective poetry it is, through its fondness for the physical world, and also

55

through its exclusion of the poet as subject matter. Góngora pauses to contemplate . . . his language, magnificent, resistent, the object among objects, the most beloved of all. It has, besides, another charm: its quality of enigma. The poem will be born of this contradiction, objective and enigmatic at the same time.

VII

How is this to be done? Góngora has outlawed direct speech. In general, he has outlawed evoking a thing by means of its own simple name. The poet's whole endeavor will go into not using that name. Reality will be only alluded to, and the resultant circumlocutions and figures of speech will create bit by bit a much more beautiful reality. A second reality that shows itself and yet does not show itself. In this respect the Gongoristic becomes identified with the hieroglyphical. In a hunting scene, falcons naturally take part. But the author does not wish to say "falcons." As a poet, he considers himself obliged not to mention this word, which could only suggest the creature as it is, or at least as it is remembered. First there will be concealment; afterward, re-creation. For beings are not going to be described, but transformed from what they are into what they really are not. This falsehood carries over enough elements common to the two identified terms to fuse them into one image possessing a broader reality. One might have written in prose: "Though idle, no less fatigued from the recent exercise (of the hunt), to the gauntlets of the master falconers complainingly came the falcons, swift Norwegian whirlwinds." Góngora, trusting entirely to the rhythm of the verse, and of enigmatic verse, sings:

> Aunque ociosos, no menos fatigados,
> quejándose venían sobre el guante
> los raudos torbellinos de Noruega. (689)

POETIC LANGUAGE

Not less fatigued, although more slothful, they
That Scandinavian whirlwinds are for speed
Upon the gauntlet, in complaint, arrived.

These swift whirlwinds are the actors in a venatorial aggression, and we must start from these particular whirlwinds in order to track down what they both are and are not: falcons. The realization of the identity of the birds, after a moment of suspense, brings with it the surprise of sudden revelation. The enigma, then, helps to dramatize a search and its denouement: this picture of a reality recast with more reality — at once fantastic and true.

Góngora does not call a spade a spade, or, in the words of the Spanish saying, he does not call bread "bread" nor wine "wine": he calls it "confused Bacchus"; and since wine is served in glass containers it becomes:

> . . . en vidrïo topacios carmesíes
> Y pálidos rubíes.   (657)

In E. M. Wilson's excellent translation:

> *Confused Bacchus did not try*
> *In burnished silver, no, nor shining gold*
> *His liquor to supply,*
> *The pallid rubies and the topaz bright*
> *In simple glass behold.*

Obviously a thoroughly Andalusian accessory could not be lacking:

> si la sabrosa oliva
> no serenara el bacanal diluvio.   (657)

> *Only the savoury olives could aspire*
> *To appease the drunken flood.*

Or, expressed in prose: "the savory olive, fruit of the olive tree (a branch of which served once before to put an end to another flood, the universal one)."

57

This play of allusion is based on what was admired at the
time as *lo culto:* a style of elevated and elegant classical refer
ence. Between the poet and life is interposed an immense
cloud of reminiscences, Greek, Latin, Italian, Spanish. This i
the tradition that has been illustrated so ably and with so
much knowledge by Antonio Vilanova in his book on the
sources and themes of the *Polyphemus.* A bookish mass weigh
down the verse, though not the artist, who moves about with
agility among pagan gods, heroes, and places: it is an archaism
essential to Góngora's art, fed by a past not wholly past. Th
culto readers seek out the reasons behind every word. Could
a Genoese ship, in the *Polyphemus,* be called a "Ligurian
beech"?

> Cuando, entre globos de agua, entregar veo
> a las arenas ligurina haya . . .   (631)
>
> *When, amid globes of water, I saw cast up*
> *upon the sandy shore Ligurian beech . . .*

Seventeenth-century commentators argued the question pa
sionately. Pedro de Ribas considers the word "beech" justified
since in vessels made of oak "the inside planking is of beech
and all the other parts . . . such as the masts . . . ; and
the greater part (of the ship) is made of beech, the poet
entirely right in calling it this." Salcedo Coronel condemr
the word, and respectfully observes: "Pedro de Rivas defend
him [in his use of the word]; I should be glad if all those wh
attack him were satisfied, but this does not seem likely." Pell
cer — Don Joseph Pellicer de Salas y Tovar! — more obli
ingly concludes: "His detractors have two objections to mak
to Don Luis. The first is that, in the time of Polyphemus, th
Genoese did not dominate shipping as they do now. The se
ond is that he called the ship "beech" when ships are not mad

58

of this wood, because it is unsuitable for building. Both problems can be easily resolved."

Here is another question: what is the wild animal that Góngora situates in Sicily?

> No la Trinacria en sus montañas, fiera
> armó de crüeldad, calzó de viento,
> que redima feroz, salve ligera,
> su piel manchada de colores ciento.　　　(621)
>
> *Trinacria in her mountains no wild beast*
> *did arm with cruelty or shoe with wind*
> *that fiercely could redeem or fleetly save*
> *its maculated many-colored skin.*

A cruel beast, shod with the wind, whose skin is stained with a hundred colors: all indications point to the tiger. That is what Andrés Cuesta and Pellicer took it to be. But Salcedo Coronel objects that the tiger "is an animal that is not found in the mountains of Sicily nor in all of Italy." How is the error to be explained? As a "blameworthy slip in Don Luis; but since this error is the result of accident, and not of artistic ignorance, it can easily be forgiven, for poets follow after verisimilitude, and are not to be condemned for following after uncertain things, if in some way there is verisimilitude in them." It is not contrary to verisimilitude to place tigers in Sicily. (Indeed, Churton, the estimable and very likable English student of Góngora of 1862, imagines this wild beast to be a "panther or pard.") According to Antonio Vilanova, this wild animal came from a passage of Claudius in *De laudibus Sitiliconis*. It was he who "suggested to Góngora the implicit inclusion of tigers and lions and wild boars and other wild animals in the island of Sicily."

The major works — all of the *Panegyric to the Duke of Lerma*, for instance — also allude to contemporary society.

One event is the baptism of Philip IV in the church of San Pablo in Valladolid, opposite the Royal Palace:

> Desmentido altamente del brocado,
> vínculo de prolijos leños ata
> el Palacio rëal con el sagrado
> templo . . .   (702)
>
> *Sublimely contradicted by brocade,*
> *a vinculum of prolix boards unites*
> *the royal Palace to the holy Temple.*

Or, as it was related by the highly curious Portuguese Pinheiro da Veiga in his *Fastiginia:* "and for the baptism they now began to make a gallery . . . or passageway leading from the palace to the church of San Pablo, which is opposite it . . . And after it had been supplied with as much wood as seemed necessary . . . it was completely covered with rich satins and cloth of gold." Góngora's words were matched indirectly but exactly to the historical truth. And always, whether the question was one of archaic and modern, or of mythological and real, the select "cultist" minority bent over Góngora's poems in vehement and solicitous pursuit of the enigmatic object. Today's scholars tell us of the discussions, often punctilious, held by the erudite of the seventeenth century. "Nor can I refrain here from defending Don Luis against a criticism made of him by his commentator Pellicer," affirms another commentator, Andrés Cuesta, "for, not being content with the back-biting of all writers, I mean passing along the back-biting he finds in the wealth of critical writings, or with seizing the occasion where it has no forelock, he does not hesitate to nip at the person he is commentating, when he should do all he can to defend him." (Cuesta accuses Pellicer of stating that Góngora was not acquainted with the temple of Galatea mentioned by Lucian. This is in connection with the line: *deidad, aunque sin templo, es Galatea* (623), "a goddess, though sans temple,

60

is Galatea." Critics referred occasionally to conversations with some cultured person. Salcedo Coronel says: "This is how I understand this place, although don Gabriel de Corral, whose wit and erudition bring felicity and honor to Spain [he was a native of Valladolid and the author of *La Cintia de Aranjuez*], told me he understood it otherwise." By this means or by others, the enigma must be cleared up. It was sustained by a text that was almost always very well organized. The enigmatic object reappeared at last as a highly precious object of language, fixed and visible in its language.

VIII

Let us turn our attention in some detail to the equestrian figure presented in the unfinished second *Solitude*. E. M. Wilson translates thus:

> *August in person, and of ancient blood*
> *   If not robust in limb,*
> *Followed a prince; and there combined in him*
> *With royal grandeur, civil modesty.*
> *His steed the spumy froth of Boetis' flood*
> *Not only drank, but the free majesty*
> *   Inspiring every wave;*
> *This glowing stallion madly bit the gold*
> *That gently held him back; arrogant he,*
> *Though not because his hide cerulean gave*
> *New starlight to the day, but that the rein*
> *In the illustrious and the sovereign hold*
> *Of a sceptre-worthy hand should him restrain.*

En sangre claro y en persona augusto
     si en miembros no robusto,
príncipe les sucede, abreviada
en modestia civil real grandeza.
La espumosa del Betis ligereza
bebió no sólo, mas la desatada
majestad en sus ondas, el luciente
caballo que colérico mordía

61

el oro que süave lo enfrenaba,
arrogante, y no ya por las que daba
estrellas su cerúlea piel al día,
    sino por lo que siente
de esclarecido y aun de soberano
en la rienda que besa la alta mano,
de sceptro digna.   (685)

In Dámaso Alonso's paraphrase: "Behind them came a prince, illustrious of blood, august of person, although more delicate of limb than strong, who abbreviated or reduced to courteous modesty the greatness of his royal lineage. The horse he mounted had no doubt drunk, on the shores of the Betis, not only the frothy swiftness of this great river, but also its easy majesty: such a horse he was, a gleaming brute angrily champing the golden bit with which he was gently held in. And he seemed to be an arrogant beast, not because of the stars studding his cerulean hide, but because he had come to comprehend what there was of illustrious and even of sovereign in the rein humbly kissing the noble hand that guided it, a hand worthy of wielding a scepter."

Let us first of all admire the harmony of this passage, which unfolds without the slightest obstacle, with few syntactical inversions, with no strange Latin vocabulary, with no mythological allusions. The description of the horseman and his mount acquires an exquisite musical quality through the flowing nature of the clause, whose tone, at once moderate and magnanimous, fits the content. There is nothing startling. We hardly know which is the real prince, whether it is the hero or the artist who with such sovereign, such infallibly superior naturalness sustains this discourse, of line so pure within its own style. ("Heroic language" is Góngora's name for it.)

The prince, portrayed in abstract, direct style, summarizes moral and aristocratic virtues: his lineage and greatness are offset — in reality, reinforced — by his modest bearing. We

62

are shown only one physical trait: the non-robustness of this hunter, perhaps not much of a sportsman. In short, "august," with a regalness that is instilled in this prince. In the Spanish text, the word *príncipe*, used without the article (an absence some critic was sure to censure), stands at the beginning of a line, with all the force of its proparoxytone. The verse moves downward from the height of its first syllable, *príncipe les sucede*, and defers with ceremonious display the presentation of the *real grandeza*, "royal grandeur," thus *abreviada*, "abbreviated," with a diaeresis that does not conceal its paradox: the word stretches itself out by "abbreviating." This is an equestrian figure. But the horse is given more space, a more poetically important place, than the horseman, who is not singled out and made to stand out like the Colleone of Venice or the Gattamelata of Padua, both of them the opposite extreme from the Charles IV in a square in Mexico, a figure so nonexistent than the statue is known as *El Caballito*, "The Little Horse."

Here is an Andalusian horse. A magnificent picture: a swift, majestic, glowing stallion. The first two excellences (*ligereza*, *majestad*) are associated with the Guadalquivir River (known in Latin, and still known poetically, as the Betis); from it the horse drank and from it they originate. This is not ancient history; there is no mythological source, even though it may seem so. There is no comparison indicating that the horse is like the river. One act was sufficient — *bebió*, "drank," also standing at the beginning of a line — to bring about the transfusion of the frothy swiftness and the free majesty to the quadruped: a swiftness and majesty at once fluvial and equine. The majesty is in accord with the rider, "illustrious" and "sovereign," a condition that his mount has come to feel and assimilate. The Spanish verses with their sinuous curve, so favored by the form of the *silva* (eleven-syllable lines interspersed

63

with seven-syllable lines, with an irregular rhyme scheme), proceed by means of repeated *enjambements,* which in themselves give fluidity and speed: *ligereza — bebió no sólo* . . . , *la desatada — majestad.* And further on: *el luciente — caballo, por las que daba — estrellas.* The horse cannot but glow and gleam, as everything of poetic importance does in Góngora's world. Now the situation is brought out: the horse, governed by the bit, obedient to it, champs at it, and with a rage that contrasts with the gentleness of the bit, a golden bit, not mentioned by name, but limited to the splendid material of which it is made: gold. Another significant diaeresis: *süave,* thus more suave, more gentle. The "stallion madly bit the gold that gently held him back": the two Spanish verses form contrasting unities (*caballo que colérico mordía/el oro que süave lo enfrenaba*). The divisions of the lines correspond in their tripartite opposition: "stallion" — "gold," "madly" — "gently," "bit" — "held back." This symmetry gives order to the picture without the slightest constriction. In the same way, "August in person and of ancient blood," "With royal grandeur civil modesty": this is an intellectual correspondence, with a tendency to be an inscription on a space. The symmetrical terms are visibly arranged like windows on a façade, and satisfy the appetite for material things that impells the Cordovan poet in many converging directions.

Our horse is acquiring more and more material vigor. His hide is resplendent — and will be brought to life by expedients borrowed from painting. But before that an epithet is placed giving a quality of attitude and, we may well say, of soul: "arrogant." The position of *arrogante,* again at the beginning of a line, corroborates its meaning. The word leaps up with an impetus called forth by an energy in abeyance. This potential energy is always to be found awaiting the person who knows how to speak the word. Here it is Góngora who, at the proper moment — as the culminating point of a clause — carries the word *arrogante* to its fullest arrogance. Arrogance coming after swiftness, majesty, anger, and gentleness, and just at the beginning of the visual representation of the hide — spotted with spots that are "stars," against a background that logic makes "cerulean," though not at night, but in the daytime. And the spots, or, rather, the stars, are not passively connected with the light of the sun. For the cerulean hide "gave" stars "to the day." The metaphor does not rely on a mere static approximation. Góngora's preference for stillness in the object does not prevent him from giving an active function to the terms of his metaphors. The fact that the spots — they are not named directly — are like stars at night situates a relation *within* an action: the hide gave its stars to the day. A metaphor based on real fact — but with an imaginary disposition: these equine stars shine in the light of the sun. A fine hyperbole! The animal is transformed into an embellished super-animal — a sort of cross between Nature and History — between the river and the stars, beneath the prince and his influence. That is why the horse is arrogant: because of what he feels that is illustrious and even sovereign in the rein. The bit he angrily resists. To the rein he submits, guessing and revering the superiority of the rider; and even the rein itself *besa la alta mano*, "kisses the lofty hand." The equestrian group is reaffirmed in its completeness. The description goes from prince to horse, and from horse to prince. And the dignity of the latter is symbolized in the hand which, while it governs the horse, is *de sceptro digna*, "worthy of a scepter." It is an ending that settles the group with moderate stateliness: "civil modesty." Rider and horse forever form an irrefutable harmony.

65

IX

Cultismos, metaphors, allusions, symmetries: everything coincides in interrupting the pure line, the simple, direct expression, subordinating ideas and words to patterns. The result is usually felicitous, and this "language constructed like an enigmatic object" succeeds in its purpose: it is poetic creation. It can also happen that a series of obstacles delays and impedes creation: the enigma does not allow the object to be seen. With so much color and such abundance of riches, sensuality is diluted under an excess of decoration. In spite of the excess, in the most tangled part of the jungle, or, if one prefers, among the gears of the machine, the mysterious *je ne sais quoi* of all poetry insinuates itself. One of the first versions of the *Second Solitude* reads:

> El gerifalte, del Trión helado
> Robusto honor . . .
> *Then the Gerfalcon, of the frozen Trion*
> *the sturdy pride . . .*

Dámaso Alonso explains: "The *Triones* are the stars of the Great Bear. Here, then, *Trion* is used for *Septentrion*." In other words: "the Gerfalcon, pride of the North." How, unless by a stroke of poetic luck, like a gift from heaven, did it occur to Don Luis to cross out those words and choose others that were very different, revealing the birds in all the sudden impulse and clamor of their flight?

> El gerifalte, escándalo bizarro
> del aire . . .   (683)
> *Then the Gerfalcon, prodigy bizarre*
> *Of heaven . . .*

Some readers are galvanized, without a doubt, as by a discharge of poetic current, by this impulse suddenly thrusting

66

itself upon them. The gerfalcon, gallant tumult of the air!
This, too, is lyricism. Pedro Salinas has a fitting formula for it:
"the exaltation of reality." "Góngora is enamoured of the real.
But he exalts it, ennobles it in such a way that the world
becomes a marvelous feast for the imagination and the senses."
This feast — and poetry, even the saddest, is always this —
will spread its canopy, its sky over landscape and things, over
plants, animals, and men. On the other hand, it must not be
forgotten that many poems — and not only the short ones;
the *Panegyric to the Duke of Lerma* has already been mentioned — are occasional poems. And the satirist that Góngora
was all his life long never ceases to pass judgment on contemporary life. But everything, whether mocking or serious, con-
cerns the external world, and never, or almost never, the inner
world locked away in the silence of this poet of impersonal
reality, which is to say of everything but his own emotions.
The two principal modes of his poetic work are set forth suc-
cinctly in two lines of verse:

> Lo artificioso que admira
> y lo dulce que consuela   (631)
>
> *Artfulness that wonder stirs*
> *and sweetness that consoles.*

Góngora arouses wonder in us more than he consoles us,
although the pathetic note is not lacking. The shipwrecked
wanderer in the *Second Solitude* exclaims:

> ¡Oh mar, oh tú, supremo
> moderador piadoso de mis daños!   (666)
>
> *"O thou, o sea! supreme*
> *And piteous moderator of my tears!*

In general, the expression of emotion is severely limited:
there is no jubilation, anguish, anxiety. What is here is a
serene joy of the spirit: a noble attitude, altered or corrobo-

67

rated at times by irony or disdain. And, if we look from the poetry to the poet, we must add one passion: pride, a pride so great that it takes offense even at praise. Cervantes recalls this in his *Journey to Parnassus:*

> Es don Luis de Góngora a quien temo
> agraviar en mis cortas alabanzas,
> aunque las suba al grado más extremo.

> . . . *don Luis de Góngora, whom I fear*
> *By such brief praise of mine to have disgraced,*
> *Although I raise it to the highest sphere.*

Not for nothing is Góngora's greatest poem called *Solitude:* in a sonnet to his first *Solitude,* which his adversaries had completely failed to understand, he apostrophizes with solemn and taciturn haughtiness:

> Restituye a tu mudo horror divino,
> amiga Soledad, el pie sagrado. (507)

> *To thy divine, mute horror once again,*
> *friend Solitude, thy sacred footsteps turn.*

Place beside these verses the portrait of Góngora by Velázquez, one version of which is to be found in the Boston Museum of Fine Arts, not far from another masterly portrait, this one by El Greco, of Paravicino, the great friend and follower of Don Luis. Don Luis, whose eyes are so aloof from what they see. But what holds us most at a distance is his mouth. It is the mouth of disdain personified, with its sunken upper lip, so lacking in relief, the antithesis of the carnal lower lip and the strong chin. The yellowish skin corroborates a biliousness of temper that refused to smile for the painter's brush; the expression is peevish, almost acid, almost melancholy. Yet under this skin, inside this small cranium, was lodged an extraordinary spiritual force. Rondelets, *romances,* sonnets, long poems — a copious work, the product of many

68

years (from 1580 to 1626), and highly successful. The successes are on many levels, the variety of which is equaled, and possibly surpassed, only by Lope and Quevedo; it ranges from the personal lyric:

> Tenedme, aunque es otoño, ruiseñores   (581)
> *Hold me, although 'tis autumn, nightingales*

to the more dramatic lyricism of the sonnet A *la memoria de la muerte y el infierno* (*To the Memory of Death and Hell*):

> Urnas plebeyas, túmulos reales.   (497)
> *Plebeian urns and royal tumuli.*

Of this complex work — *La vida es ciervo ferido* (147), (Life is a wounded deer) — we have studied here the poems placed on the heights of greatest rigor. Góngora proposes to himself and to us — without any statement of theory, for this would have made him blush — a goal of perfection, or, more strictly speaking, as much of perfection as can be achieved by scrupulous endeavor. "Don Luis, of whom it is told that he used to linger several days over one line, in imitation of Vergil," Andrés Cuesta says of him. The poet must follow his way of self-perfection — which is not a "road to divine perfection." This was not an unusual attitude among his contemporaries, who were accustomed to setting down their inspirations in the best handwriting they could achieve. Góngora surpasses them all; he was an exacting master, as Velázquez was in painting. Let us remember these great Spaniards enamored of "perfection" — of work painstakingly wrought — to counterbalance the common, superficial view of the Spanish temperament capable only of spontaneous and irregular outpourings of genius.

Poetry of the kind that Góngora wrote requires inspiration, effort, culture. This culture, the culture of a sixteenth-century humanist, is incorporated, assumed also as experience, into his writing. Erudition in quantity in the long run accumulates a burden difficult to manipulate with safety. Don Luis himself warns that learning is deceptive:

No es sordo el mar: la erudición engaña.   (667)

The ocean is not deaf. Our learning feigns.

That erudition represented an order that had ended, but had been resuscitated. It is natural that the multitude of Graeco-Latin reminiscences should weigh heavily today and chill our pleasure in the reading of texts so learned. Góngora scholars have explained his situation clearly. The poet must submit to a canon and continue a style. Góngora makes the style his own by intensifying its magic and multiplying its artifices. But no cunning of composition stands out as entirely new in Góngora's poetry. Everything has an antecedent, distant or immediate, Greek, Latin, Italian, or Spanish. Góngora is not a dawn but a sunset, the most opulent of sunsets. In him the humanistic poetry of the *Siglo de Oro* is filtered and purified, fluted and worked to its maximum complexity, for Góngora is a termination, which is to say perfection, ripe, mature perfection in this general historical sense. And it is in relation to this that we should see his individual perfection.

x

Everything converges toward rigor of language and of poetry, achieved by means of the purification and intensification of already existing means of expression. Góngora is an artist who submits the forms of his art to examination and expurgation, and does not fling himself into creation without due consideration. Although we are scarcely acquainted with his general ideas, everything in his writing postulates this preliminary self-criticism. Our great Andalusian must have em-

70

bodied the type of man who first imposes a problematical stage on the foundations of his art. So that the poetry of his predecessors remains as a period of preparation, for there poetic elements were combined with others belonging to the styles of the orator and the historian. It will be necessary, then, for Góngora to eliminate what is common and reinforce what is genuine and distinctive. In this he approaches the distant, very distant poet Mallarmé: "I have created my work," the latter wrote in a letter in 1867, "only by *elimination*." And Mallarmé underlined the word "elimination."

The total result achieved is new, completely new, scandalously innovative. In it the primordial factor is the divine something, the genius of that man, who is the incarnation of a very Hispanic type of person: the extremist of tradition. The heritage of a past so cultured, so talented, so refined, is preserved with such exquisiteness that the center of equilibrium of tradition is displaced. The poet inhabits his own Finisterre, his Land's End, and in it he writes specialized poetry for specialists. Specialists because of their culture, not in any sense initiates of a cult. There is no mystery here but the mystery inherent in all poetry. Góngora's manner is far removed from the Orphic. It is based on clearly defined knowledge and understanding. Let no one enter here who has no knowledge of geometry, no familiarity with humanistic poetry. Many are the writers, in many different lands and periods, who have written for a more or less restricted public. Góngora restricts his audience considerably, and brings to light a new factor in Spain: a minimum minority, living in the shadow of the church, the palace, and the university. Churchmen, courtiers, scholars, and writers are the players in this game: "the communication I hope for with persons so well-born and so cultured," Góngora writes in a letter to Tamayo de Vargas (899). His poetry will present difficulties; for that very reason

71

it will be attractive. To the experts, Góngora will be difficult; to the inexpert, he will remain forever obscure. "Obscurity," in this connection, indicates only the dividing line between the "masses" and the rest. The rest are those "foreigners" to whom T. S. Eliot referred when he said: "One of the more obscure of modern poets was the French writer Stéphane Mallarmé, of whom the French sometimes say that his language is so peculiar that it can be understood only by foreigners." Góngora is as obscure as . . . Einstein, which is another way of saying that the *Polyphemus* is as clear and precise as the theory of relativity. This Spaniard, a genius, an ingenious inventor, an engineer, constructs each poem — and each is a world, a garden, and a machine — in that Land's End in which he dwells, so admirable, so remote, so rare.

No being can be defined without its limits, both negative and constituent. We should not reproach a work of art for lacking certain things that contribute to its most positive affirmation. In Góngora's great poems we should not look for references to God, the soul, man's destiny, because these poems are not developed along religious, metaphysical, psychological, or moral lines. Don Luis offers us nothing more nor less than a beautiful vision of Nature. Nature — with the capital N of the humanists — that takes on cosmic proportions. It is the most central theme one could choose, and Góngora treats it according to the tradition inherited by his period and his country, without extravagant deformations of sensibility or of taste. His infinitely numerous poetic discoveries spring from the soundest, most balanced vision of the reality he accepts and enjoys.

The introduction of disturbing elements does not interfere: "This panting impulse, this jostling of telluric forces, an urge expressive of all that is strong, widespread, dark, and monstrous" that Dámaso Alonso has examined so perspicaciously.

72

And he emphasizes "this new contribution of Góngora's century" with a cheerful vehemence far superior to that of Polyphemus, the character who represents and sums up the "new spirit": "a force opposing tradition . . . , which momentarily bends and even contorts it, but cannot break it," he concludes. Góngora is not his Polyphemus. The beauteous idol — that he humbly worships — remains erect. Beauty is not a mask for truth, and being is never more fully being than when its reality is raised up to harmonious fulfillment. To Garcilaso, water is never more truly water than when it is *Corrientes aguas, puras, cristalinas,* "Flowing waters, pure and crystalline," and the comparison with crystal doubles its transparency: it is the most intense way water has of being water. Góngora sees a place where the ocean thrusts into the land as if it were a centaur:

> centauro ya espumoso el Oceano
> — medio mar, medio ría — (663)
>
> *The Ocean now a spumy centaur, see,*
> *— Half sea, half estuary —*

This learned image embellishes not by falsifying, but rather by revealing a geographical truth. To be sure, things will not be seen thus in the new perspective of the seventeenth century; there appearances will always be deceiving. The blue sky will neither be sky nor will it be blue. One of the Argensola brothers then formulates this contradiction between the true and the beautiful (in complete antithesis to the phrase of Keats):

> ¡Lástima grande
> que no sea verdad tanta belleza!
>
> *What a pity*
> *that there should be no truth in all this beauty!*

But was Góngora the major poet a *desengañado,* a disillusioned man? Let us have confidence in his artist's faith. Let us exult with him in light, in color, in gold: appearances will not deceive us. (Only in his marginal elegiac verse does he warn of the danger to be found *en seguir sombras y abrazar engaños* [526], "pursuing shades and toying with deceits.")

Our poet, whether in his major or his minor verse, can no longer be accused of formalism. Formalism implies vacuous rhetoric. And it has been proved beyond a doubt that form, in Góngora, corresponds to a plethora of content. That form, so lucidly and delectably erected to the greater glory of God and the Castilian language, is in itself seductive, like a beautiful body valued for its own sake — and always functioning as a sign. The arrow of meaning strikes its mark, but it throws off so many sparks in the process that at times the target is not perceptible at first glance. All great texts, as we know, require more than one reading; as for poetry, if it is not reread, it has not been read at all. Góngora's texts begin by offering us an enigma, and it sometimes happens that the enigma dissolves our reading into separate moments that progress too slowly. We have to struggle with this language that is different from our ordinary language. This discriminative refinement ultimately sustains the poem on a lofty eminence — from whose heights Góngora looks out over the royal roads of literature. Within the poem, only the poetic will be found; the prosaic will camp outside the walls. This insistence on distinguishing between poetry and prose carries a very grave implication: that of purity. For purity is cruel. The poet wishes to create a poem wrought of genuine elements, only the most genuine, and this intransigent severity must operate during the whole course of the poem, always on the same high level of poetry that is poetry. A noble, a very noble ambition, but . . . is "poem" the equivalent of "poetry"? Góngora would never have conceded that "in a poem of any length there must be transitions between passages of greater and less intensity," as

74

POETIC LANGUAGE

T. S. Eliot affirms. The same thing that attracts us to Góngora is, without a doubt, what separates us from him: his terrible purity, his poetic language.

This is well. It was well worth doing, for someone to stake his life on such a card. No one has ever staked his life more fortunately than Góngora, who was wonderfully successful. It is no less a wonder that Spanish poetry, in a Century that was truly Golden, beginning with Garcilaso, its dawn, should embrace such distances and offer such polarity and such wealth — from Fray Luis de León and San Juan de la Cruz to Góngora and Quevedo, with so many other remarkable lyricists along the way; and, in the middle, Lope. There is no bland eclecticism in admiring all the peaks of a great mountain range. Before us, and for us, rises, immortal, the pinnacle that is Góngora.

3

THE
INEFFABLE LANGUAGE
OF MYSTICISM

San Juan de la Cruz

The Ineffable Language
of Mysticism

San Juan de la Cruz

I

No Spanish poet inspires more unanimous admiration today than San Juan de la Cruz. It is true that his works in prose, which are highly important, have contributed a great deal to his international reputation, to his glory on earth as in heaven. Even his name has been translated, and with outstanding success: Saint Jean de la Croix, San Giovanni della Croce, Saint John of the Cross. Saint Teresa and he, with their translated names, stand out in the eyes of the world as supreme representatives of the great Spanish mysticism of the sixteenth century.

An increasingly intense religious concentration, in San Juan de la Cruz, turns into mystic experience. This experience is communicated in two ways: in doctrinal exposition and in poetic expression. Life, doctrine, and poetry are the three areas in which San Juan de la Cruz unfolds. A rather extensive explanation of the doctrine accompanies a poetic output which is very brief. San Juan de la Cruz is the briefest great poet in the Spanish language, perhaps in world literature. If we leave aside the compositions of doubtful authenticity and a few of minor interest, San Juan's poetic expression is condensed into seven poems: like the Pleiades, a small but brilliant constellation. No one could be less the professional rhymer than he. However, he must have written more poems than we know. It is not conceivable that the *Noche oscura* and the *Cántico espiritual* should be the early works of a novice. But poetry never came to be his principal task; it was something extra, overflowing from a life consecrated to religious zeal, the true name for which is none other than "sainthood." The highest pinnacle in Spanish poetry is reached not by an artist who is primarily an artist, but by a saint, who ascends to this height by his most rigorous road to perfection; and the *Noche oscura,* the *Cántico espiritual,* and the *Llama de amor viva* are the work of a person who never wrote the word "poetry." This is curious: San Juan often has recourse to the terminology of the arts and trades, and uses the words "rhetoric," "metaphor," "style," "verses," and others of the literary craft. In one passage he applies the word "poet" to the author of the *Book of Proverbs* (*Ascent* 3, XX, 6). Yet the word "poetry" never appears.

Three poems stand forth from the seven, unique. The three form a series which is perhaps the highest culmination of Spanish poetry: *Noche oscura del alma* (*Dark Night of the Soul*), *Cántico espiritual* (*Spiritual Canticle*), *Llama de amor viva* (*Living Flame of Love*). In order to feel and understand these texts purely as poems, we must approach them directly, not as if they were anonymous, but still disregarding for the moment the supplementary information available about them, such as the historical circumstances of their origin and their transcendental interpretation. It will be a good exercise in "ascetic" criticism to leave until later the saint's own explanations, and to read the poems attentively as if we knew nothing about the author. Later, when reading is followed by study, the time will come to consider the nonpoetic aspects of this poetry.

80

II

What do these three marvelous poems offer us? Or, rather,
what are they? On this point there can be no doubt: we know
at once that they are truly poems, and that they are truly
marvelous. The original text, the Spanish text, imposes itself
without any possible equivalent in translation. We are all
aware of the most obvious condition for the poetic word: its
uniting of meaning and sound. The one cannot exist without
the other. Although abstractly they are separate, they present
themselves as a single force, which is both body and soul.
Mallarmé's phrase is by now proverbial: "It is not with ideas
. . . that poetry is made. It is with words." Exactly! Yet any
formalistic interpretation, even one that came from Mallarmé
himself, would be erroneous. For a word in a poem is also an
idea — with a whole constellation of associations, allusions,
and suggestions. If the Spanish word *administración* corresponds roughly to "administration," *luna* is not the equivalent of *lune* or "moon." And how can one express in any other
way:

> ¿Adónde te escondiste,
> Amado, y me dejaste con gemido?

It is this and only this the Bride says, and not:

> *Where can your hiding be,*
> *Beloved, that you left me thus to moan?*

In our reading of the three poems, let us pay no attention
as yet to the titles, which incline us toward the author's interpretation. And the author at this point is not explaining: he is
saying, telling, singing. They are three love poems. This love
shapes a world with its atmosphere, its nights, its half lights,
its days, its fields, its caverns; in a solitude that welcomes the
lovers; in a remoteness where they reign over themselves and
over Creation; and in the most secret way, protected by the

81

most impregnable walls. The first poem is the poem of nocturnal adventure.

> En una noche oscura,
> Con ansias en amores inflamada,
> ¡Oh dichosa ventura!
> Salí sin ser notada,
> Estando ya mi casa sosegada.

> *Upon a gloomy night,*
> *With all my cares to loving ardours flushed*
> *(O venture of delight!)*
> *With nobody in sight*
> *I went abroad when all my house was hushed.*

A woman, moved by love, has slipped out of her house. And, before morning comes, in the hour between night and dawn, the lovers meet, and their love is consummated in the most profound fulfillment.

> Quedéme, y olvidéme,
> El rostro recliné sobre el Amado,
> Cesó todo, y dejéme,
> Dejando mi cuidado
> Entre las azucenas olvidado.

> *Lost to myself I stayed,*
> *My face upon my lover having laid,*
> *From all endeavor ceasing:*
> *And all my cares releasing,*
> *Threw them amongst the lilies there to fade.*

This first poem is perhaps the purest of the three great poems. (And "pure" refers here to a quality devoid of any suspicion of rhetoric.) This is why the images appear in organic function. At first, between silence and solitude, moving through darkness to darkness, the amorous woman repeats her exclamation: "O venture of delight!" And we feel her whole being suspended, concentrated in eagerness — which holds itself back,

82

tensely, when it is on the point of bursting forth: "O venture of delight!" Delight with adventure, with boldness, but without disorder. "I went abroad when all my house was hushed": this is the last line of both the first and second stanzas. The nocturnal departure depends on this sure repose, which opens toward love — with no light other than the light from the heart. ("Blessed is that secret place of the heart that is of such great price that it possesses everything." Letter to Mother María de Jesús, 1589.) This light illuminates so clearly that it is brighter, in the midst of darkness, than "the light of noonday" and "dawn." Never has dawn been suggested with more tender clarity than in this verse:

¡Oh noche amable más que el alborada!
Oh night that is more kindly than the dawn!

And the deep peace of consummated love — *Allí quedó dormido*, "There he lay asleep" — abandons itself to the slow rhythm, in an atmosphere of beauty and rapture. The lover sleeps on the beloved's flowering breast. And she "regales" him, *regala*. No expression could be more delicately voluptuous. The decorative elements, robust and graceful — *el ventalle de cedros*, "the airs with which the cedars wave," oriental and Biblical; *el aire de la almena*, "Over the ramparts . . . the fresh wind," medieval and Castilian — are not limited to a decorative role and collaborate in the action: the airs with which the cedars wave act as a fan; the fresh wind from the ramparts is now a hand that suspends the senses, and even more, wounds the neck of the beloved. The violence of the verb "wounds," which might have destroyed the harmony of the moment, is made subject to this harmony, and everything is absorbed by a love absorbed in itself, consummated. This is shown in a crescendo of reiteration by the series of verbs of increasing negation: *quedéme, olvidéme, recliné, cesó, dejéme,*

83

"stayed," "lost to myself," "laid," "ceasing," "releasing." *Dejéme*, literally "I abandoned myself," is followed immediately by *dejando*, "abandoning," in a lightly explanatory tone, less elevated, more prosaic. The level rises again with the oblivion among the lilies: a final picture that is precise, concrete, physically and spiritually pure. Seldom, very seldom has love's consummation been sung as it is in this final stanza, so compact, with its abandonment that is fulfillment.

The same story, passing through the same stages — seeking, finding, consummation — is told again in the second poem, which is considerably longer. (It has two hundred lines; the first, *Dark Night of the Soul*, has only forty.) A *Canticle*-eclogue. It was also called *Canciones de la Esposa* (*Songs of the Bride*), according to a letter to Mother Ana de San Alberto, 1586. The lovers here are shepherds, and the eagerness of the Bride takes her by sheep-folds and river banks, through woods and meadows. Finally the lovers are joined.

> Mi Amado, las montañas,
> Los valles solitarios nemorosos,
>
> *My Love's the mountain range,*
> *The valleys each with solitary grove.*

Against this depth of great landscapes, and not just in immediate rural surroundings, the action unfolds, and its bucolic elements always manifest the most genuine states — spiritual and sensual — of love: absorption, abandonment, rapture, perfect union, perfect bliss. Nature allies herself with passion; and the pastoral details, borrowed from literary texts, are combined with a story that is very much alive.

> ¡Oh cristalina fuente,
> Si en esos tus semblantes plateados,
>
> *O brook of crystal sheen,*
> *Could you but cause, upon your silver fine*

INEFFABLE LANGUAGE OF MYSTICISM

The word *plateados*, as San Juan himself tells us, is one he had read in Psalm 67 of the Vulgate: "It is as the wings of a dove covered with silver" (*las plumas de la paloma serán plateadas*). But no source could lead by itself, without the intervention of a great poet, to that exquisite *semblantes plateados*. Everything here is symbolic: everything is what it is, and something more. The amorous Bride, in stanza 13, is a dove, and the Bridegroom calls her this, and with her flight — "fanned by the wind . . . of your flight" — she cools the Bridegroom, a wounded stag. This eclogue, then, is highly dramatic, full of movement, with gradations in intensity which have been superbly analyzed by Dámaso Alonso. Broad spaces, withdrawn and solitary, — with mountains, valleys, islands, streams — are followed by pictures of smiling, early morning brightness: garlands of flowers, flowers interwoven with strands of hair, dewy mornings, clusters of roses. The mountain, *montaña*, becomes a hillock, *montiña*, and not merely because of the exigencies of the rhyme. All is love: "And only now in loving is my duty" (*Que ya sólo en amar es mi ejercicio*). This exercise, or "duty," gives rise to audacious visions: "Which my Beloved browses with his mouth" (*Y pacerá el Amado . . .*). Everything takes place in the open, but without ever losing the reserve of intimacy. The Bride has now fallen asleep; the Bridegroom adores and watches over her sleep. (An admirable theme: to watch love sleeping.) Wishing to protect her sleep with a conjuration, the Bridegroom invokes and evokes the most seductive of all profane music: the song of poets and of sirens.

> Por las amenas liras
> Y canto de serenas os conjuro
> Que cesen vuestras iras,
> Y no toquéis al muro,
> Porque la Esposa duerma más seguro.

> *By the sweet lyre and call*
> *Of sirens, now I conjure you to cease*
> *Your tumults one and all,*
> *Nor echo on the wall*
> *That she may sleep securely and at peace.*

This wall, thick and solid, is the boundary and the barrier between the world at large and the other world created by love for itself. And the word *muro*, "wall," rises up with prodigious material density impregnated with spirit. No, let "the wall" not be touched, the complete wall protecting the complete couple, withdrawn as always into their fortified castle. Then the couple returns to the fields — the mountain slope, the fountain, the caverns — amid gentler elements: the nightingale, the grove. "The waving charm/Of groves in beauty seen" (*El soto y su donaire*), with its incredible grace. It is now serene night,

> Con llama que consume y no da pena.
>
> *With fire that can consume yet do no harm.*

This line in the next to the last stanza of the *Canticle* announces the third poem (the shortest of the three, with twenty-four lines), which refers only to the final stage of the lovers' relationship. This poem is all astounded exclamation and fire, fire that illumines love while it burns in it.

> ¡Oh lámparas de fuego,
> En cuyos resplandores
> Las profundas cavernas del sentido,
> Que estaba obscuro y ciego,
> Con extraños primores
> Calor y luz dan junto a su querido!
>
> *Oh lamps of fiery blaze*
> *To whose refulgent fuel*
> *The deepest caverns of my soul grow bright,*
> *Late blind with gloom and haze,*

INEFFABLE LANGUAGE OF MYSTICISM

But in this strange renewal
Giving to the belov'd both heat and light!

We are immediately fascinated by these forms that do not break with the laws of our world. And yet this is another universe, with its own autonomous harmony, sustained by passion and contemplated by the spirit, to the sound of a music that is at once image, feeling, and beauty. By the close interlocking of all these components we are made to feel with persuasive force the intensity of each word, each line, each stanza — without ever losing sight of the closely knit whole. In the poem it may be either night or day, but the language is always luminous, and this light illumines a mystery without making it any the less inaccessible. The melody rises above a silence of solitudes. In this way, with this restrained decorum, the absolute nature of the passion is brought into sharper relief — a passion that seeks, awaits, finds, and at last is fulfilled. Who are these lovers? They are given only generic names: the Bride, the Beloved. Where do they live? Here in these poems, in the world created by these words. The things that happen, throughout the *Canticle* and the *Flame*, are set before us in a very real present. This is not a past already concluded that the poet reconstructs. Nothing in the poems is alien to the burning actuality which here and now — within the compass of the poem — sets forth its present acts of love.

Poetry is achieved by means of art: the art of the poem. It must be pointed out that San Juan de la Cruz has found the supreme equilibrium between poetry of inspiration and constructed poetry, unlike so many modern writers for whom poetry and art represent an irreconcilable contradiction. (For them any voluntary attempt at fitting or adjustment, any effort to compose, would ruin or nullify the inspiration of the poet, who abandons himself with complete passivity to his muse, or, to say it with scientific pretensions, to his subconscious.) San Juan de la Cruz does not fall into the heresy of quietism either when searching for the treasure or when wishing to display his find. His poem is erected like the most subtle work of architecture, in which each piece has been worked with the most elaborate care in the hope of achieving perfection; and artistic perfection is joined to spiritual. "The soul that walks in love wearies not neither is wearied." Only thus, by loving, artful labor, could he create the marvel that is the *Dark Night of the Soul*, a poem of even greater purity perhaps than the *Spiritual Canticle*, which is a peerless epithalamium. Who can say at what invulnerable distance, on what heights or in what depths, the marriage of the sublime lovers takes place? Not for a moment does San Juan de la Cruz cease to insist on the three notes which he exalts as no one else has: remoteness, solitude, secrecy. Each word he uses is felt in all its crystalline purity, infinitely refined as the result of a thrusting up from unknown depths. But this deep rooting in no way obstructs or dulls the final accomplishment. Was not the fire sufficient to reach the diamond? Rapture, reserve, serene security . . . These are poems of great love, which has the extremely rare privilege of being happy love. "And where there is no love, put love, and you will find love," was the recommendation of that ardent man. Here there is nothing to do but to find love. As Pedro Salinas says so well: "Everything in San Juan de la Cruz presents an obvious case of clear mystery . . . The trajectory of San Juan's poetry is like that of a bright flash of lightning, shooting like an arrow from darkness to darkness, piercing it and disappearing, leaving the shadows dissipated behind it, and darkness illuminated. The mysterious will continue to be mysterious, because San Juan in his poems does not explain anything logically, but it will now be clothed in the brightness of the light that pierced it like the light of

88

grace." And Salinas adds: "The final impression is one of pure flame in which absolute poetic unity is attained." But how can we analyze or sum up this poetry if it is also, and especially, like the air, which, according to San Juan, "when you try to close your fist on it, escapes"?

III

We know that San Juan de la Cruz conceived these poems in accordance with a Biblical tradition (the supreme eclogue of the *Song of Songs*) and the Graeco-Latin-Italian tradition flowering in the eclogues of Garcilaso de la Vega, who was the point of departure for all Spanish poetry of the sixteenth century. These various reminiscences having been fused in San Juan's "integrating lyricism," we find here three magnificent expressions of human love, love in absence and in presence, in anxiety and in fulfillment. The poems, when they are read as poems — and that is what they are — signify nothing but love, the intoxication of love, and their terms of reference are invariably human. No other "poetic" horizon is perceptible.

Are these poems, then, anything more? To be precise: are they anything extra-poetic? We would have no way of knowing if the author had not added to his verses, which are autonomous, his own explanations. The saint informs us that to his poetry there corresponds a personal experience and a doctrinal interpretation. First of all came the experience. But this origin, a mystical one, must not be confused with its result. Let us avoid any intrusion of the "genetic fallacy." In this case especially, one cannot imagine a greater distance between an experience and its expression. On the other hand, the doctrine rests on the poems. Yet this second meaning, an allegorical one, remains separate from the primary text. Poetry and allegory are developed along parallel lines which, if each is held to its definition, cannot interfere with or obstruct one another.

89

LANGUAGE AND POETRY

The moment has now come to listen to the author speaking as a critic, viewing his own work from without. One can always find, corresponding to the poetry of every great poet, a more or less well-organized and well-formulated poetics, a general point of view about the poetry already written or still to be written. Even though San Juan de la Cruz does not refer to poetry by that name, in the prologue to his *Spiritual Canticle* we discover a complete poetics. Before expounding in prose the mystic doctrine implied in the poem, the author warns us: "it would be ignorance to think that sayings of love understood mystically . . . can be fairly explained by words of any kind. For the Spirit of the Lord . . . makes intercession for us with groanings which cannot be uttered, pleading for that which we cannot well understand or comprehend, so as to express it ourselves. For who can write down that which He reveals to loving souls wherein He dwells? And who can set forth in words that which He makes them to feel? And lastly, who can express that which He makes them to desire? Of a surety, none; nay, indeed, not the very souls through whom He passes. And it is for this reason that, by means of figures, comparisons and similitudes, they allow something of that which they feel to overflow and utter secret mysteries from the abundance of the Spirit, rather than explain these things rationally. These similitudes, if they be not read with the simplicity of the spirit of love and understanding embodied in them, appear to be nonsense rather than the expression of reason, as may be seen in the divine Songs of Solomon and in other books of the Divine Scripture, where since the Holy Spirit cannot express the abundance of His meaning in common and vulgar terms, He utters mysteries in strange figures and similitudes. Whence it follows that no words of holy doctors, despite all that they have said and may yet say, can ever expound these things fully, neither could the

90

be expounded in words of any kind. That which is expounded of them, therefore, is ordinarily the least part of that which they contain." And further on: "the sayings of love are better left in their fullness, so that everyone may pluck advantage from them according to his manner and to the measure of his spirit, than abbreviated to make sense to which not every taste can accommodate itself. And thus, although they are expounded after a certain manner, there is no reason why anyone should be bound to this exposition. For mystical wisdom (which comes through love, whereof the present stanzas treat) needs not to be comprehended distinctly in order to produce love and affection in the soul; it is like to faith, whereby we love God without comprehending Him."

This is an admirable page. Here is proclaimed the essential ineffability of "poetry," or, more exactly, of its origin, of the pre-poetic state. San Juan de la Cruz affirms, directly or indirectly, that: 1. Love is his theme. His subject is "sayings of love." 2. Love cannot be said, it cannot be expressed in words, it is ineffable. (Since language requires so many logical conditions, some part of what is not rational thought cannot be fitted into the sentence or discourse.) 3. From this inevitable impossibility of finding an equivalent in words is deduced the necessity for poetry. When love is expressed, its object escapes. But in a partial attempt it can be caught. How? By poetic circumlocution; and thus, with "figures, comparisons and similitudes" one can suggest something of the "secret mysteries." Poetry, then, will be resolved in figurative language: comparisons, metaphors, symbols. Language then overflows its intellectual limits. 4. From this it follows that, in the light of reason, a "figure" can seem to be "nonsense." A poem is never "the expression of reason." 5. Therefore it cannot be completely understood or completely explained. The understanding of a poem does not exhaust its content. To the essential ineffability of a poem there corresponds an essential unintelligibility. San Juan de la Cruz does not pretend to limit his "song" to its "declaration" or explanation. The commentary is presented modestly, with no pretense of dominating the verses being commented on. As a consequence, each reader will enter fully and at his ease through the gates of poetry. "The sayings of love are better left in their fullness."

San Juan de la Cruz's allusions to the impossibility of expressing such and such a state of spirit in verse or in prose are numerous. "For only he that passes this way can understand it, and even he cannot describe it," he forewarns in the prologue of the *Ascent of Mount Carmel*. "It is like one," he says again in *Dark Night of the Soul*, "who sees something never seen before, whereof he has not even seen the like; although he might understand its nature and have experience of it, he would be unable to give it a name or say what it is," even if he had perceived it with the senses; "how much less, then, could he describe a thing that has not entered through the senses!" And he sums up: "the language of God . . . transcends every sense." Further on he explains it: "the language of God to the soul [is] addressed by pure spirit to pure spirit," so that "naught that is less than spirit, such as the senses, can perceive it . . . , neither can they say it." The soul can only have recourse to insufficient "general terms." On the other hand, experiences "of a particular kind, such as visions, feelings, etc.," affect the senses, and therefore do not resist expression. But "how base and defective, and, in some measure, how inapt, are all the terms and words which are used . . . to treat of Divine things," which are always secret. The unintelligible is ineffable: "for, as it is not understood, so neither can it be expressed — although . . . it can be felt." And in the prologue to the *Flame*: "spirit transcends sense and it is with difficulty that anything can be said of the substance

92

thereof. For it is hard to speak of that which passes in the depths of the spirit." Experience is as far removed from expression "as is a picture from a living person." This reservation is found at every turn. If the mystic experience is situated beyond reason and imagination, then from the incomprehensible nature of the divine must follow the inadequacy of the human voice. Thus, in his commentary on the stanza of the *Flame* beginning: "Oh lamps of fiery blaze," the saint affirms: "All that can be said in this stanza is less than what there is to be said, for the transformation of the soul in God is indescribable."

In this respect, the Spanish mystic claims to be continuing Biblical tradition. The Old and New Testaments are his great masters in poetry also. "For the incapacity of man to speak of it and describe it in words was shown by Jeremiah, when, after God had spoken with him, he knew not what to say, save 'Ah, ah, ah!' This . . . incapacity . . . was also demonstrated in the case of Moses, when he stood before God in the bush . . . [there] did he say to God that after speaking with Him he knew not neither was able to speak." A similar example: "Let us say what Christ said of it to Saint John in the Apocalypse, using many terms and words and comparisons, on seven occasions: since "that" cannot comprehensively be described in one word, or on one occasion; because even after all those occasions much still remains unsaid."

IV

These Biblical examples corroborate an experience. And what an experience! San Juan de la Cruz began by living a most extraordinary adventure, and from the emotion it caused emerged the poem. This friar, so slight in build, whom Saint Teresa called *Senequita*, "Little Seneca," did not, to be sure, take part in the conquest of the Indies, nor suffer the hardships of the open road in rough weather, nor even leave his own little corner, or himself. And because of this, not in spite of it, he has a great deal to tell. How does he tell it? Not only through poetry. He also thinks it out in the form of concepts, and this analysis he sets forth as "mystical theology." This theology, "the science of love," "a most savory science," is held immeasurably apart from the adventure that was lived so deep within him.

No one, perhaps, has traveled further than San Juan along the road to mysticism. No one has analyzed it more profoundly than he has in his four treatises, especially in the first two, so audacious, so extreme, so ferocious: the *Subida del Monte Carmelo* (*Ascent of Mount Carmel*) and the *Noche oscura del alma* (*Dark Night of the Soul*). San Juan surrenders himself to his vocation, the most daring one of all, even though he is well aware of the principles opposing it: "it is lawful for no creature," he states in the *Ascent*, "to pass beyond the limits that God has ordained for His governance after the order of nature. In His governance of man He has laid down rational and natural limits; wherefore to desire to pass beyond them is not lawful, and to desire to seek out and attain to anything by supernatural means is to go beyond these natural limits." In another passage he emphasizes the same idea: "For it is this that Solomon meant when he said: What need has a man to desire and seek the things that are above his natural capacity? As though we were to say: He has no necessity, in order to be perfect, to desire supernatural things by supernatural means, which are above his capacity." A trenchant affirmation. But San Juan interpreted it in his own way, and did not hesitate to embark on this supernatural journey. Clinging to religious tradition and reinforcing his personal observations with quotations from Holy Scripture, which is to say without ever permitting himself any possible deviation

94

from orthodoxy, San Juan recounts his ascension toward God, to God, the most dolorous and difficult ever attempted by man. "All that the imagination can imagine and the understanding can receive and understand in this life is not, nor can it be, a proximate means of union with God." To the intelligence of the favored person those things remain secret which always lie beyond all clear and distinct intellection: "Be thou never willingly satisfied with that which thou understandest of God, but rather with that which thou understandest not of Him." But will there not be, on the road toward God, some supernatural revelation to appeal to the imagination or fancy? No, not this either: "God is not communicated to the soul by means of any disguise of imaginary vision or similitude or form . . . ; but mouth to mouth — that is, in the naked and pure essence of God." The soul progressively nullifies "the forms and imagining of things." Jean Baruzi, a friend whom I remember with fervent affection and admiration, called them "distinct apprehensions." (For San Juan they are "distinct kinds of understanding" in *Living Flame* III, 48.) Not even revelations are received with pleasure: "How much more precious in God's sight is one work or act of the will performed in charity than are all the visions and communications that they may receive from Heaven, since these imply neither merit nor demerit." Nor are the "locutions" heard during prayer admissible, however spiritual they may be. San Juan insists that "all the visions, revelations and sentiments of heaven . . . are of less worth than the least act of humility." To sum up: "These things may hinder the soul greatly in its progress to Divine union because, if it pay heed to them, it is led far astray from the abyss of faith, where the understanding must remain in darkness, and must journey in darkness, by love and in faith, and not by much reasoning." No mystic is so austere, so unencumbered by supernatural anecdote as San

95

Juan de la Cruz, who is violently opposed to visions of any kind, always fearful lest they proceed from the devil and always hostile even on the hypothesis that they are inspired by the Divinity. And why should we trouble to distinguish whether they are demoniacal or divine? The saint concludes emphatically and almost with impatience: "By paying no heed to visions, and refusing to receive them, all this is prevented, and the soul acts as it should."

We must detach ourselves from things and causes in order to arrive at the First Cause. "Wherefore, though all things smile upon a man and all that he does turns out prosperously, he ought to have misgivings rather than to rejoice." And Ecclesiastes corroborates the saint in this: "The heart of the fool, says the Wise Man, is where there is gladness, but that of the wise man is where there is sorrow." Let there be no road that does not lead to night, "even though the world perish." Everything is dissolved into night, or rather, into a succession of nights. "The first purgation or night is bitter and terrible to sense . . . The second bears no comparison with it, for it is horrible and awful to the spirit." In this second night, the spirit is "as one who has been imprisoned in a dark dungeon, and is bound hand and foot, and can neither move nor see, nor feel any favour whether from above or from below, until the spirit is humbled, softened and purified, and grows so keen and delicate and pure that it can become one with the Spirit of God." Total night, absolute night: "the darkness which it here suffers is profound and horrible and most painful, for this darkness, being felt in the deepest substance of the spirit, seems to be substantial darkness." So that "in the horror of nocturnal vision," as San Juan quotes from the Book of Job, first comes the emptying of the soul of any particular content, in supreme indistinctness, thus preparing it for the supreme contact and the supreme metamorphosis. "This cup is the

96

death of the natural self, which is attained through the soul's detachment and annihilation, in order that the soul may travel by this narrow path." The terrible word "annihilation" is repeated: "the one thing that is needful, which is the ability to deny oneself truly, . . . giving oneself up to . . . total annihilation." Does this lead to "the destruction of the natural use . . . of the faculties" and reduce man "to the state of a beast"? Man, reduced to his own nature, would be worth nothing. And yet, "One single thought of a man is of greater worth than the whole world." The spirit is of such great worth that "God alone is worthy of him."

The creature has now been purged of his condition as a creature, and life is reduced to the consciousness of an emptiness which is inhuman — and which is to become, at last, superhuman. For now the light of God arrives at the frightful rendez-vous. What happens then? "A deed so heroic and so rare" as the soul's being "united with its Divine Beloved." There is no vision, no exploration. The soul does not prepare to see or to know: it wishes only to love — in a way beyond the ways and acts of a human creature, who destroys himself as a creature to the greatest degree compatible with the preservation of life and of consciousness. Almost lost in what is almost Nothingness, he will be united with the Beginning of All. An ill-treated son, he will be absorbed into the Father. And if God is man in Christ — the mystery of the Incarnation — man will unite with God and will be God — the mystery of what is almost a De-Incarnation — when, the will of the soul having been transformed into the will of God, all is now the will of God, and "the soul is made Divine and becomes God by participation." This is the final "serene night," the end of the other, the dark night: it is "total transformation in the Beloved," "even as when the light of the star or of the candle is joined and united with that of the sun, so that that which shines is not the star or the candle but the sun, which has absorbed the other lights in itself." The creature in San Juan de la Cruz, the most daring in all Creation, has been redeemed, while still on earth, of its condition as a creature: it now enjoys the "swiftness that is needful for one that would attain to Him" to rise from the Spiritual Betrothal to the Spiritual Marriage. Then the soul becomes "a Paradise watered by springs Divine," and "with great readiness and frequency the Spouse reveals His wondrous secrets to the soul, as to His faithful consort . . . He communicates principally to it sweet mysteries concerning His Incarnation and the ways and manners of human redemption." Incarnation, De-Incarnation: an absolute circle. "For in this state the soul sees that God truly belongs to it, and that it possesses Him with hereditary possession, with rightful ownership, as an adopted child of God." Thus the mystic life reaches its fulfillment: through a gradual, very long, very arduous operation of enthusiasm. "Enthusiasm" in its etymological meaning: "Deifying [the] substance [of the soul] and making it Divine, wherein the Being of God absorbs the soul above all being." And just as if it were human love, which is to say exclusive, "it believes that He has no other soul in the world to favour thus, nor aught else wherewith to occupy Himself, but that He is wholly for itself alone. And, when it feels this, it confesses its feeling like the Bride in the words of the Songs: *Dilectus meus mihi et ego illi.*"

v

Neither on the negative journey of purgation nor at its affirmative conclusion in union, neither in the horror nor in the bliss are there revelations that can be communicated. There could hardly be any in this poetry, which is not presented as a travel diary or as a direct psychological document. San Juan de la Cruz does not impart a vision that has been

98

lived, as does the visionary bard, for none of the symbols in these poems is a "vision"; nor does he communicate his dreams, like the dreamer of a later period. And surely it would be absurd to think in terms of an all-important subconscious. San Juan's inner life, always super-conscious, never brings forth formless bits or fragments that are base, ugly, or capricious. Our poet will never remain content with

> Un no sé qué que quedan balbuciendo.
> *A nameless "something" they keep stammering.*

This verse, famous for its triple repetition of the syllable *que* (obviously intentional), expresses most felicitously one stage in the real experience — a stage that must be excelled by poetry. The saint has found "a most lofty understanding of God, which cannot be expressed, and for that reason is called a 'something.'" But the poet does not confine himself to "stammering." For "to stammer" means "to talk as do children, and not to convey and express perfectly that which they have to say." San Juan de la Cruz is the least infantile of poets. Poetry cannot be either stammering or a mere interjection. (Though the interjection, a word without intellectual content, may suit the inexpressible content very well: " . . . the soul would fain speak, yet speaks not, but keeps this esteem in its heart, and in its mouth the wonder implied in this word 'Oh,' saying: 'Oh, delectable wound!' ")

Nothing could be further removed from San Juan de la Cruz than any form of automatic writing, so often found in mystics. The Blessed Angela de Foligno (1248–1309) dictated in her *Memoriale* to Fray Arnoldo, her relative, confessor, and secretary, what she called her "secret mysteries." Of all her words Fray Arnaldo understood only *le più grosse*. When he read back to her the text he had taken down, the Blessed Angela considered it quite inadequate: "but of the most precious things my soul has felt, you have written nothing." Or, as her secretary said in his rude Latin: *sed de precioso quod sentit anima nihil scripsisti.* Fray Arnaldo had to set down in great haste words that were spoken in a trance. Thus the *Memoriale* is the product of a double agitation: that of the woman who was inspired, and the scribe's. Saint Catherine of Siena (1347–1380) also dictated while in ecstasy. There were three, perhaps even more than three secretaries writing whenever she soared "into abstraction, having lost all her senses, save that of language," one of her disciples assures us. Thus was composed "in a short time" her *Libro della Divina Dottrina, volgarmente detto Dialogo della Divina Provvidenza.* In this sublime manner, "carried away from her physical senses," the nun of Siena composed her mystical treatise. The *Aurora* of Jacob Böhme (1575–1624) was also the result of automatic composition. "Art has not written here," the author himself tells us. "All was set down according to the directing of the Spirit, which often came swiftly. The burning fire often advanced with great velocity, and the hand and pen had to move before it with anxious haste." Inspiration was imposed, then, "like a sudden storm." San Juan de la Cruz, on the other hand, does not let himself be carried away. No one dictates his words or suggests his images to him. He is the exact opposite of such a visionary poet as William Blake (1757–1827), who, through his "celestial friends," wrote "twelve or sometimes twenty or thirty lines without premeditation and even against my will." San Juan never felt himself, like Blake, "really drunk with intellectual vision," nor did he pretend to be only a secretary. His habits as a writer and his Christian humility would not have allowed him to say of his poems: "The authors are in Eternity."

It is important to emphasize this contrast, for it makes more obvious the originality of San Juan de la Cruz, who is a perfect model of a creator when he sets out to suggest what does not admit revelations. How could one convey something of this love that is without ideas, without images, without words, but by a re-creation that is totally independent, based on the words, images, and ideas of the human creature? From the ineffable state we leap lightly to the most rigorous creation. San Juan de la Cruz is forced to invent a world for himself, and his inexpressible intuitions will be objectified in images and rhythms. They are "a solitude full of sound" (*soledad sonora*): "without imagination there is no feeling." It is indeed amazing that a single human being should have achieved the conquest of perfection in these two realms: the religious and the poetic. For, if San Juan as a saint can hardly be judged an apprentice, as a poet his professional mastery astounds us. It does not seem likely, as the exquisite French musician Eric Satie used to assert, that many great artists have been amateurs. San Juan wrote very little, and never considered himself a professional poet; but no trace of amateurishness is to be found in these masterful poems.

From the mystic origin come the impulse, the passion, a sublime quality of soul. That inner crisis which the saint calls "love of God" is not comparable to any habitual erotic phenomenon, and the reader — necessarily humble, if he is a good reader, whether or not he is a good believer — bows before the unique and always unknown character of that process that begins in night and ends in flame. Without this real process there would be no poem, even though the impossible revelation is only indirectly transferred to the poem — so indirectly that only the emotions and their modulations are transferred, not their subject matter. The sacred part of the experience remains fundamentally unknowable to the profane reader. He is separated by an abyss from the metaphoric harmonies, which "reveal" nothing. The three great poems contain nothing but images: unreal, concrete representations relating a story of love. Nothing abstract intrudes on their story, which is reduced to the motions and emotions of a pair of lovers. The action is completely free of explanatory accompaniment. We behold the Bride and the Bridegroom, we behold their transports. And the narrative is autonomous, sufficient unto itself as a narrative in almost all the verses. What meaning is hidden beneath this marvel? For the moment, we behold only the marvel with its first horizon and its infinite distances and poetic resonances.

Can any traces of abstraction be discerned? In the *Spiritual Canticle* we find:

> Nuestro lecho florido,
> De cuevas de leones enlazado,
> En púrpura tendido,
> De paz edificado,
> De mil escudos de oro coronado.

> *Now flowers the marriage bed*
> *With dens of lions fortified around it,*
> *With tent of purple spread,*
> *In peace securely founded,*
> *And by a thousand shields of gold surmounted.*

This web of images, highly plastic ones, reveals only one abstract component: "peace." "In peace securely founded." Conceptual antithesis is even more rare. In the *Flame:*

> Matando, muerte en vida la has trocado.
> *And change my death to life, even while killing.*

This antithesis, if isolated, does not sound to us like San Juan de la Cruz, because he does not usually inject intellectual play or ingenious word-crosses between our fascinated attention and the life he has made immediately concrete. If as a mystic he was forced to disassociate his night and his love from any trace of the anecdotal, later as a poet he was forced to

102

have recourse to the sternly rejected "imagination or fancy" in order to allude to the ultimately inconceivable and inexpressible indistinctions. By means of this contradiction San Juan was able to make the transition from his life to his poetry. The mystic relegated to the category of possessions of the senses that "interior fabric of the imaginative discourse" that is to be the fabric of the poem. *Oh ninfas de Judea*, "Oh nymphs of Judea!" exclaims the saint in one verse of the *Spiritual Canticle*. What do these historically hybrid women signify? "By Judea she means the lower part of the soul, which is that of the senses. . . . And by nymphs she means all the imaginations, fancies and motions and affections of this lower part," he explains in the commentary. Although the saint shut these nymphs outside, "in the outskirts" — "And do not dare to pass across our threshold," — the poet calls out from the threshold to the creatures thus rejected; and, thanks to them, the verse comes into being. In the verse there "finds a foothold" what is referred to in the *Flame* with stern disdain as *el gitano del sentido*, "the Egyptian of sense," which is another way of saying "the gypsy of sense." Just what can the degree of mysticism be of a work that has been forcibly "gypsified"?

VI

Images, symbols, allegories . . . Jean Baruzi, distinguishing perspicaciously between the functions of symbol and of allegory, sees among the symbols used by San Juan some that are intimately related to the mystic experience itself. Successive states of the first stage are held in a single image: "dark night." A psychologist would need many pages to explain the reason for the darkness of this night. Similarly, a series of spiritual happenings is caught up in a single primordial intuition, "flame." "Oh living flame of love." In both these cases, the

103

symbol originates from the vital impulse itself, without bene-
fit of any elaboration. San Juan de la Cruz has not sought out,
with a sheet of paper before him and pen in hand, the similes
of night and flame. In reality, in his most profound reality, the
mystic turned poet — for how can the two be separated at
such a moment? — has lived his dark night and his flame of
love. "There must have been so intimate a fusion of image
and experience," Jean Baruzi says, "that we could no longer
speak of an effort to depict an inner drama visually. Symbolism
would reveal to us, perhaps directly, a fact that no other way
of thinking would allow us to grasp. And as a result there
would not be translation of an experience by a symbol; there
would be, in the strictest sense of the word, *symbolic experience*." Among the unreal images used by the poet, if this hypothesis is true, these symbols have imposed themselves upon
him: they are the only points of immediate continuity between
his life and his poetry. (A continuity doubtless not unknown
to other poets less carried away by inspiration.) In any case,
this kind of image is to be found only at the bubbling up of
the fountainhead, and its study belongs to a story of genesis.
Within the poem, "night," "flame," and who knows what
other components are set apart free of any trace of biography,
and they will appear transferred and made subject to the completely new atmosphere created by the other images that are
purely invented, whether under the dictates of fate or as the
result of free choice.

And what of allegory? The mystic experience has been followed by crystal-clear consciousness, and many hours' reflec-
tions are gradually ordered into a systematic interpretation.
Later, with the ineffable experience, the first symbols, the first
intellectual outlines as his point of departure, San Juan de la
Cruz composes the poem. He also draws up a commentary in
which he develops the doctrine implicit in it, and adds other

further speculations. The commentary reveals that beneath the poetic meaning there lies another occult and allegorical one adjusted to the doctrine. These two meanings, very carefully fitted together and dependent on each other, do not interfere with one another. The more abstract thought — what could be called, using a coarse and in this case brutal word, the didactic foundation — does not diminish the grace of the fountainhead as it bubbles forth. It is incredible, but true: all this lyricism conceals another side which is meticulously reasoned out. This is what San Juan calls *el acomodado sentido*, "the accommodated meaning." ("But the accommodated meaning of this line is that the soul . . .") The poem unfolds as if it were invariably subservient to the most calculatedly premeditated allegory. Can such surprising wealth of poetry have been born in the shadow of such premeditation?

Let us recall, in the *Spiritual Canticle*:

> Ni temeré las fieras,
> Y pasaré los fuertes y fronteras.

> *. . . nor for fear*
> *Of prowling beasts [I'll] delay,*
> *But pass through forts and frontiers on my way.*

This dramatic narrative has another meaning underlying it: "In these lines the Bride speaks of the three enemies of the soul, which are world, devil and flesh . . . By the 'wild beasts' she understands the world; by the 'mighty' ['forts'], the devil; and by the 'frontiers,' the flesh." This correspondence between image and meaning rests on a rational foundation. The thinker-poet gives a reason for everything. "She calls the world 'wild beasts' because . . ." — and a prolix discourse follows. "Evil spirits . . . she calls the mighty, because with a great display of strength they endeavour to seize the passes of this road; likewise because . . ." And so on. By "frontiers," "she indicates the repugnance which the flesh has of its nature to the spirit and the rebellions which it makes against it." This mutual adaptation of the poetic and the nonpoetic, which are fitted together so logically, is constant. At times theory seems to have favored the creation of the image:

> Y pacerá el Amado entre las flores.
> *And the Beloved shall pasture among the flowers.*

The author observes: "And it is fitting to note here that the soul says not that the Beloved will pasture 'upon' the flowers, but 'among' the flowers"; "it is upon the soul itself that He pastures, transforming it into Himself, when it is prepared and seasoned and made fragrant with the aforementioned flowers of virtues and gifts and perfections . . ."; "for this is the habit of the Spouse, to unite Himself with the soul amid the fragrance of these flowers." Is it not probable that this vision, this "among," alludes to an experience that has been thought out intellectually? Let us also remember the *Song of Songs*. The author himself indicates his sources. "My Beloved is gone down into His garden . . . to pasture . . . and to gather lilies." "I am my Beloved's and my Beloved is mine: He feedeth among the lilies." It is impossible to know, however, what the precise source of the final image was: "And the Beloved shall pasture among the flowers." Does an act of creation really have a source?

San Juan de la Cruz wishes to introduce what he calls, in his philosophical vocabulary, "the imaginative fancy," "the two natural faculties . . . which are those of wrath and concupiscence," "the three faculties of the soul — memory, understanding and will," and "the four passions of the soul — namely: joy, hope, grief and fear." Obviously it would not be feasible to invent suitable images through rational deduction.

106

The creator must fling himself into pure, unreal space. And he exclaims:

> A las aves ligeras,
> Leones, ciervos, gamos saltadores,
> Montes, valles, riberas,
> Aguas, aires, ardores,
> Y miedos de las noches veladores:
>
> *You birds with airy wings,*
> *Lions, and stags, and roebucks leaping light,*
> *Hills, valleys, creeks, and springs,*
> *Waves, winds, and ardours bright,*
> *And fears that rule the watches of the night:*

What lightness and agility in a setting of the brightest profusion! Yet everything signifies, in addition, something else: "He calls the digressions of the imagination birds of swift wing, since they are light and subtle in their flight first to one place and then to another." Here we have the allegory and the reason for the allegory. "By the lions He understands the acrimonies and impetuosities of the irascible faculty, which faculty is as bold and daring in its acts as are lions. And by the harts and the leaping does is understood the other faculty of the soul, which is the concupiscible — that is, the power of the desire." Up to here, it is easy to perceive the allegoric structure. At other times the relation is very distant. "Mountains, valleys, banks. By these three names He denotes the vicious and disordered acts of the three faculties of the soul, which are memory, understanding and will." And "the affections of the four passions, which, as we have said, are grief, hope, joy and fear" are represented in the last two lines of the stanza: "Waves, winds, and ardours bright, / And fears that rule the watches of the night." This unexpected and flashing nocturne, still trembling and phosphorescing, has surged up in the bosom

107

of creation *in order to* close a series of enumerations of a theoretical nature. Or did creation come first, and theory afterward?
Thus the greatest of mystic poets gives a running explanation
of his poetry, or rather of his allegories: images entwined with
concepts, translatable into abstractions.

In some way that we cannot determine, the poet has acted
along with the thinker. Actually, in order to penetrate into
the terrain of the poet, do we need the permission of the
thinker? The poet sings in human terms in such a way that
they captivate in and by themselves, for the mystical-allegorical
meaning remains outside, anterior and posterior to the poetry
itself, to its own poetic being. As we read the *Spiritual Canticle* let us heed its only values, the symbolic values, within a
terrestrial atmosphere, without thinking of the possible conceptual allegories, which are wholly, or almost wholly, foreign
to the poetic sphere.

VII

> ¿A dónde te escondiste?
> *Where can your hiding be?*

And the Beloved appears in a simile:

> Como el ciervo huiste.
> *While like the stag you flee.*

This animal and his flight, amid waves of poetic suggestion
whose farthest reach cannot be determined with exactness, are
expressing the dolorous situation of the enamored bride without her beloved. The bride suffers as if she were wounded:

> Habiéndome herido.
> *Leaving the wound with me.*

The symbolic import of these verses is clear. It is entirely
within the order of the profane, for this poetry does not offer

108

any other. The reader, alone with the poem, cannot pass beyond to the order of the divine. It is not here, in such symbols as these, that the allegory is to be found which the author, and only the author, can indicate, for it exists only in his private mind, and not objectively in the text. In his commentary the saint takes us into his confidence and tells us that "beside many other different kinds of visit which God makes to the soul . . . He is wont to bestow on it certain hidden touches of love, which like a fiery arrow strike and pierce the soul and leave it wholly cauterized with the fire of love; and these are properly called the wounds of love."

Here is another example. The symbol of the caverns, or caves, transports us with moving resonances to the retreat to which the lovers have withdrawn.

> Y luego a las subidas
> Cavernas de la piedra nos iremos.
>
> *Then climb to lofty places*
> *Among the caves and boulders of the granite.*

But the allegory tells us: "The rock of which she here speaks . . . is Christ. The lofty caverns of this rock are the lofty and high and deep mysteries of the wisdom of God which are in Christ . . ." ("Caverns of the rock," as San Juan himself indicates, appears in *Exodus*.)

> Y allí nos entraremos,
>
> *And, entering . . .*

"There shall we enter — that is, into that knowledge and those Divine mysteries . . ."

> Y el mosto de granadas gustaremos.
>
> *And revel in the wine of the pomegranate.*

"The pomegranates here signify the mysteries of Christ, and the judgments of the wisdom of God, and the virtues and attributes of God." Let it be observed, moreover, that God "is signified by the spherical or circular figure," typical of the pomegranate, "because it has no beginning or end."

Only the author can present these elucidations. From the poetic phrasing it is impossible to infer the allegory, for it is not located within, like the marrow of its bones, but is mounted on air. This free-standing edifice, allegory, corresponds to the other edifice, poetry, the only one set securely on the reality of words. Has there been mutual influence between creation and construction — the creation of poetry and the construction of a system? We do not possess enough information about the genesis of these works to say. To what extent has the rational interpretation of those ineffable mystic states intervened in the inspired process of poetic composition? Love lived, exalted in verse, and scrutinized in prose: the relation among these three modalities must have been one of unprecedented complexity, the knowledge of which escapes us. San Juan, mystic, poet, thinker, resolved them all in consummate unity.

This unity is achieved without any of its elements — life, poetry, doctrine — getting in each other's way. This explains why the second meaning, the allegorical, belongs to the realm of intention. And intention, as Croce has demonstrated more than once, is reduced to an act of will "by which it is decreed that this must signify that." Sometimes the two things are kept close together: "lion" refers to "strength," "fox" to "cunning." San Juan de la Cruz is unusually successful in keeping his poetry almost completely uncontaminated by allegory. It should be noted that what is operating here is not the intention of the poet as a poet. San Juan declares his intention — as a psychologist — of adding a conceptual meaning to his lyrical expression. This, then, is a poem of mystic origin (biography) and of mystic intent (allegory). Strictly speaking it

110

is a nonmystical poem, and irremediably so, for the ineffable experience and the theoretical mechanism both remain outside it.

Even so, there are exceptions. There are moments when this continuous metaphor of human love cannot withstand the violence of the occult love that is its origin, and something new bursts into the poetic sphere at a height that is not human.

> ¡Oh noche que juntaste
> Amado con Amada,
> Amada en el Amado transformada!

> *Oh night that joined the lover*
> *To the beloved bride,*
> *Transfiguring them each into the other!*

The last line expresses the great metamorphosis in the same words as the prose sentence of the *Dark Night*. Such an affirmation could not appear even as hyperbole in any story of purely human love.

> Oh bosques y espesuras,
> Plantadas por la mano del Amado.

> *Oh thickets, densely trammeled,*
> *Which my love's hand has sown along the height.*

The Beloved does not appear here as a simple shepherd in a bucolic setting. He is a Beloved who plants, that is to say, who creates, thickets and woods. The tacit meaning overshadows the unfolding of the human story, which is already superhuman in some verses difficult to decipher without the divine key:

> ¡Oh cristalina fuente,
> Si en esos tus semblantes plateados,
> Formases de repente
> Los ojos deseados,
> Que tengo en mis entrañas dibujados!

Oh brook of crystal sheen,
Could you but cause, upon your silver fine,
Suddenly to be seen
The eyes for which I pine
Which in my inmost heart my thoughts design!

Let us remember the "Reply of the Creatures":

Mil gracias derramando,
Pasó por estos sotos con presura,
Y yéndolos mirando,
Con sola su figura
Vestidos los dejó de hermosura.

Diffusing showers of grace,
In haste among these groves his path he took,
And only with his face,
Glancing around the place,
Has clothed them in his beauty with a look.

This, if it were to be taken as praise in the usual sense, would be only a rhetorical exaggeration of no particular interest. But its lyrical interest increases greatly if we understand it as love of God, as it is known and felt by a Bride who is already more than human. On one occasion the allegory is patent. Stanza twenty-nine of the *Spiritual Canticle* permits no interpretation but the religious one of original sin and Christian redemption.

Debajo del manzano,
Allí conmigo fuiste desposada,
Allí te dí la mano,
Y fuiste reparada
Donde tu madre fuera violada.

Beneath the apple-tree,
You came to swear your troth and to be mated,
Gave there your hand to me,
And have been new-created
There where your mother first was violated.

112

The saint elucidates with great precision: "even as by means of the forbidden tree of Paradise she [the soul] was ruined and corrupted in her human nature through Adam, even so upon the tree of the Cross she was redeemed and restored, by His giving her the hand of His favour and mercy, through His death and passion, and raising the barriers that came from original sin between the soul and God." The commentary on the individual lines makes even clearer the only meaning the stanza offers: " 'Beneath the apple-tree.' That is, beneath the favour of the tree of the Cross, which is here understood by the apple-tree." " 'And thou wert redeemed where thy mother had been corrupted.' For thy mother, human nature, was corrupted in thy first parents beneath the tree, and there likewise wert thou redeemed — namely, beneath the tree of the Cross." Under this heavy burden of allegory, it must be admitted, poetry has difficulty in subsisting.

In some passages it is the author-critic who establishes the correct reading.

> Con llama que consume y no da pena.
>
> *With fire that can consume yet do no harm.*

"To consume signifies here to complete and to perfect." In other words, "consume" means "consummate."

> En la interior bodega
> De mi Amado bebí . . .
>
> *In the inner cellar*
> *Of my Beloved have I drunk . . .*

No, there is no question of drinking in the inner cellar of the Beloved. San Juan means, and indeed says: "In the inner cellar I have drunk of my Beloved." In other words: "even so is this communication from God diffused substantially," and, the soul having been transformed into God, "the soul drinks

113

of its God according to its substance and its spiritual faculties."
The metaphor presupposes, then, a spiritual experience, a
knowledge of wine, and a reading of the Bible. To be sure,
there would be no metaphor if all these precedents and components had not been fused and illuminated by poetic grace.

At times the commentary clarifies the primary meaning of
the verse.

> En par de los levantes de la aurora.
>
> *Before the dawn comes round.*

In other words: "the night at the time of [the] rising [of the
dawn] is neither wholly night nor wholly day, but, as men say,
'between two lights.'" In exceptional cases, the literal meaning is not sufficiently autonomous to be clear, as here in the
final stanza:

> Que nadie lo miraba,
> Aminadab tampoco parecía,
> Y el cerco sosegaba,
> Y la caballería
> A vista de las aguas descendía.
>
> *With none our peace offending,*
> *Aminadab has vanished with his slaughters:*
> *And now the siege had ending,*
> *The cavalcades descending*
> *Were seen within the precinct of the waters.*

What does this mean? It is an enigma that cannot be deci-
phered until we seek enlightenment from the only person possessing the allegorical key. According to the saint, the Bride
"says five things. The first thing is that her soul is detached
and far away from all things. The second, that the devil [Ami-
nadab] has now been conquered and put to flight. The third,
that the passions are now held in bondage and the natural desires are mortified. The fourth and fifth, that the lower and
sensual part of the soul has now been reformed and purified

114

and has been brought into conformity with the spiritual part."
Without this counterpoint we should not understand the ending of the poem, for the ending is purely mystical, carrying us
beyond the pastoral narrative, and to a greater height — from
the point of view of religion, though not of poetry — than the
human level on which the eclogue of love has been unfolding.

VIII

Although the mystic spirit thus imposes itself in the field
of erotic images, the *Dark Night of the Soul,* the *Spiritual
Canticle,* and the *Living Flame of Love* exist as a group of
independent songs, or almost independent, with an almost
complete coherence of metaphor, so continuous that it ceases
to be metaphor and becomes the relating of adventures and
exalting of emotions, especially in the *Dark Night* and the
Flame. This brings us, then, to the conclusion that San Juan
de la Cruz, the greatest poet of all the mystics, composed
poems which it is customary to consider mystical for reasons
that are biographical and allegorical, on the basis of a combined reading of the prose and poetry which superimposes the
commentaries on the verses. Our purely poetic reading does
not take anything away from the poems, which are indeed
poems, and admirable ones, without biography or allegory.
Their poetic value is not heightened by being turned toward
the conceptual. Let us recall the nocturnal scene in which the
Betrothed goes forth to seek her Beloved "In darkness . . .
Concealed from other eyes." This exquisite nocturnal atmosphere would be dissipated if the soul that traversed it were
"in hiding and in concealment from the devil and from his
wiles and stratagems." In the *Spiritual Canticle,* the "wall"
that is so significant and suggestive when it protects a woman
dissolves poetically when "by the wall is understood the fence
of peace and the rampart of virtues and perfections wherewith

the same soul is now fenced around and guarded." Let us turn again to the *Flame,* and the exclamations of that summit of love:

> ¡Oh cauterio suave! . . .
> ¡Oh mano blanda! ¡Oh toque delicado,
>
> *Oh cautery most tender! . . .*
> *Oh gentle hand! Oh touch how softly thrilling!*

But we cease to hear these sighing "oh's" of bliss when they are explained thus: "The 'burn' is the Holy Spirit, the 'hand' is the Father and the 'touch,' the Son." Even the images, sometimes so surprising, that appear in the commentary suffer the same fate: "the fragrance of the water-lilies from the sounding rivers, which we said were the greatness of God."

But if the allegory is not perceptible to the reader, and its rational content does not increase the poetic attainment, the biography — that is to say, the fact of the actual mystic trance — does cling to the poems. The mere knowledge that the author wishes to express something else, and that this purpose is based on a profound experience, is enough to cause the formation of a sort of spiritual accompaniment, though not a conceptual one. An air is insinuated into the verses that gives them a significance at once human and divine. Everything appears circled by a halo, and a mysterious reality maintains communication with the first horizon, which, whether nocturnal or diurnal, is always extremely human. The three poems then are enfolded in an atmosphere that would be very difficult to disperse, and a substantial resonance is added to the song of love. The song in this way is distorted, twisted, turned aside from its strict meaning — not without being enriched in the process. For impurity enriches. We find certain religious harmonics existing along with the composition's own music.

116

While "the music without sound" or "the solitude that clamours" sound unceasingly, from the darkness comes a solemn organ accompaniment. Its solemnity is not defined, and thus, gravely, it vaguely prolongs the mystery of those extraordinary words the Bride speaks as if she were not breaking the silence.

> Mi Amado las montañas,
> Los valles solitarios nemorosos,
> Las ínsulas extrañas,
> Los ríos sonorosos,
> El silbo de los aires amorosos.

> La noche sosegada
> En par de los levantes de la aurora,
> La música callada,
> La soledad sonora,
> La cena que recrea y enamora.

> *My Love's the mountain range,*
> *The valleys each with solitary grove,*
> *The islands far and strange,*
> *The streams with sounds that change,*
> *The whistling of the lovesick winds that rove.*

> *Before the dawn comes round*
> *Here is the night, dead-hushed with all its glamours,*
> *The music without sound,*
> *The solitude that clamours,*
> *The supper that revives us and enamours.*

How should the first of these lines be written? Literally translated, it reads: "My Beloved the mountains." Should we put a comma or semicolon between "My Beloved" and "the mountains"? Or supply, as a grammarian would say we should, the verb *to be*? To write "My Beloved is the mountains," adding nothing further — might that not be an absurdity that could be considered heretical? But the solution found in some translations is worse: "My Beloved is like the mountains," an

117

interpretation both incorrect and vulgar. Nevertheless, "is" appears in the explanation of the individual lines. Since "each of these grandeurs which are spoken of is God, and they are all of them God," San Juan states in his commentary, "these mountains my Beloved is to me." But all that matters to us in the poem is its poetry. Let us hold to the verse just as we find it, with a pause that has no equal: *Mi Amado   las montañas,* "My Beloved   the mountains." If we read religiously, though without teleological lucubrations, this blank, this moment of silence, between the Beloved and the mountains designates and offers something transcending earthly love. Seen in this light, the mountains, islands, streams, and lovesick winds are not gathered solely to weave the garland that is dedicated to the Eros of each new spring. These expressions thus related and directed are situated on a level superior to man's love. When they transport us with a tone of prayer, these poems can indeed be called mystical. Strictly speaking, with complete theoretical rigor, they are not, they cannot be mystical. The almost perfect autonomy of the images, so continuously referring to human love, admits neither the evocation of the experience, which is not conceivable or revealable, nor the interposing of thought upheld by allegorical scaffoldings outside the poetic structure. In spite of the truth, in a synthetic reading — synthesizing all the writings of San Juan — the "loving desires" which poetically are profane will become, when directed to God, "a pillar of smoke that issues from the aromatic spices of myrrh and incense." Smoke in an aura. An aura, very light and mysterious, surrounds, conceals, and yet does not conceal this conjunction of a soul with the universe and its divine beyond. The saint wishes to relate his adventure; and through his earthly images, if we heed his wish, we hear a revealing voice. The voice wishes to reveal, and says . . . What?

118

IX

Revelations? What the voice in the verse says is something else. In the eyes of San Juan the poet, divine non-vision and human vision are mutually exclusive. This is an antithesis that did not trouble Dante. In the last canto of the *Paradiso*, the vision of the Divinity imposes itself at the end of a journey in which a human creature, without ever renouncing his identity as the Florentine Alighieri, wishing only to explore and venerate, without any thought of union or of fusion, confronts the eternal light, *alto lume*, with its *tre giri di tre colori e d'una contenenza:* the Trinity and Unity of God. Not even this mere contemplation can be reduced to language; Dante is faithful to the tradition of ineffability of all mysticism:

> Oh, quanto è corto il dire e come fioco
> al mio concetto!

His theme, which is mystical to a certain extent, can be poetry now because it has not previously been experience. San Juan's extraordinary adventure, his fusion with the Absolute, leads him to write, in the most relative and concrete manner, poems of human love — some of the most beautiful the world has known. San Juan begins by rejecting his own being and nullifying within himself all other being. For him, as for Angelus Silesius, *Mundus pulcherrimum nihil* (a phrase written by the German mystic in the notebook of a Paduan friend). At the end of his experience, on the return voyage, San Juan complies in advance with this distich by Angelus Silesius:

> *If you possess the Creator, all things run after you:*
> *Man, angel, sun and moon, air, fire, earth and water.*

San Juan does not seem, then, to have indulged in that "escape from reality" indicated by Pedro Salinas: "San Juan renounces all this and escapes into his soul." For his inner life

119

gives rise to the most lofty affirmation of the world and its creatures; and humbly taking the ineffability of experience as his point of departure, San Juan achieves one of man's greatest triumphs over language. A whole world arises within his soul, in the greatest plethora of intimacy that has ever been felt, shutting itself off from our world, away from the world that belongs to everyone. This reality so completely closed to communication brings about a corresponding lack of communication in language — this language that is so useful to many of us. It is an extreme case of conflict between individual life and social life. Man cannot say anything when he is alone with God. The name of God does not reveal God. In this speechless plight, when the spirit is silenced by all that it has to express, no language will serve, unless something completely new can be invented. Picture the man in this moment of tragic muteness. Neither his saintliness nor his virtues nor his marvelous experiences will come to his aid. But the soul is capable of creating a new form of speech. In the journey toward light, creation of language and creation of poetry emerge as one: profound expression will take the form of a poem. Everything that has been so intimately lived will now be just as expressively invented. Shortly before San Juan died, on the night of the thirteenth to the fourteenth of December 1591, some of the lines of his immortal *Spiritual Canticle* returned to the mind of the dying saint and poet:

> Gocémonos, Amado,
> Y vámonos a ver en tu hermosura.
>
> *Rejoice, my love, with me*
> *And in your beauty see us both reflected.*

Gocémonos, Amado! These words, which can just as correctly be translated "Let us have joy of one another, Beloved," are an audacious exclamation of a love completely fulfilled. San

120

Juan de la Cruz is the one who realizes absolutely the type of poet Baudelaire was to dream of three centuries later: "Like a perfect chemist and a sainted soul" (*Comme un parfait chimiste et comme une âme sainte*). San Juan de la Cruz is precisely that, a sainted soul and a perfect chemist. Saint and poet: the twofold authority makes itself felt in each one of his verses, which are among the best, perhaps the best, in the Spanish language.

> Entremos más adentro en la espesura.
>
> *Let us enter deeper into the thicket.*

When has there been so happy a fusion of soul and art? San Juan de la Cruz achieves a poetry that is everything: illumination and perfection.

4

THE
INEFFABLE LANGUAGE
OF DREAMS

Bécquer

The Ineffable Language
Of Dreams

Bécquer

I

THE mystic poet is unable to express his knowledge, his suffering and his ecstasy, and words provide but an inadequate solution. Even when the point of departure is an inner life not based on the supernatural, the profane poet is equally unsuccessful in finding adequate words to transmit visions and emotions. For the "dreamer" of the nineteenth century, the problem of expression arises again under conditions analogous to those of the mystic. In Spain we must pass from San Juan de la Cruz to Bécquer.

Gustavo Adolfo Bécquer, an Andalusian with Nordic given names and Germanic surname, appears as an outcropping foreign, in part, to Spanish history, where the visionary, the purely secular visionary, is rare. Critics have always related Bécquer to German literature. Nothing could be more exact if this relation is presented as an affinity, and not as subservience to specific "sources," although influences of detail are not lacking. Bécquer's predecessors are undoubtedly those poets in Germany who, beginning at the end of the eighteenth century, proclaimed the primordial importance of dreams. And not because the philosophy of idealism dared to consider the dreamed world equivalent to the real world, both pure phenomena within the mind. What was important above all else was the

125

profound relation that exists between the soul, when it dreams, and the world of greatest substance, the spiritual. All is Spirit.

Jean Paul says: "Only in ourselves do we perceive the true harmony of the spheres, and the genie in our heart can only teach us these harmonies — as one teaches birds — by making our terrestrial cage dark." For this reason he also affirms: "Wakefulness is the prose, dream the airy poetry of existence, and madness is poetic prose." It is not a question of fantasies composed in the style of the dreamer, but of spontaneous dreams that invade the sleeping person: "Sleep," Jean Paul thinks, "buries the first world, its nights and sorrows, and brings to us a second world, with the forms we have loved and lost, and scenes too vast for this little earth." He devotes himself to dreaming, then, "in order to delight in the great Night as if it were Day"; but this Night is a Day which is much more profound and essential.

This Germanic concept is summed up in a phrase of Novalis: "We are more closely bound to the invisible than to the visible." In another place he assures us: "In truth, the spiritual world is already open to us, it is already visible. If we should suddenly acquire the necessary flexibility, we would see that we are in the midst of this world." Greater or less flexibility is achieved for us by dreams: "Then our soul penetrates within the object, transforming itself immediately into this object." "And what is poetry," Novalis concludes in another fragment, and with the poet his contemporaries, "but the representation of the soul?" The soul thus centers the universe. This vague faculty called "soul" must embrace, then, much more than just reason, and not only for Hölderlin, the sublime madman: "Man is a god when he dreams, a beggar when he thinks."

Such nocturnal activity is conducive to poetry, and the sleeper prepares the materials of the poem by dreaming. Thus, for example, Tieck, an intense dreamer: "Tieck was accustomed to dream a great deal during his sleep. Sometimes, especially in his earlier years, these night-dreams were most tormenting. They threw him into a fever in which he was half asleep, half awake." In one way or another, the dreamer ends by writing poetry. Tieck himself tells us: "I would fall into a state of dreaming, and I could not rest until I had put my dreams down in writing." That other great genius of the imagination, E. T. A. Hoffmann, also suffered severe nocturnal crises. It is told that "often, late at night, he would shake his wife awake and make her sit beside him, terrified by the spirits his imagination had called into being. No amount of reasoning could calm his tremulous anxiety." Dreaming was obviously a very serious matter. E. T. A. Hoffmann sincerely believed that through dreams we enter into communication with "the soul of the world," with "the spiritual principle of things." As a result, "we come to believe that dream is our real existence." All of life, then, is taking on the shape of a dream, and the phrase of Calderón — the Calderón so admired by these same Germans — acquires a completely positive value. Yes, life is a dream. Hoffmann is affected not only by "the dream which appears as sleep is softly stealing over us, but by the dream we dream our whole life long."

A history of the visionary dreamer, especially during the first half of the nineteenth century, would be long. In France, even such a poet as Vigny affirms: "The Invisible is real." It is not strange that Charles Nodier should point out the bonds that exist between dreamed fantasies and written fantasies: "What surprises me is that the poet when awake should so seldom have profited in his poetry from the fantasies of the poet when asleep, or at least that he should so seldom have admitted his borrowings." It was to be expected that the French imagination should attempt to maintain rational clarity. "Sleep," according to Charles Nodier, "is not only the

most powerful but also the most lucid state of thought." Lucid
thought and forceful imagination join forces vigorously in that
splendid trajectory that goes from Hugo to Baudelaire, from
Baudelaire to Rimbaud. Suffice it to quote from the most de-
lirious — and, in a sense, the most Germanic — of these authors. At the beginning of *Aurélia*, Gérard de Nerval says:
"Dreaming is a second life. I have never been able to pass
without a shudder through those doors of ivory or of horn
that separate us from the invisible world." For Nerval too a
profound relation is established between that external, invisible sphere and the inner life during sleeping and wakefulness.
In these depths of the spirit lies the source of every poem.
Coleridge, representing the great lyric poets of his country
and his time, affirms as a fundamental truth: "One character
belongs to all true poets, that they write from a principle
within, not originating in anything without."

And this brings us to Bécquer. Representing the culmination of the poetry of sentiment and fantasy in the middle of
the nineteenth century, the exquisite and profound Gustavo
Adolfo is the Spaniard who assumed most authentically the
role of visionary poet. "When matter sleeps, the spirit
watches." Within the spirit of the sleeper arises the "magnificent, prophetic vision, real in its substance, illusory only in
its form." But this poet did not indulge in rambling and effusion, as some supposed who gave credence to the bard-like
figure that abetted his great celebrity. Bécquer has left us
poetry and a poetics, and his faith in dreams and their fantasms
goes hand in hand with a luminous consciousness.

II

The most important pages in which Bécquer expounds his
ideas on poetry are the *Cartas literarias a una mujer* (*Literary
Letters to a Woman*), the prologue to *La Soledad* (*Solitude*),

128

and the *Introduction*. Since Bécquer feels and understands love and poetry together, it is not surprising that it should occur to him to give an account of his cavilings to the woman with whom he is in love. Perhaps it was she herself, Casta Esteban, who had dared to ask him: "What is poetry?" After the first and second letters, of December 20, 1860, and January 9, 1861, there also appeared in *El Contemporáneo* on January 20 another reply to the same question: the prologue to *La Soledad*. Here Bécquer cannot help commenting on the contrast between the Andalusia evoked by the songs of his friend Augusto Ferrán and the snow-covered Madrid in which he is writing. Seville "appeared as by enchantment" before his eyes; "and I heard the songs the girls sing to themselves as they sew behind the lattice windows, half hidden among the leaves of the blue morning-glories; and voluptuously I breathed in the fragrance of the honeysuckle." Meanwhile, the writer sees a "Madrid, dirty, black, ugly as a fleshless skeleton, shivering under its immense shroud of snow." During that winter the poet's theory takes concrete form. Bécquer proposes to continue composing, in that epistolary and wandering fashion, addressing himself to the woman he loves, a whole book, which can be neither very erudite nor very long. He does not pretend to give lessons to anyone nor to set himself up as an authority. He limits himself to saying what he knows by intuition and by experience. "I know nothing, I have studied nothing; I have read a little, I have felt a lot, and I have thought a great deal, though I cannot say whether well or badly." Bécquer speaks in the name of the future poet he is beginning to be. He hardly was one in public: in 1861 he could not have had more than three poems already published. Nevertheless, his attitude and tone presuppose a poetic activity already well under way. Like the character he is to invent years later, Bécquer "was a poet and had faith in poetry," very different from "those defeated and uncultivated philosophers" he sees gesticulating and murmuring to themselves in the Retiro. On April 4 and April 23 he published in *El Contemporáneo* two new "literary letters," but did not fulfill the promise he made: "To be continued." (It is curious that this break coincides with Bécquer's marriage to Casta Esteban, which took place on May 19, 1861.) The book remained interrupted, but the author did not cease to refer to the same subjects in several articles and legends, in some poems and in the *Introducción sinfónica*, "symphonic" according to the manuscript, June 1868. Not only can several concordances be established between the *Rimas* and the other writings; very evidently all the texts converge toward a constant line of theory. Without allowing himself any contradiction or distraction, the poet has held himself faithful to his criterion.

In its first meaning, the word *poetry* does not allude to the work of man but to that which in the real world is poetic. "There may not be poets; but always / There will be poetry," *Rima IV* proclaims. Man puts himself in contact with the realities, and while this initial stage lasts he invents only in the primary meaning of this action: he finds and recognizes the mines hidden from the eyes of those not inspired. Here, very skillfully reduced to prose terms by José María de Cossío, is the idea of *Rima IV*: "Poetry has an objective existence, independent of the poet who captures it. The air-wave exists without the antenna. It resides and is produced in three main sectors, which Bécquer delimits perfectly and methodically. The world of the senses: images, lights, sounds, perfumes. The world of mysteries: the origin of life, the destiny of mankind, the unknown universe. The world of feeling: discord of the heart and head, hopes and recollections, love." Poetic values are possessed, then, even if no one ever converted them into a poem, by the Creation with its beauty and its mystery, the

130

Soul with its beautiful and mysterious emotions. One could even speak of "poetry in action," for instance, in a "period of great passions . . , of upheavals, of dangers and combats." All this is poetry, and the one who discovers it and makes it his is a poet.

How does he make it his? For the moment, "poetic," in a second meaning of this qualifying word, is applied to a very singular state of soul that has not yet ceased to be internal. Poetry then is revealed as feeling. What will the person do who is thus moved? "Follow the movements of your heart," whispers the wind that precedes the gnome. And since the impulse is ascending, one must "rise to the heights to find love and feeling." In general, "feeling" means "love," inasmuch as love "is the supreme law of the universe; a mysterious law by which everything is governed and directed, from the inanimate atom to the rational creature." With love situated, according to this metaphysics, in the center of the world and at the heart of every thing, it is love that guides the poet toward the two highest ends: by supraterrestrial ways, toward God; by human ways, to woman.

"Love is poetry; and religion is love," for "our religion, especially, is love too, the purest, most beautiful love, the only infinite love that is known." Like "those figures whose long shadows were projected on the walls and pavement" of San Juan de los Reyes, it is to God that "earth's emotion turns its eyes, as to a pole of love." And from God proceed, besides "those thousand unknown thoughts" that are already poetry, all the arts. Reflecting on the architecture of Toledo, Bécquer deduces "an influence that religious beliefs exercise on the imagination of the peoples who create a new style." For that reason, "Neither Rome nor Byzantium had an architecture that was absolutely original and complete," because "only a new religion can create a new society, and only in this is there

131

sufficient power of imagination to conceive a new art." On the other hand, "Catholicism has made use of it [art] as a powerful interpreter in order to reach to the depths of the soul by means of the senses." Therefore God, "the eternal and ardent focal point of beauty," will stir the poet to this final depth of his soul.

Another focal point exists, another great beauty. "Poetry . . . is you." Why? "Because poetry is feeling and feeling is woman." In man, feeling constitutes an accidental phenomenon, while in woman it is identified with her very organism. That is why poetry, "a faculty of the intelligence in man," in woman "could be said to be an instinct." The intelligence of a true poet will then have to feminize itself to a certain point, and enter into contact with this impulse of the instinct. In spite of everything, poetry will always be "in man purely a quality of the spirit." "In woman, however, poetry is as though incarnate in her being"; she herself is "the poetic word made flesh," manifested by those inexplicable phenomena that alter the soul. And how can one weigh "all this inexhaustible treasure of feeling" if it is allied to beauty? "So long as there exists one beautiful woman / There will be poetry." Or, expressed in a more intellectual way: "I . . . believe in all sincerity that a beautiful woman civilizes as much as a book." This conviction is to remain unalterable in Bécquer: "The silhouette of a woman standing out light and graceful against the sheet of foam of the sea and the vast horizon of the sky," he writes in the last year of his life, "what feelings does it not awaken? What poetry does it not contain?" Woman, emotion, poetry: this is the essential trinity — up till now.

III

Thus, the "poetic state" of the soul is gradually being determined. If the emotion is sufficiently sharp, it usually awak-

132

ens associations of ideas. So rapidly do these flit by that they can scarcely be called ideas, dimly formed among vague images and outlines. One afternoon, on the plain of Toledo, before some ruins, Bécquer is assaulted by "a thousand thousand thoughts," tumbling over one another, mingling together and dissolving. Again in Toledo, giving up the task of sketching a picturesque old building, he leans against a wall in order to give himself over "completely to the dreams of the imagination," that is to say, to "many confused things," "of the kind that after they are thought cannot be remembered." Another day it is in front of a cross — the devil's cross in Bellver — that the traveler is swept by "a world of ideas," "of light, swift ideas." On another occasion he finds himself in the Collegiate Church of Roncesvalles, and as he sees a monk passing by in his long, dark cloak with the green cross, there arise in his memory "I know not what confused recollections of centuries and of peoples"; tradition surrounds him in that place like an atmosphere, and as he breathes it in he feels a beginning of intoxication of his soul, "ever more disposed to feel without reasoning, to believe without arguing."

This world of light, swift ideas cannot be called chaos. A "thread of light" runs through it, illuminating and sustaining it. With pleasure in reiteration Bécquer reverts to this metaphor. The thread of light can extend from the landscape — "the profound solitude of those places, the deep silence of the incipient night" — to the subject — "the vague melancholy of my spirit." Again it is the wanderer who assembles his fantasies in his mind "by means of a series of ideas like a thread of light," and, struggling with obscurity and confusion, "relates . . . the most distant points . . . to one another in a marvelous way."

In these prepoetic states, along with the emotions images arise. The dreamer — not yet the poet — feels, sees. These

133

are not, of course, unrelated phenomena. Vision and feeling are born in a state of fusion. They have one thing in common: their irrationality. At such times one does not think. Bécquer has clearly perceived the peculiar nature of a situation that may well be called a trance: a sort of profane aesthetic ecstasy. None is more significant than the one analyzed, and very well analyzed, in the third of the letters written *Desde mi celda,* "from my cell," in the Monastery of Veruela in Aragon, so perfect a setting for the solitude and soliloquies of a contemplative stroller. A chance excursion leads him to a tiny village cemetery. Between its "four walls of humble adobe" stretches a plot of ground invaded by wild vegetation: thistles, poppies, daisies, coral dragonweed, "yellow five-pointed stars," and other wild flowers. The visitor is conscious too of butterflies, bees, linnets, a lizard . . . After investigating everything, in detail and in its entirety, Bécquer tells us that "I sat down on a stone, filled with that emotion without ideas that we always experience when some little thing impresses us deeply, and seems to overwhelm us with its newness or its beauty." The formula is significant: "emotion without ideas." Bécquer explains it: "In those fleeting moments, when sensation fertilizes the intelligence, and in the depths of the brain there occurs the mysterious conception of the thoughts that will one day come forth conjured up by the memory, there is no thought, there is no reasoning; the senses seem completely occupied in receiving and keeping the impression they are to analyze later." This is the trance, which the poet calls *sopor,* "stupor." "Still feeling the vibrations of this first agitation of the soul, which submerges it in a pleasant stupor, I sat there for a long time."

This disposition to ecstasy, surely of great importance in the history of Spanish sensibility, develops according to a well-defined process. First of all comes the sensation, or, in a more general way, the very deep impression which is defined as

134

"emotion without ideas." The subject passively allows himself to be "fertilized," and it is pointed out that his passivity requires no aid other than that necessary to keep this passive reception free of impure intrusions of the intellect. There is no reasoning. The pureness of the crisis resides in this submission to the influence of the sensation. And the sensation proceeds, for the time being, to the memory. There it settles down, without more ado. The recipient of the emotion is aware that recollection is being prepared. The present moment takes on the depth of a perspective of the past. Man glimpses the worth of present reality, and the present guarantees that future in which it will appear as a past resuscitated with nostalgia. Another aspect of this trajectory is to be noted. While the sensation is operating, it already knows where it is going. Without losing itself in obscure byways, when it takes refuge in the memory it seeks out the intelligence. Does this mean that all this irrational movement is to have a rational outcome? "Intelligence," for Bécquer, must mean "poetic consciousness"; it will struggle to reduce to forms of expression — that is to say, intelligible form — this wealth of sensations. Pure sensations, intact, which in their own humble way transmit a revelation. Hence the ecstatic delight, the "pleasant stupor," beyond superficial and conventional life, with the soul embracing the real world, those "arteries" through which the "fluid" of the Creation circulates. Bécquer does not dream only when he is asleep and at night. It is well to emphasize that for this Andalusian poet immediate contact with things, when he was wide awake, was also a beginning of transcendent clarification.

There is an affinity, partial but not slight, between Bécquer and another writer who knew the ecstasy of sensation: the one who finally found his *temps perdu*. Proust takes as his point of departure sensations that provoke an involuntary recollection. A recollection that resuscitates, without the intervention

135

of the intelligence, a moment already lived. There is no need to examine here a process elucidated by Proust and his commentators with such precision. We are concerned only with noting that in Bécquer and in Proust certain privileged sensations lead to ecstasy. Ecstasy? Yes, this is the word for it. They find access to the absolute: transcendent reality, the realm of the spirit, authentic life. Proust remains immersed in a moment of the past because sensation functions as memory. Bécquer, too, trusting in his "emotion without ideas," waits for the present to be transformed into past, when memory may call it back. The feeling for the supernatural is stronger in Bécquer, a religious soul, so much at home among dreams and spirits. In Proust the objective discovery brought by involuntary memory reveals no more than the moments he lived just as they were lived within the monad each man represents: the radical subjectivism of the end of the nineteenth century. The *madeleine* revives no more of Combray than the images of Combray reflected by the spirit of the narrator, now identified with that childhood suddenly brought to life by the taste of the *madeleine*. A happening as slight as this is sufficient to enable Proust to rise to a height beyond time and to feel the rapture of the absolute, beyond death. How distant now appears San Juan de la Cruz, so determined to cast off everything concrete in order to rise to absolute truth. Bécquer here uses this communication with something concrete — a certain afternoon, a certain cemetery, that little village of Aragon — as a means of entering "deeper into the thicket." Later, when "the vibrations of this first agitation of the soul" have died out — the *sopor* of ecstasy — what Bécquer calls "relative ideas" will arise, in contrast with the preceding spiritual revelation. Spiritual, but not rational. Nevertheless, consciousness will close the process, as with Proust, and memory will recall, aided by imagination. This will be the genesis of

136

the poem, or more exactly of the "state" which is to lead to expression: the expression of a world revealed, remembered and dreamed.

IV

Will poetry, still limited to this inner state of feeling, be no more than a sentimental effusion? Bécquer has gone further, has penetrated much deeper. Taking pleasure in the paradoxical tone of the phrase, and disagreeing with a commonplace attitude of his time, he affirms: "When I feel, I do not write." Which is to say that when he is ready to write, feeling no longer subsists in him with the actuality it originally had. The act of writing is posterior to the life which inspires the writing. The writer remembers, and if memory is the cradle of poetry, the material that has been lived will reappear calmed by recollection. Bécquer shows himself faithful to the best tradition of the nineteenth century. Friedrich Schlegel was of the opinion that "when the artist finds himself under the sway of imagination and enthusiasm, he is not in the proper condition to communicate what he has to say . . . In this situation, he will be tempted to say everything. One who yields to such a temptation fails to recognize the value and merit of *self-restraint*." It is to this self-control of the artist, the master of his emotions and insights, that Achim von Arnim refers when he maintains that "no poet has written a lasting work . . . under the domination of passion." When passion is concluded, it will be possible to reflect what it was. Novalis, the angelic Novalis, the poet of inspiration par excellence, is very firm on this point. "The young poet can never be too cool and deliberate. A truly poetic and musical style requires calmness and concentration. When a tempest is raging in the poet's heart, making it bewildered and confused, nothing comes forth but a meaningless twaddle." That is why

137

Bécquer writes only when he feels himself to be "pure, tranquil, serene." One cannot fail to be reminded of the phrase of Wordsworth. Bécquer, then, keeps in his memory the "light and ardent daughters of sensation . . . until the moment when my spirit, pure, tranquil, serene, and clothed, so to speak, in supernatural power, calls them forth . . . and they pass before my eyes again as in a luminous, magnificent vision." From this paragraph shines forth one of the most lucid explanations ever given by a Spanish artist. "Then," Bécquer adds, "I no longer feel with agitated nerves, with straining bosom, with the organic and material part of me stirred by the harsh impact of sensations produced by passion and the emotions."

Poetry is born from memory. From there, life having now been transformed into vision, that is to say, into contemplation, someone calls it forth. But he is no longer the same person who suffered or rejoiced. He no longer feels with agitated nerves or with straining bosom. He is now — let these three characteristics be remembered — "pure, tranquil, serene"; he is now a poet. This raises the question: will only those "few beings" be poets to whom "it is given to keep the living memory of what they have felt"? Will the writer face always toward his past as if this were his only object? The spirit is already "pure, tranquil, serene," and — let it not be forgotten — "clothed, so to speak, in supernatural power." In this experience submitted to contemplation, transfigured into vision, something new is born. Nothing less than a supernatural power appears as the dominant force. Before the surprised gaze of the seer passes a parade of images that cannot be reduced to mere recollection. This vision is being dreamed by the poet, and to dream is to create that "world of visions" that "lives outside us or moves within us." Such are the intimate bonds between the dreamed and the real. Poetry, then, as a dream: "If you only knew how diaphanous, how light, how impalpable

138

are the gauzy golden veils that float in the imagination, enfolding these mysterious figures it creates." The imagination creates beyond memory. The poet will be, therefore, a dreamer, and doubly so: because he dreams while awake, and in this watchful half-sleep resides his proper function; and because he dreams while asleep, and the world thus pictured aids the other, serving as a constant point of reference and as a perfect model for it.

Bécquer would love to "be king, lord of lords," like the chieftain of the red hands, whose lordliness consists in "seeing pass before his eyes, like visions in a dream, pearls, gold, pleasures and joy." The spectacle of reality often presents itself to him as a "vision in a dream," words he takes pleasure in repeating. The Good Friday procession in Toledo, "like a vision in a dream, floats between the real world and the imaginary." Everything about the wizard of Trasmoz "seemed like something from an illusion or a dream." Even architectural monuments have this effect on him. "Arabic architecture is like the daughter of a dream of a believer who has fallen asleep after a battle in the shade of a palm tree." Sometimes the dream implies an escape: the musician of *El Miserere* "believed himself outside the real world, living in that fantastic region of dreams where everything takes on strange and phenomenal shapes." The dream serves, in short, as the highest form of comparison. It was bound to enter into some compliment to a woman. "And that woman," Manrique meditates, "who is as beautiful as the most beautiful of my adolescent dreams." Bécquer also remembers "those nameless hours that preceded my dreams when I was a child, those hours in which the genii, flying about my crib, would tell me wonderful tales which, enchanting my spirit, gave rise to my golden delirium."

Thanks to dreams, the soul finally accomplishes its liberation: "Man's intelligence, dulled by its contact with matter,

139

cannot conceive the purely spiritual." This is one of the convictions that are part of Bécquer's very nature. Fortunately, "there are moments when the soul overflows." In a sleeping person, "the spirit frees itself from matter and flees." Toward what? Toward a luminous emptiness that is not stretched over the earth nor in the sky. It is a marvelous, limitless space that leads "to the regions where love dwells," when dreams soar above sleep to serve "as an invisible link between the finite and the infinite, between the world of men and the world of souls . . . to draw down the powers of Heaven and to elevate those of Earth until they touch in space," in that extraordinary emptiness large enough to hold all fantasms. "When matter sleeps, the spirit watches." The body of the Indian chieftain lies in a lethargy, and "his soul clothes itself in an imaginary form and escapes from the bonds holding it prisoner, to hurl itself into the ether; there it is awaited by the creations of Sleep," which make an imaginary world for him. This world offers a "magnificent vision" that is "illusory only in its form," because these beings also live "with the life of the idea," with that ideal life — the best, no doubt, to Bécquer — toward which his energies and his nostalgias flow. "Dreams are the spirit of reality with the forms of untruth." One must keep in mind *Rima LXXV*: the spirit flees from its prison, sheds its human form, breaks its earthly bonds, and, "a guest of the mists," rises to the empty region, to the silent world of the idea, where it dwells with its loves and hates. It is the "world of visions reserved for the sleeper."

Through the efforts, obscure or luminous, of the spirit, we enter "deeper into the thicket" of the universe, "and all mingled together, we shall be the motive force, the vital ray of creation, circulating like a fluid through its subterranean arteries." There is no nature without spirit. "In the silvered leaves of the poplars, in the hollows of the rocks, in the waves

140

of the water, the invisible spirits of Nature seem to talk with us, recognizing a brother in the immortal spirit of man." These daily or nightly manifestations place us, however, in an ambiguous zone of fluctuation and conflict. "I believed myself transported I know not where," Bécquer exclaims while wide awake at an inn not far from Seville. Why? That impression "can only be compared to the one we feel in the kind of dream where, through some unexplainable phenomenon, things both are and are not at the same time, and the places where we think we are are partially transformed in a freakish and impossible manner." This "unexplainable phenomenon" of certain dreams is repeated during waking hours. Bécquer's prose and verse are constantly referring to dreams, states of insomnia, nightmares, half-dreams between sleeping and waking, voluntary daydreams.

From all these mines comes forth the poem. Or, what amounts to the same thing: Bécquer does not succeed in being Bécquer except when he is surrounded by dreams. To many situations the phrase of the *Introduction* must have applied: "Insomnia and fantasy continue, and continue procreating." It is a procreation half sought, half autonomous. The poet aids in the growth of that fantastic existence that quarrels over "the atoms of memory as if they were the scant liquid of a sterile earth." Memory, though reduced to the status of an impulse center, is inescapable in those moments of semilucidity so characteristic of Bécquer. While he is visiting the castle of Olite, his fantasy begins to roam as if he were dreaming while half asleep. What form appeared for a moment at the window? Perhaps it was a shred of mist, or a lingering ray of twilight . . . "But who can prevent us from dreaming it is a woman in love, hearing once again the echo of a song pleasing to her ear?" One night in Soria the poet is unable to sleep, and he turns over and over in his imagination a tale heard in that city. The tale will later become *El monte de las ánimas*. From other "poetic insomnias" come *Tres fechas*, and so many other stories "whose vague outcome floats . . . indecisively in the point that separates waking from sleeping." Bécquer is attracted by the dividing line between light and shadow, and like Garcés, fascinated by the white roe deer, likes to "swing for a moment in that vague space which is half-way between waking and sleeping," that limbo "in which objects change shape," according to *Rima LXXI*.

In the same way he mentions the "light and fitful dreams of morning," which are usually "rich in smiling images," although they may also take on extravagant aspects, as they did in the famous dawn on the road to Tudela. It must not have been unusual for the poet to awaken "still filled with the stupor one feels when he comes to suddenly after a deep sleep." As he awakens, a dim vestige floats, similar to "the last cadence of a dying melody lingering in the ear." "I do not know what I dreamed in the night just past," he confesses in *Rima LXVIII*, even though that is the usual gathering-time for "the vague ideas" he has dreamed, and once gathered they begin to form "an immense and dolorous poem." Nevertheless, "After a night of insomnia and of terror, how beautiful is the clear, white light of day!"

But the fictitious world does not vanish. "Common sense, which is the barrier to dreams, begins to weaken," and imaginary elements mingle with the real. The result: "It requires an effort for me to tell which things I have dreamed and which have actually happened to me." He has seen certain specific green eyes: "I do not know whether in my dreams, but I have seen them." And when he glimpses the professed nun illuminated by "the resplendence of all the lights" he stifles a cry and says to himself: "I knew that woman; I had never seen her, but I knew her from having gazed upon her in my dreams,"

142

by divination or reminiscence of another spiritual universe. Another day, also in a church in Toledo, he observes a woman kneeling by the tomb of Garcilaso. His emotion is so strong that he has to reassure himself: "I did not dream this woman." But then he wonders: "Had I really seen the tomb of Garcilaso? Or was it all a story invented by my imagination, about a very ordinary tomb?" He could consult a guide to Toledo. Bah! "It was just as good to think I had seen it as to see it." Which are the phantoms, which are the real persons? "But I know that I know many people / Whom I do not know." Bécquer's friend Narciso Campillo could well affirm: "Gustavo was one of those men who dream when they are awake even to the point of watching as spectators the real drama of their own lives."

v

And what will the dreamer do with the creations that multiply and swarm unceasingly through "the shadowy nooks" of his brain? Can depths so nocturnal be brought into the light? Not even on awakening can he find a way to relate, "in all its inexplicable vagueness and poetry," what he has dreamed. The phantoms wish to emerge into the light and to find a means of existence in language. "It is necessary to open a way for the deep waters, or they will end by breaking down the dike." The cycle of deepest life must come to its final stage: expression. "I do not want you to appear again in my sleepless nights, passing before my eyes in weird procession, urging me with your gestures and contortions to bring you out into the life of reality from the limbo in which you live, like phantoms without substance." Phantoms, then, *in cerca d'autore*, that would not be satisfied with mere recollection: only in expression can they find meaning and rest.

And now the great problem arises. "How can words,"

143

Bécquer asks himself in the *Cartas literarias a una mujer*, "how can crude and wretched language, inadequate at times to express material needs, serve as a worthy interpreter between two souls?" Immediately he answers: "Impossible." Language is crude, poor, wretched. Bécquer has no confidence in words, which will be only "like the nebulous trail marking the passage of an unknown comet, like the scattered atoms of a world in embryo." The infinitely complex, and formless, embryo of the soul. He would like to chisel a phrase as he would a golden vase. "But it is impossible." If everything revolves around what he has dreamed, it will be impossible to express what he has dreamed in words. From which it follows that intuition and expression represent two distinct nonequivalent moments that never succeed in becoming identified. Why? Because dreams are very different from words, and, especially, much richer than words. In consequence of this, dreams grope their way toward poetry, stumbling over the obstacle of words.

This latter assertion is in opposition to an essential tradition. Poetry is words in their plenitude, and without this plenitude what can the poet do, if he conceives and feels only through words, by managing to extract some part of their refined potential energy? But Bécquer, the visionary, the dreamer, the pure spirit, does not trust in words. He has dreamed, and his dream is ineffable. "But alas! Between the world of the idea and the world of form there is an abyss that can be bridged only by words; and words, timid and lazy, refuse to aid in the effort." This is what happens to Manrique, who is in love with a ray of moonlight: "for Manrique was a poet, so much so that he had never been satisfied with the forms in which he might enclose his thoughts, and he never had enclosed them when he wrote them down!" Only an imaginary creature would be capable, thanks to his capricious creator, of achiev-

144

ing the desired form. Maese Pérez, at his organ, one single night, rises to the heights of "the songs the spirit perceives and the tongue cannot repeat . . . the unknown music of heaven which only the imagination can comprehend," similar to the *Miserere*, "which cannot be explained and can scarcely be conceived."

The author himself, on the other hand, declares his impotence, like the successor to Maese Pérez at Santa Inés. It is "nameless vagueness" that engulfs him before the panorama of Toledo, or before one of its palaces. Often he has a thought which he cannot remember, and "even if I remembered it, I could not find words to say it." But the very vivid remembrance of the woman of stone, who so impressed him, cannot be reduced to "comprehensible terms" either. The woman of stone in her solitary corner formed "an inexplicable whole." When the whole embraces a complete atmosphere, the difficulty increases: the same thing happens, for instance, in the market place in Tarazona as in the Retiro or the Pradera de San Isidro in Madrid, or at the fair in Seville. The physical world can be as ineffable as the immaterial, and for the painter as well. "Where not even the painter's palette can reach . . . how can my pen reach, with no other means than words, so poor, so inadequate?" With words one cannot produce "the effect" of line, chiaroscuro, light, color, movement, life. Bécquer has to resign himself to not being able to describe the marketplace in Tarazona and its "over-all effect," just as he does to not being able to portray the appearance of the Virgin to Don Pedro Atarés, even though he has seen the market place very clearly, and he imagines the appearance in all its splendor. Besides, "The time of day at which an object is seen, the light it receives, or the horizon against which it is drawn, modify its appearance to such an extent that it would

145

be difficult to fix its true character if one were to isolate it from its surroundings or contemplate it from some other point of view than the one that suits it best."

And how is one to interpret the language of "the invisible spirits of Nature, which recognize a brother in the immortal spirit of man?" Bécquer shares the good fortune and misfortune of Manrique: "In the clouds, in the air, in the depths of the forests, in the crevices of the rocks, he imagined that he saw mysterious forms or heard mysterious sounds, forms of supernatural beings, unintelligible words that he could not comprehend." Deep down in his intuition, what he has seen, what he has felt, what he has dreamed, all resist, ineffable. To be sure, it is dreams that offer the greatest resistence to language. In order to emphasize the fragility of "those light, swift phantoms, inexplicable phenomena of inspiration," of "those light and so to speak impalpable fantasies," the writer twice has recourse to the simile of a butterfly which, escaping, leaves between one's fingers the golden dust of its wings.

This conflict between inspiration and language implies another, parallel one between inspiration and reason. This is the subject of *Rima III*. On the one hand, inspiration, depicted as a shock and a murmur, with its deformed outlines and its landscapes seen through a veil; still more, as a nervous attitude, a madness, an intoxication. This is inspiration independent of reason, which therefore has neither meaning nor rhythm. On the other hand, reason. Order and light triumph with her, a golden rein to check, an intelligent hand to construct, a chisel, and finally a rhythm, a universe of atoms upheld by a hidden attraction. But order, light, and rhythm come substantially later than the shock, murmur and intoxication. The hand with its chisel and its rein applies itself only to a previously existing formless material.

Bécquer needs, in the well-chosen images of Rafael Alberti,

146

to escape from the mist, to be the guest of light, to flee from the phantoms, or better yet, to succeed "in feeling, in grasping with his hands, in pinning down" these phantoms of his mist. But how? Bécquer never ceased to be tormented by this drama, a painful variant of the fundamental contradiction of spirit and matter. With spirit go emotions, dreams, intuitions. On matter are built the rational machine, the apparatus of logical language, the mechanism of art. This contradiction, many times famous, that has been a cause of anxiety for so many, Bécquer makes his own, with all his being. Joaquín Casalduero has analyzed it admirably: "An inner need of annihilating matter, of fleeing from reality, but at the same time the need of a form, a reality, to satisfy the exigency of being. Poetry must be expressed, the poem must be created; poetry is there, demanding life, form, desiring to cease being a germ and to see itself bloom. I have already indicated the sensation of movement, of lightness, of immateriality produced by Bécquer's poetry through this impulse to fuse itself and be one with the spirit; now, when Bécquer catches by surprise this longing for being, we feel the primitiveness of life, because he stops us on that fascinating borderline between being and non being, sleeping and waking — for everything sleeping desires to awaken. Bécquer captures the moment in which a tear is *just about to fall*, a phrase just about to be spoken; and he does the same thing with respect to poetry. All is repose: a drawing room, a harp covered with dust and silent, in whose strings the notes are sleeping; but these notes sleep in the strings *as a bird sleeps in the branches*: poetry is ready, waiting to soar at the slightest touch." Here what is called poetry is the prepoetic realm, which, properly speaking, is still limited to being "content," vital content. There will be poetry only when spirit becomes form, the plenitude of the word. Of the ineffable, of course, only the author can speak. The reader is con-

147

cerned only with the text, which is incompatible with any comparative study of the prepoetry of the Creation and this second creation which is the poem. Bécquer is, in short, one of those people who are aware of the "incomprehensible phenomena of our mysterious nature, of which man cannot even conceive"; phenomena of the inner life that are not only inexpressible but inconceivable, like universal nature, possessing an "incomprehensible language" which the poet strives to translate.

VI

What, then, will the poem be like? The first line of the *Rimas* asserts: "I know a hymn . . ." It is the emotions and dreams of the soul. "I should like to write it / With words that would be at once / Sighs and laughter, colors and notes of music," in a language not exclusively logical and rational, a language that would take on values allied to the ineffable: passion, color and music. It would be necessary, for the purpose, to master "rebellious, wretched language." "But it is vain to struggle; for there is no device / Able to contain it . . ." The poet, in spite of everything, struggles to carry the word beyond logic, in accordance with the intuitive impulse of the word itself. What will these new qualities be, according to Bécquer? In the prologue to *La Soledad* he writes: "There is a magnificent, sonorous poetry . . . that decks itself with all the pomp of language, that moves with cadenced majesty." Our Andalusian, living remote from the Sevillian School, takes no pleasure either in magnificence, or sonority, or pomp. Further still: "Bécquer," observes Luis Cernuda, "was obscurely aware of all that separated him from the majority of Spanish poets." Referring to this high-sounding style, Bécquer adds: "It is everybody's poetry."

But there is another kind of poetry: "There is another,

148

natural, brief, plain, that rises from the soul like an electric spark, that strikes the emotions with a word and flees, and, naked of artifice, unhindered within a free form, awakens, with one word that touches them, the thousand ideas sleeping in the bottomless ocean of the fantasy." A paramount declaration! None has underscored its importance more ably than Dámaso Alonso: "The essential element in Bécquer's words is the distinction between poetry that is pompous, ornate, fully developed, and poetry that is brief, naked, unhindered in a free form, that touches lightly a moment and flees, *leaving the strings vibrating with a harmonious humming*. All our poetry, except for folk poetry, before Bécquer . . . belonged to the first type, and the great find, the great gift of the author of the *Rimas* to Spanish poetry is the discovery of this new manner which with only a touch of the wing awakens a chord in the depths of the heart and, when the voice has died out, leaves it — a diapason gently stirred — full of resonance." If emotion and fantastic vision are ineffable, it will only be possible to suggest, not to express directly. Poetry, then, of the indefinably spiritual, as vague suggestion rather than as strict communication. The word in all its radiant and musical efficacy will find its response in the collaboration of the reader. The poet is unable to describe a pair of green eyes for us, and he compares them to drops of rain on the leaves of the trees in summer, after a storm. "In any case," he adds, "I count on the imagination of my readers."

On the other hand, "Works of the imagination always have some point of contact with reality." But immediately, as soon as we have touched the blessed ground, we must move off and keep our distance. When one walks in the mountains, like Bécquer on the Moncayo, picturesque little villages are glimpsed in the distance; these, when they are seen on arrival, often belie their appearance, and "poetry is turned into prose."

149

Poetry in no way incompatible with reality, if reality submits to the condition of distance: that imaginative distance which the new-found art of photography, for instance, had not succeeded in establishing. According to Bécquer and the opinion of his time, photography lacks "the taste necessary to select what best suits the character of an object, that mysterious spirit, in short, that stands out in the work of a painter, which does not always make the object appear just as it really is, but as it appears to the imagination." Only thus can the special result be produced, special though undefined, that obliges us to recognize that "inspiration has passed this way."

Bécquer defines in general, and attempts in his work, the poetry of ineffable love: something which at first was feeling changes to memory, then to dream, and finally to verse, suggestive words. If Bécquer seemed at first glance a literary laggard, he now is revealed as a precursor of the modern movement. He will not fall either into irresponsible spontaneity or into discipline without fire. One road exists that is completely intuitive, irrational to the point of absurdity, hostile to any touch or retouching of consciousness. There is another road subjected to intellectual calculation and the most severe abstraction. Which path does Bécquer choose? *Rima III* suggests an alliance, almost chimerical perhaps and therefore all the more tempting, the alliance between inspiration and reason. A literature thus conceived "speaks at the same time to the intelligence and to feeling, and from the sweet harmony created by the combination of the two strings vibrating at the same time in the heart and head of the spectator comes that deep, calm, indefinable pleasure produced by true works of art." A deep, calm, indefinable pleasure corresponding to the "pure, tranquil, serene" instant of conception. "I am the invisible / Ring that binds / The world of form / To the world of idea." This image of the ring signifies union. But it is a

150

union between two points discovered successively and in hiatus; whence the distress felt by the poet, conscious of the ineffable moment. No matter. It is an ideal of perfection: skill and insight, a spark flashing in the darkness and the mastery to capture that spark, at once luminous and mysterious. No, this poetry of the soul will not be nullified by the principle of contradiction, even though it may be ineffable, even though there may be no voice that can express it with absolute fitness. Feeling is elevated to memory, memory is elevated to dream, and achieves, finally, its verbal form, forever form in spite of all — with its power of suggestion. Here we have a successful example of this union, the poetry of Bécquer.

Nevertheless, these poets of intense inner life, religious or profane poets — in Spain San Juan de la Cruz and Gustavo Adolfo Bécquer — teach us to be modest, to be aware of our limitations. Something of our emotions escapes us, something that is irreconcilable to logical symbols rationally articulated. At this barrier set up by the inability to equate the soul and the word, many pause. Though deeply moved, they do not know what to say. But in spite of all these difficulties, the poet — dissatisfied, perhaps, but still the supreme sayer — delivers to us at last his victorious expression.

VII

The most important elements of Bécquer's work — all but one, the love theme, which is extremely important — are found in the letters written "from my cell." It is pleasant to imagine Bécquer in the year 1864 in the Monastery of Veruela, an ideal retreat for a nineteenth-century poet. Between the Abbaye-aux-Bois of Chateaubriand and the Tower of Muzot of Rilke, it would be difficult to find a more beautiful setting for an artist. It is not sumptuous, like the palaces of Byron and Browning in Venice. It does not possess the picturesque ele-

151

ments of the Valdemosa of Chopin and George Sand. The twelfth-century monastery, then without monks, facing the great mountain of Aragon, the Moncayo, allowed Bécquer to live in accordance with his destiny, among the most discreet harmonies: a historic spot, an archeological monument, evocation of the past, landscape — a mountainous northern landscape, popular traditions, typical village customs. And all of it wrapped in solitude, the solitude of a Gothic cloister, of shadowy tree-lined walks, of paths hardly worthy of the name. Bécquer dreamed and strolled through the freest of hours, following his whim in the most idle kind of rambling. From this indolence all kinds of things were to emerge: observations, impressions, meditations, legends, dreams. (And, by way of contrast, all of it was to be consigned to articles, because this poet was not, for instance, a professor, like some of his successors, but a newspaperman.) Bécquer wore a long cape and a hat with a very broad brim, and, thus garbed, he rested on occasion under the branches of a huge tree; it is thus that we see him in the sketches of his painter-brother Valeriano.

"When the north wind blows, snow falls, or rain lashes the window-panes of my cell, I hurriedly seek out the ruddy, cheerful glow of the fire, and there, with the dog curled up at my feet by the blaze, as I watch the thousand golden sparks glancing off the copper pots and utensils hanging in a dark corner of the kitchen reflecting the fire's gleam, how often have I interrupted the reading of a scene from Shakespeare's *Tempest* or Byron's *Cain* to listen to the sound of the water boiling, covering itself with foam, its plumes of vaporous blue steam lifting the metal cover and making it tap against the edges of the kettle!" Picture Bécquer ensconced in this village kitchen with its fire-lit objects worthy of a still life by Zurbarán or the young Velázquez. Do not forget the companionship of the boiling water with its blue steam. The poet flees from the

152

cold and dedicates himself to good reading. Retirement to a cell or explorations of historic and wild scenes engender such constant dreaming, whether the poet be awake, half awake, or asleep. And the writings will alternate between legendary narratives in prose — sometimes a prose-poem — and very brief lyrical condensations; *märchen* like the German ones of the first half of the century, or ballads in the style of the sentimental poetry of the period in Spain, whose affinities with the German — and the Andalusian — are obvious. The main stream shows the influence of these general affinities rather than influences of detail, so difficult to establish, and definitely quite secondary. Within this atmosphere, in the fifties and sixties, there is diffused a tone that has already been suggested by various poets prior to Bécquer. This tone crystallizes in Gustavo Adolfo Bécquer, writing under the fateful shadow of his three names.

Along with the Bécquer who is sentimental and very popular, the "pretty" Bécquer with his fragile tears, there is concealed a very pure poet. An excellent lesson: almost never are the best elements found in isolation; they are mingled with other inferior ones. Purity is a thing or quality of Heaven. Bécquer is not guilty of pretensions to angelic perfection; he is a gallant with a melancholy air and a cape, who composes poetry as brief as it is intense, in which the phrase acquires a lightness of soul visible through a form that seems vaporous, so radiant is the material of these words, conductors of vision in light. Professor Edmund King has shown the capital importance of light in Bécquer's vision: "light which is the aspect of reality most nearly corresponding to what he sees in his own mind." And there is no doubt: "The ideal is light." Thus is revealed a transcendent world. And the Spirit gradually makes itself manifest through a thousand spirits agitating dreams, nights, lakes, mountains: a spiritual quivering like an irides-

153

cent ray of light in the forest, over the river. And the nerves, or the strings of the harp, vibrate.

Even without giving up the sentimental manner, addressing his beloved, Bécquer tells us: "I saw you an instant" (*Te vi un punto*). It is *Rima XIV*. It alludes to Her, or rather, to her eyes. The theme could not be more susceptible of vulgar associations. What will the poet write? A madrigal, a rosary of gallant comparisons? These eyes, by the end of the poem, will be a sort of *ignis fatuus*, a will-o'-the-wisp. And not by means of a metaphor. We are beholding a truly visionary operation. Now the rest of the face is not distinguished, nor even the more or less vague outline of the woman. The eyes, alone, independent now, remain floating "Like the flame-wreathed spots that blind / The eyes that watch the sun too closely." Somber, fervent eyes, turning their gaze on the poet, who is obsessed. All this takes place in the bedroom corner where Bécquer so loves to dream. From that dark corner of his room, he sees the eyes shine, "disembodied." When he sleeps he contemplates them too: then they "hover / Up above me, open wide." Eyes drawing the poet with an irresistible power, like the *ignis fatuus*. This is what "may lead a traveler to his death." It is not two bodies that are being compared, but their actions. That is why these eyes have the effect of carrying one away: they are at once a fatality and an enigma. "In the course of the poem," José Pedro Díaz aptly observes, "we have moved from the world into dream, and this dream has given shape to another, transcendent world, with laws which are the laws of destiny, with orbits of which the poet feels himself a part." A great nocturne, in short; and these eyes are truly disembodied, living, and they hallucinate, with magnetic power — thanks to a total act of creation. "The seductive power of the ineffable, under the form of light," Edmund King concludes, "is the substance as well as the controlling image of the poem."

154

INEFFABLE LANGUAGE OF DREAMS

Te vi un punto, y flotando ante mis ojos
la imagen de tus ojos se quedó,
como la mancha oscura orlada en fuego,
que flota y ciega si se mira al sol.

Adonde quiera que la vista fijo
torno a ver sus pupilas llamear;
mas no te encuentro a ti, que es tu mirada:
unos ojos, los tuyos, nada más.

De mi alcoba en el ángulo los miro
desasidos, fantásticos lucir;
cuando duermo los siento que se ciernen
de par en par abiertos sobre mí.

Yo sé que hay fuegos fatuos que en la noche
llevan al caminante a perecer;
yo me siento arrastrado por tus ojos;
pero adónde me arrastran, no lo sé.

The following translation was made for the present volume by
Edmund King, a great expert on Bécquer and on the English
language:

I saw you an instant; your eyes remained
Before my eyes, an image floating
Like the flame-wreathed spots that blind
The eyes that watch the sun too closely.

No matter where I fix my eyes
I see your eyes aflame once more;
But not yourself, only your gaze,
A pair of eyes, your eyes, no more.

I see them in my bedroom corner,
Disembodied, ghostly, shining;
In my sleep I feel them hover
Up above me open wide.

Phantom fires, I know, may lead
A traveler to his death at night:
I feel your eyes compelling me
To follow. Where? Who knows? Not I.

155

The poet is now a sylph, an exhalation wandering and roaming, incorporeal, invisible, throughout the universe. "In a shoreless sea, a thundering wave; / In empty space, a roving comet." The poet reaches his own center: the universal center. "I am the secret stairway / That joins heaven to earth . . . I, indeed, am the spirit, — Unknown essence . . ." Spirit. Sylph. Essence. Universe. Poetry of love, poetry of dreams, poetry of the universe. This world of visions — profane ecstasies — still holds its magic for us. An admirable transition between Hispanic poetry of the nineteenth century and that of the twentieth, the work of Gustavo Adolfo Bécquer still stands today pure and youthful, the work of a poet who, though half asleep, was wide awake: an Andalusian visionary.

5

ADEQUATE LANGUAGE

Gabriel Miró

Adequate Language

Gabriel Miró

I

A LITERARY work is defined both by the attitude of its author toward the world and by his way of feeling and understanding language. A writer's words are sometimes fitting, sometimes inadequate. One cannot express well an inner life as rich as that of the mystic or the visionary. But this situation does not arise frequently. There are many poets, perhaps a majority of them, who see their language as their best friend. Góngora was one of these. Without his great faith in words he could not have sought and selected them with the fervor he did. In this same fervor and faith, none among modern Spaniards surpasses an admirable lyric writer, the novelist Gabriel Miró (1879–1930). The first third of the twentieth century in Spain produced outstanding cultivators of prose. Unamuno, Valle-Inclán, Azorín — to reduce unjustly to three names an enumeration that could be a long one — cultivated their Spanish language diligently, and they as well as their principal contemporaries refined their style intensively. It is in this magnificent period that Miró wrote, with an extraordinary capacity for expression. He may very well be chosen to represent, in our brief gallery of writers, the opposite pole from the poets of the ineffable.

Miró himself asserts: "Perhaps through the word I may be granted fullness of contemplation." It is not simply that contemplation may find adequate expression for itself. Miró says

159

more than this: the contemplative act is wholly realized thanks
to the verbal act. Then the cycle of experience is completed.
Until it is "pronounced," this experience is not fully lived.
Poetry is not an ornament to be superimposed on existence, but
the culmination of existence. Profound life must come to be
expressed life. Without language — "the most precious human
reality," according to Miró — there could be no possession of
the other reality. Of course every true writer knows this. With
real insight Miró points it out: "There are emotions which are
not wholly felt until they receive the lyric force of the word,
their own full and exact word. A wide plain on which stood
a single tree lay before me, but I did not feel that it was
mine until I said to myself: 'Parched earth and cool tree.' A
bird was singing in the smooth, still heat of an afternoon, and
the song penetrated it, possessed it completely, when someone
said: 'Brightness.' And it was as if the bird were transformed
into a shining pane of glass that reverberated even at a distance." Thus, man comes to be man thanks to expression. In-
tegral man means, in this light, expressive man, expressed man.
No, there is no need to translate in a second column a text that
is already complete in the first column. This would amount to
repetition, and the arts cannot be reduced to a mere matter
of more or less elegant redundance. The vital act reaches its
final stage and is consummated at the very moment of its
verbal metamorphosis. During the nineteenth century, more
than one writer was to wrestle with that problem which is so
false: which is preferable, life or art? These words designate
two distinct moments in close interdependence. An artist like
Miró cannot oppose them to the point of preferring one to
the other. Are they not successively distinct and necessary
in a single trajectory? After the vital act the poet must continue to live and live prodigiously in order to realize the final
act: the word.

ADEQUATE LANGUAGE

There is the countryside in the afternoon heat, there is a bird, and suddenly, through the stillness, the song of the bird. What else is there? A man who feels it and who fuses, between his eyes and his soul, countryside, heat, and bird. This intuition would not reach fulfillment if it were not for a word: "Brightness." "Brightness" is something which is also very real: a focus of idea and suggestion. And everything is guided, illuminated. The separate beats, "bright-ness," resolved into a single resplendence, "brightness," enrich a moment of meeting — the meeting of spirit with world — and are form. And form, the revelation of content, is something more than revelation. Form discovers — and remakes, creates. The word "brightness" adds more light to the light of the sun, and that country spot on that bright afternoon receives permanent brilliance when that man, Gabriel Miró, pronounces the word "Brightness." Expression, then, constitutes a spiritual conquest, which will ultimately be aesthetic creation. Life with spirit plus form in single, indivisible unity: is not this poetry? To begin with, some few authentic elements are extracted from reality by the poet. This is the reason for his great value as a witness. His testimony will refer to external reality — a certain time of the afternoon in the country — and to inner reality, the impact of a spirit with the world. For the poet does not pretend to eliminate his reactions from the picture he paints for us. The sensuousness, sensibility, and sentiment of a Gabriel Miró form a world, rather than deforming ours, and this is what we ask of an artist: his personal testimony. These raw materials now are preserved by means of a marvelously decisive transformation: a series of significant, suggestive, allusive sounds. "For the word," Miró affirms, "like music, brings realities to life, gives them value, exalts and refines them, raising to a 'precisely ineffable' purity what, when it was neither felt nor said in its nuances, in its exactness, was lying dormant

161

within the dusty exactness of the same gaze, the same speech and concept that are possessed by everyone." The ineffable state, then — according to this discerning interpretation — follows speech, it does not precede it. Thanks to the expressive word commonplaces are transcended, and a degree of existence is achieved which is then truly ineffable, situated beyond the word and sustained by it. The language of the author will then be the language of the reader. The reader takes possession of a virtual treasure which only in this way, by being shared, exists aesthetically. From a private zone one emerges to a height common to the author and to his readers. "Brightness" conveys an idea and suggests a picture, and without these general, clearly understood values "brightness" would lie like a dead, dull term, illuminating nothing. The world of the artist, however unique and new it may be, is visible only when it rests on known components, on experiences lived by the reader. Total novelty would neither be comprehensible nor of any interest. We are interested in the world invented by this man from the distant Mediterranean coast of Spain, Gabriel Miró, because it partakes of universal human experience, through a form which is now free, separate, at last, from its genesis.

II

"Awareness of things," Miró believes, is given us "under the influence of the word." Awareness of things and of feelings. Sigüenza, the alter ego of Miró, "has heard himself pronounce the words: 'Let us be happy.' And as he said it he began to be so . . . Because in those words there was a beginning of the will to happiness and awareness of happiness." This height of awareness, accompanied by determination, is reached only by formulating an idea in words and actually pronouncing the syllables by which the idea is identified with

162

its form. The phrase "Let us be happy," Miró concludes, "constitutes an aptitude and a purpose that bring closer to us and make easier for us the possession of a whole, of a panorama of feelings." In the mouth of this man phrases acquire material density, just as they did in the lady who made candy, Mrs. Oloriz: "Everything she pronounces has form and a contour of tender sound, so delectable that you gather it into your whole body, and are left savoring her words as if they themselves were exquisite candy." The literature of Miró is just this: a contour of tender sound savored on the palate. Even in tacit monologue, "The things that are most a part of our life, we must say these too, to ourselves." And when a youth in love thinks of his absent beloved, the image of the absent one involves words first of all, "the words that María Fulgencia would have on her lips." "She too would look at the water, the trees, the sky, and would say: river, tree, sky. When the pigeons left their roof terrace to fly through the vegetable patches, she would see them and pronounce the words: pigeons, air, sun." Most especially it is the poet who pronounces words: "I compressed into words," Miró tells us, "the things that I most loved, that I felt most belonged to me; and I pronounced them." And since they dissolved in the air, "in order not to lose them I wrote them in stones," beside the sea. And he threw them into the sea and into the sea they sank; "and the sea throbbed gloriously." Fortunately, Miró did not repeat that fantasy of his adolescence, and wrote on everlasting paper.

Frequently he causes us to witness the birth of a word at the very moment it springs forth. A peasant exclaims: "In the shade, in the shade!" "And the word 'shade' took on a new coolness, as if he had just created it." Similarly: "Joy in the revelation and pronunciation of the word 'village.'" All of Miró is in this insistence on using the word "pronunciation"

163

beside the word "revelation." Intelligible sound is discovery as well as form: discovery of the world through verbal form. In language our lyric writer finds "maximum profundity." And the more concrete it is, the more profound it will be. Hence the great fascination of place names. Ibi, Tibi, Famorca, Benisa, Jávea — these names of villages in Alicante would intoxicate Miró if they were not solid substances that nourish and fortify him. "Is it delight in a word for its own sake?" Miró asks himself. But: "The fact is that a word would not be delightful if it did not signify a quality." And he likes to hear these names pronounced in the villages themselves by their own inhabitants in order to dig as deeply as possible into the dense, compact clods of the most concrete. "And these rural names in the mouths of the local people leave a taste of fruit," and this fruit carries with it the whole tree "and its garment of earth, and the air and sun and water that touch and soak it." Thus the name, of almost no worth as an ideograph, takes on full value as an image. Let us look, too, at the other side of this concrete picture. Sigüenza sets face to face a very beautiful landscape and certain "atrocious words," atrocious because they are abstract, or at least urbane and general. Sigüenza begins to shout. He shouts words of two syllables, then of three, then of four: "Judg-ment! Me-thod! Vis-count! De-fine! De-pu-ty! Dis-tin-guished! Pro-vi-sion-al! And even formulas of courtesy like My-dear-Sir!" And he scatters "the poor concepts in the motionless, diaphanous air, torn only by the wings of the falcons." Those ridiculous nouns are no longer anything but "poor concepts," the antithesis, for instance, of "Alcalalí," another village in the same region. " 'Alcalalí,' without thought of etymologies, 'Alcalalí,' tiny and sharp as a bell." Geographical reality and verbal reality are fused, and we find each of them in the other: Alcalalí! "Now he joins the image to the word," Miró adds. According to him, these names, like those of the gods to Plato, are without any doubt "the exact expression of truth." (Miró is referring to the passage in the *Cratylus* in which Socrates praises Homer because he distinguishes the names used by men from those used rightly by the gods.) All roads lead to so much faith in language.

Miró did not like to be considered a poet. Even the most modest of "singers" feels that he is something of a demiurge, and Miró, a lyrist — this title did please him — did not aspire to this. His efforts were directed toward capturing a reality revealed by means of the senses and the feelings. For this he needed, obviously, the richest language, the most copious register of words. Miró's vocabulary is immense, and even the most cultured Spaniards find unfamiliar terms in his writings, which are in perfect accord in this respect with those of his great contemporaries. Which writer uses more words: Valle-Inclán? Azorín? Miró? The Castilian language flourished, during the first third of this century, with fabulous splendor. Writers sought and found the exact word; they embellished their phrases with a lexicon of rare words. Miró was not behind the others, and even, on occasion, expressed himself just a shade too carefully. But this in no way detracts from the essential vigor and efficacy of his language. It is a language more opulent than the reader's, and not merely because of the verbal inadequacy of the latter: his world, too, is poorer. "The *arimez* of the flat roof." *Arimez*? The reader turns to his dictionary: "*arimez*, Arabic, *alimed*, support. Projection found on certain buildings." Miró applies himself to "cramming" the phrase with all the substance it can hold, and devotes less thought to the harmony of the whole. This accumulation of elements will not be deterred even by a superabundance of genitives: *Un Mediterráneo de urna de consola de los señores de Guadelest*, "A Mediterranean like the one on a console urn

of the Lords of Guadelest." The cascade of de's seems to please
Miró. What he seeks is precision, exactness. "Sigüenza," at
that point Miró, the writer, "is beginning to feel distrustful
of the oratorical turn of his thought . . . He needs an earnest
effort at precision in order to be able to accept himself. He
will strive for exactness." And while he strives he will observe
everything — without ceasing his reading of the ancients,
without forgetting his dictionaries. And from a sharply felt
experience expression will be born, inseparable from the experience to such a point that the experience would not be
what it is, truly, vitally, without its expression.

III

What does Gabriel Miró say? "And I loved life madly, im-
mensely, even in my furthest posterity. That is why, since
then, I walk, tramp, climb mountains, scramble over the
rocks and sands of the seashore, cross the fields, hear the roar
of my blood like a torrent inside me; and when I cannot go
any further, I lie on the ground looking up at the sky." This
declaration by one of his characters sums up not so much the
incidental life as the destiny of our poet. Blood, torrential
blood, earth, sky — and perpetual avidity. "Oh life, life, life
of mine!" This is what he exclaims every morning. "We are
strong! and it is a fine, hot day. Let us live upward! Isn't that
it?" But Miró, insatiable as a man and as a novelist, will take
on existence at all its levels, and not just the highest. The
same character, the painter in *La Novela de mi amigo* (*The
Story of my Friend*), alluding to certain meannesses he permits himself, says: "This voluntary or forced degradation does
not distress me. I consider it the virtue of clasping every level
and kind of life." No, let us not imagine Miró's world as an
eclogue or an idyll. The sun, far more than the moon, illumines
that splendid Mediterranean coast of Spain known as the

Levante and its whole scale of beings, from a beautiful woman to a monster. The blue of the sky stretches over the leprosy of Parcent. "Oh life, life, life of mine!" And through this individual life, that of everything and everyone. "Look at the air; all I'm asking you to do is look! Can't you see, can't you discover anything in it? Why, it is seething with germs anxious for life!" The first source of these writings is without doubt a fountainhead of good health, accompanied by a deep awareness of that health: "Don't forget that I am alive and healthy by the impulse and virtue of willing it." More clearly: "I live knowing I am alive and wanting to be alive, and alone with myself, with my tissues, with my bones, with my blood." And he loves life as if it meant "clasping all that is created." Note the word "clasping," which refers to the sense of touch. An all-pervasive sense of touch. That is why he adds: "I imagine that I have roots and that they penetrate everything. What joy must be felt by enormous, centuries-old trees: to feel themselves throb and shudder and live by their distant roots!" Life, and therefore fruitful. This tree incorporates also the feeling of paternity and of posterity. Miró will not be like that Don Alvaro who "stooped under the glory of life as if he were afraid of bumping his head in a cave."

This glory assails him, naturally, from the material world, but not as it did Saint Anthony, "Flaubert's Saint Anthony," who would have liked "to descend to the depths of matter, to be matter." This was the last temptation, at the end of that horrendous nocturne. "Sigüenza is not Saint Anthony." Miró is impelled toward matter by that "sensitive divination with which delicate lives are gifted." He knows "how deep and magnificent is the sensation of things." A sensation that may be far-reaching. "Oh, sensuousness, how you transfix us with infinite longings!" There before us lies what we call Nature, or, to say it pictorially, the landscape. There is no bet-

167

ter landscape painter than Miró in all of Spanish literature. He possesses as no one else does that power of contemplation that he attributes to the waters of a spring: "They say it is sleeping water. How can water be sleeping when it catches sensitively all that comes near it and reflects it, even when there is no one to see it! . . . And leaves, treetrunks, rocks, clouds, blue sky, birds, everything can be seen in it, and frequently we know it is beautiful only because the water says so. Then everything takes on the mystery and life of its emotion. It is now beauty contemplated; it is the concept and formula of a beauty produced in this solitude as if in the soul of man, and the water is like the mind that has invented this landscape. Landscape beside the clear, naked water; submerged, tall landscape, how your heart trembles and bows in the face and depths of the water!" If previously the symbol of the poet was the tree, now it is water, which feels, understands, and composes everything that it reflects around it. "Beauty" summarizes the positive values of the landscape. The latter, without man, does not exist. For us it exists only when it is humanized. Miró notes the contrast with sorrow: "All this . . . that is what it is through our concept, our recollection, our lyricism, will continue to exist without our emotion, without our eyes, without us." Poetically there is nothing but the tremulous image in the water. In water in a certain specific place. Miró's landscape is always local, completely local. "The biological and aesthetic necessity of having belonged and always belonging there, with the ethnic, exclusivist feeling of the blood of Israel." So profoundly does the man submerge himself in this bit of Nature that he penetrates even universal Nature. "Many a time Sigüenza has proclaimed with Somoza that it is our native landscape that sustains our emotion in and understanding of all landscape." José Somoza, the delightful Castilian writer (1781–1852), had written: "A countryside that is not

168

in my country is not comprehensible to me, nor does it give me any pleasure to speak of." "But," Miró continues, "a landscape, for a lyric writer, is the landscape, the evocation of them all . . . A landscape, our own especially, extends the gaze from the lineal, from the most subtle detail, to the essence of limitless countryside." Miró makes use of a dangerous notion: essence. In any case, he will never take as his point of departure a more or less Platonic idea, an abstract original perfection. In this universalized landscape flourish in full daylight the attributes of its most specialized differences — along with the differences of soul, the unique soul, of the landscape painter. In a word, "Miró's landscape seems to be a personal experience," as Pedro Salinas observes; "it is not something he has seen but something that has happened to him, that has befallen him, like an adventure, a love affair."

Our adventurer takes possession of this immediate world with his five senses. He has an enormous capacity for sensation. His sight, hearing, taste, smell, touch operate unceasingly, and often their functions are combined. Sight and touch redouble their strength when they are joined. Perhaps the sense of smell intervenes most delicately. Odors are not only smelled but imagined, and even the soul and abstraction come to have their odor. "He remarked that the month of June was the most beautiful month of the year. It smelled of happiness." But someone else corrected him: "It is happiness that has its own smell; it smells of the month of June." Another similar scent: "Flowers almost always smell of a moment of happiness that is no longer ours." And in another passage, the jasmine, roses, orange blossoms, all smell that afternoon "of a happiness that is unfulfilled." Things no one has ever smelled have an odor. "Don Arcadio . . . breathed in with emotion the odor of faded paste." The repertory of odors in Miró's works would make a very lengthy enumeration. "Have you noticed the

169

chimneys? I smell the smoke from their kitchens." His sense of smell is extremely imaginative: "And it even seems to me that I smell the bedrooms, the cupboards and bureaux in the houses, and I feel that I am living and being a part of all the families." Sensation is not confined within limits, and surpasses matter. The artist, of necessity a whole man, always confronts a human world in which the material and the spiritual are indivisible. Miró's sense of smell scents in the air all its depth of life made up of innumerable lives: men, women, children — and animals, plants, things. Sensuousness is spirit. Joaquín Casalduero explains it perfectly: "Sensuousness is situated on a spiritual plane, which does not in the least diminish the beauty that is purely tactile and olfactory, visual and gustatory, thermal and muscular . . . In Miró's totality we find face to face physical and moral brutality and *Caritas:* beauty and love."

IV

Landscapes which have been and are being lived in so much appear before Miró's eyes with great depth: depth of space and of time. Miró looks out the window or scans the horizon from a hilltop, and perceives, feels, divines what he is to call in his last book "years and leagues." They come as a single vision. "The leagues and the years one can see there!" From intimate contact with present things and present time arises the consciousness of time past, which is lying there awaiting resurrection. "Sigüenza's past moves toward him, breathing in the exactness of his awareness of the present." Only thus is the essential continuity of a person fulfilled. Without this continuity there is no person, one cannot coincide with oneself. "Not to participate, not to belong to one's own past, is an absence, a syncope of the soul, which would be unpardonable in Sigüenza, who lives by reason of the continuity of his in-

170

ner self." This is the basis of what Miró considers "his essential lyricism." But this past is not only man's past. Everything is submerged in time. "He penetrated deeper into the solitude of the hill . . . And as soon as Sigüenza appeared, everything began to breathe within the orbit of time" — which is not the time of the person contemplating: "the time of these solitudes, counted now by Sigüenza's pulse." The contemplator discovers there a time outside himself: "and when [the goats] disappear, time without any living being settles on the mountains." Indeed this time is truly spatial. Don Miguel de Unamuno has already pointed it out: "Miró reaches the contemplation of how space and time are merged, and thus he reaches the eternal now." Even the future is surveyed in the panorama. In the distance an old peasant woman follows the ups and downs of the path. "With a single glance Sigüenza covers many hours of that path; so that he can watch the future of the little old woman until she reaches home late at night." "Future" is not exactly a happy stroke. Miró is to be obsessed always by this perspective of space-time. It may present itself in a very limited interior. Certain rooms "keep . . . an ancient darkness, a restful, suspended darkness, a darkness of former years." In the open air: "The golden hours of the fields" stretch "across a luminosity of many years." There is material contact between these two orders. "The days too rolled over Oleza." Every space has its time. "Big, harsh, noisy cities still have some spot with its own quietness, its own time reposing under some garden wall." This quietness preserves the years in which those who enjoyed and watched over the garden lived there. But Miró does not limit himself to the knowledge that through that garden people, generations of people, have passed. For Miró the past is incorporated into his present vision, and he contemplates it thus: past and present, a past that has come to an end within the moment that is now passing. "To feel

171

oneself in another time and now. The fullness of the present sustained by a distant beginning. The clear emotion of our awareness of depth of days." Thus man matures and ceases to be a child: remembering. "To be no longer a child would be that: to depend on past feeling, on the memory of it."

"I have just discovered a delightful spot asleep among the years," Sigüenza tells us. It is not a ruin, the melancholy ruin of the 1830's, nor an ancient monument maintained against a background of History. Sigüenza discovers the abandoned garden of a ruined house, Nature and Time. He describes it thus: "No one. Silence, with the breathing of everything. When he came, the nightingales, swallows, and blackbirds flew away. One could hear the jasmine blossoms dropping, the fine nerves of the plants rustling, the big lizards with their dazzling, icy skins like damp, embroidered silk scurrying into hiding." This abandoned garden, revealing its abandonment in the "dropping," "rustling," and "scurrying" of so much vegetable and animal life, proffers to the visitor a disordered profusion, encouraged, as it were, by those deserted hours that no one claims. Plants, birds, lizards — lizards felt by the eyes and by visual touch in a unique sensation manifested by heterogeneous touches which, nevertheless, are skillfully blended: "dazzling, icy skins like damp, embroidered silk." Once the fright caused by Sigüenza's arrival has passed, the garden returns to its cheerful confusion: "Little by little the birds came back; the salamanders ventured out into the greenish sunlight of the stones; the locusts warmed up again; the swallows, on a dead cypress, began killing their lice, and a bee buzzed in every jasmine blossom." All the purely zoological, botanical, mineral archaism of that corner vibrates in the green that joins sunshine and stones, described in reference to the reptiles: "The salamanders ventured out into the *greenish* sunlight of the stones." But

172

with the swallows and the cypress, noble inhabitants worthy of dwelling in the noblest poem, a discordant note is introduced: discordant in respect to possible decorum, but exact, and very expressive of the wretched reality sheltered among the ruins of the garden: "the swallows, on a dead cypress, began killing their lice." Immediately comes the compensation: "and a bee buzzed in every jasmine blossom."

"Everything, everything was the same as when the outsider came. He looked on the garden as if it were his own, not through purchase, but through ancient possession based on lineage and wishes. He would have inherited it from a great distance of years, from the time when all that had begun to decay; and now he was visiting his inheritance, grieving and feeling grateful to it for the abandonment in which it had left his possessions." The garden lies, then, submerged in time, in its "distance of years," which become for the visitor an inheritance: not to be confused with any illustrious past, either private or public. Human life has withdrawn from that garden. And there remains only an emptiness that permits time to float there like one more factor in the landscape, absorbed by the landscape and perceptible only to the soul of a solitary wanderer in that bit of Nature, not of social History. There are also seven cypresses in a row, two oleanders, and a jasmine vine. "A jasmine vine blinded the window gratings and half the wall . . . A long time ago it too had collapsed from the weight of its shoots and stems, and yet it stays green and tender. It is a torrential, motionless mass, with a virginal odor." What a far cry from the elegies of the Generation of 1898, from the gardens of Castile as described by Azorín! Instead of an elegy, we are treated to an idyllic description of a whiteness that comes dangerously close to being excessive: "All the earth around about is fluffy with snow from the flower. The air is dense

173

with a bride's perfume, a good one, but so strong that the bride is multiplied into a dovecot of maidens stifling us with sweetness. Sigüenza's temples and eyelids were drenched with odor. He suffered an attack of dyspnoea from drinking that sensual odor of chastity." Perfume, bride, dovecot, maidens, sweetness! But at least it is sweetness with irony: "stifling us." The scientific name for asthma, *dyspnoea*, serves as an even greater counterweight, leading to the ironical mixture at the end: "drinking an odor," paradoxically symbolic of a virtue that has no odor: "that sensual odor of chastity."

Finally: "Another aged element of beauty in that enclosure was a laurel tree." It would seem that we are to be favored, under the auspices of beautiful agedness, with a classical or neoclassical decoration. No. "A laurel tree in all its beauty, fit for a god to make his own, but a laurel tree that is completely vegetal, in no way predestined to mythological or allegorical themes . . . It has grown up free, pure, and handsome, without anyone's expecting any more of it than that: that it should live big, beautiful, and secluded." Any thought, then, of a museum composition has been carefully set aside. "And this laurel tree is not only its trunk and its crown, spreading their moist, bluish cloth of shade, but also its impetuous suckers, which split the earth and emerge from the ruins and explode over the wall, so that the plant multiplies itself in baroque profusion without losing its classical unity. It is there in itself and piercing the flagstones and transmitting its note of serenity in its life with the cypresses, the oleanders, the jasmine, and on a terrace dotted with orange trees with a border of grapevines and rose bushes." What springtime vigor, what pressure in this abandoned garden with its "distance of years!" A distance courting the attention of an infinitely sensitive passer-by.

174

V

This passer-by is sensitive not only in his senses but in his memory. It is the subtle alliance of sensation and recollection. Turn to the prologue of *El humo dormido* (*Slumbering Smoke*), published in 1919 (the date is significant). "From the harvested fields, from the ripe earth, from the distant stillness, a blue smoke drifts upward, hangs in the air, and slumbers. A tree, or the outline of a house, emerges; a road, or the cool splendor of living water, passes by. Everything quivers in its nakedness. — Thus the landscape lies before us weary or filled with the days that were left behind us. Concretely, it is not our own past; but it belongs to us, and we make use of it to revive and give substance to episodes that break through the slumbering smoke. The distance holds a deep silence that pauses and listens to us. A remembered word, like a honey bee, goes about opening everything up and setting it to trembling. — Do not think that these fragmentary pages are intended as memoirs; but as you read them you may hear from time to time the bells of the city of Ys, whose fable was retold by Renan, — that more or less peopled and primitive city that all of us carry submerged within ourselves." Renan does tell us of a city of Ys surviving within his heart; according to the Breton legend, from the city covered by the sea the muffled sound of bells arises. "I have taken special pleasure," Renan adds, "in gathering up those remote sounds from a vanished Atlantis." Today's readers are reminded by this submerged world of the great French "rememberer" previously mentioned in connection with Bécquer. The protagonist of *A la Recherche du temps perdu* carries submerged in his memory that town of Combray that was resuscitated by means of a sensation. Proust and Miró? Yes, sensation and recollection, sensation to the point of recollection, or, better yet, recol-

175

lection through sensation; herein lies the essential analogy between these two masters of evocation of "time lost," of "slumbering smoke." ("To associate the names of Proust and Miró is natural," Baquero Goyanes observes.) Over the leagues of a space much traversed and much lived in, the years linger like a haze of reality, at once external and internal; and the deepest substance, which is the most concrete, will be preserved thus, gathered into the memory. "One day we saw a stranger . . . ," Miró remarks. "Now we say: 'We never saw him again!' thinking of how he departed and was lost to us . . . ; and yet, even as we say it, we see him break forth from the slumbering smoke, more clearly, more sharply than we could see him if we had him near us; for that would only mean repeating the first glance, without deepening or enlarging it." As one probes deeply into recollection, into the mass of that "smoke," one comes to possess a reality more substantial than the one that has merely been lived and not yet remembered: "for there are incidents and parts of our lives that cannot be seen wholly until we relive them and contemplate them through memory; memory applies our fullest awareness to them." It is clear that there is more world because there is more spirit, a spirit that acts by *submerging* itself in the exact recollection of sensation, of one's own genuine sensation. It is natural that in such consummate artists as these, their enormous appetite for realities should involve this exacerbation of their inner life.

Sigüenza drinks water in a village, the same water he had drunk from twenty years before. "As he drank, he sensed on his tongue precisely the same taste — of the water and of his own thirst — as in those days." Here the same sensation is reproduced in the same place, and by the same cause. For Proust, it is a question of sensations aroused by different objects in different places. An unevenness in the paving stones in Paris resuscitates Venice. The important point is that from sensation the profound past should arise. "And now all those years, all twenty of them, came as docile as lambs to drink and look at themselves in the old watering trough where the sky was tremblingly reflected." Just as, in Proust's famous phrase, "all of Combray and its surroundings, all that can take on form and solidity emerged, the city and its gardens, from my cup of tea." To be sure, in Miró the notion of "involuntary memory," of sudden recall, does not appear. Neither has he experienced that more or less escstatic trance that brings Bécquer and Proust together. The slumbering smoke could be defined by another expression of Miró's: "spatial recollection." It is typical of Miró to contemplate a landscape with which he has long been familiar. "Now he lies down and stretches out in the imprint of spatial recollection, which is still warm with himself." This, at last, is the approach to felicity. "The foliage receives and sends back and forth the movement of the breezes with their maritime sounds of surf, and it smells of the village, and the repose, of twenty years ago. Sigüenza's past moves toward him, breathing in the exactness of his awareness of the present." But, since Sigüenza does not limit himself to feeling, and wants to see clearly in the world discovered by sensation and evocation, he adds (and this attempt at psychological analysis also characterizes the troubled Sigüenza and brings him closer to Proust): "To feel oneself clearly, — was it to feel oneself at a distance or in one's present form? . . . And as he deduced himself and extracted himself from the past, satiating himself with his vanished image, was he not acquiring a predisposition to a happiness that did not exist then when it could, nor does it now because it has already passed? — and was he not, being without realities, and because of not having any, finding a formula for fulfillment?" A fulfillment, then, that is "ideal," in accordance with an "idealistic" standard that Miró adopts provisionally, with questioning and uncertainty.

Miró takes over, for just a moment, a supposition that is not consistent with his usual attitude: that the realm of pure spirit is superior to that of the incarnation of the spirit in its bodies, works, and acts. This dubitative interrogation marks only a moment of transition, a very brief hiatus between the present and the remembered image. In short: "One has to be, as far as is necessary, one's own predecessor. What filters through, only what filters through." There is, then, in Miró a resistence to the excessive influence of memory. Recollection will resuscitate the past, it is true, but without excessive domination. And everything joins together in the present. "Now I see how they say that God contemplates past, present, and future, in a *continued present*." This does not attenuate the force of recollection. "Recollections, to me, do not dwell just in the memory but in my whole flesh." Or what amounts to the same thing: "My flesh is made of memories!" Memories which are also tied to the land where one has lived, to the flesh of the landscape. A fleeting hour does not pass. And when Sigüenza returns to the countryside he traversed twenty years before, he realizes that "that hour" has remained motionless for him ever since then. "And he even made a slight gesture as if to touch it, to push it." If this landscape identical to itself sustains a motionless hour, by paths different from those of Proust time penetrates time to a certain extent. "This afternoon might have been some other afternoon centuries ago. Sigüenza feels himself carried backward in time . . . This afternoon could just as well have been a September afternoon in 1800, in 1700, in 1600." This chronological equivalence, across the years, gives rise to an eternal synthesis within time, not outside it — as in the ecstasy of Proust, freed then from temporality and, therefore, from death. Miró is more modest. "Sigüenza is experiencing an emotion caused purely by the eternity of the countryside." An eternity situated in

Nature rather than within man. The afternoon becomes eternal by the superposition of many afternoons. At times the moment becomes more personal, and the contemplator achieves "the reiteration of himself," as if he had already lived that moment: a state well known to psychologists. The past is not lost: it floats in the slumbering smoke.

VI

Miró's contemplation involves something more than just a number of objects. All of them are joined together by an atmosphere, both physical and spiritual. In *Slumbering Smoke* we see a double garden, glimpsed through an iron grille, and reconstructed within the house by means of flowers and fruit: "We reached his house. An ancient, lordly house of dark stone blocks with sculptured lintels. Everything was pleasantly dimmed by green shutters, which seemed to extract all the coolness and scent from summer. For you felt that outdoors the raw elements of summer were thickening as it were into a crust, while indoors there was only that delightful, refined intimacy. In the vestibule, the living rooms, the dining room, there were numerous vases, bowls, baskets, and jars overflowing with magnolias, gardenias, fruit, and jasmine; and through the half-open inner gates one caught a rapid glimpse of the afternoon garden, shadowy and familiar. I realize that in July many houses have magnolias, jasmine, fruit, gardenias; but they are this and nothing more: flowers, flowers because someone picks them and too many are dropping in the garden; and fruit: peaches, plums, pears, apples . . . and we instinctively know which one we would bite into. There it was different: there flowers and fruit constituted a tonic note of lordliness and of beauty, an emotion of summer living and of woman. They were not peaches, plums, pears, apples, by classification, but fruit for the emotion inspired by fruit, as

179

well as its evocation of delightful baroque motifs; and that particular fruit, the feel of its skin as you merely looked at it, and its aristocratic enameled coloring; and flowers that had to be precisely magnolias, gardenias, and jasmine for their whiteness and their fragrance, the fragrance of a happiness remembered and inconcrete, in which it almost seems as if hearing has a part, because the emotion inspired by some music expands like an intimate perfume of magnolias, of gardenias, of jasmine, which do not have a specific perfume as do carnations."

A double garden: outside, "the raw elements of summer," inside, in that "ancient, lordly house," the quintessence of summer and garden, "pleasantly dimmed by green shutters, which seemed to *extract* all the coolness and scent from summer." It is a summary, but of the senses, not intellectual. The various sensations are merged in a whole: "that delightful, refined intimacy" inside, and outside "a rapid glimpse of the afternoon garden, shadowy and familiar." Sensations, an impression of the whole, and emotion, which is unifying also. In other words: creation.

The representative elements are flowers and fruits, named repeatedly and assigned to a setting: that particular summer afternoon in that particular garden. There is no question — and the poet analyzes his impressions very clearly — of rational distinctions: "They were not peaches, plums, pears, apples, *by classification*," objectively classified. Neither is there any attempt to embellish reality by associating it with works of art: "as well as its evocation of delightful *baroque* motifs." Even less are these flowers and fruits exhibited from a practical point of view: "I realize that in July many houses have magnolias, jasmine, fruit, gardenias; but they are this and nothing more: flowers, flowers because someone picks them and too many are dropping in the garden; and fruit: peaches,

180

plums, pears, apples . . . and we instinctively know which one we would bite into." Here these flowers and fruits are offered to us united in a creation: "there flowers and fruit *constituted a tonic note* of lordliness and of beauty, an *emotion* of summer living and of woman." Contributing to this emotion are a social background, lordliness; a display of Nature with its season, summer, and it light, afternoon; the proximity of a woman; and all is in delicate balance. These components are then re-created by the association of various senses. Touch with sight: "that particular fruit, the feel of its skin as you merely looked at it." Sight with smell: "magnolias, gardenias, and jasmine for their whiteness and their fragrance." Smell with hearing: "fragrance . . . in which it almost seems as if hearing has a part, because the emotion inspired by some music expands like an intimate perfume." And at this point, as a purely spiritual synthesis, sensation is linked to memory: "the fragrance of a happiness remembered and inconcrete." So intimate is this happiness that it is uncommunicable. From the concrete we have passed to the inconcrete, to the sort of ineffable state that follows intuitive and expressive experience. It is the complete scale of Miró: "fragrance — of a happiness — remembered — inconcrete." Sensation, emotion, memory, ineffable delight.

In this way Miró contemplates interiors and landscapes. Naturally many of them possess or acquire that repose to which a contemplative spirit predisposes. Baquero Goyanes has observed that "Miró likes to situate himself in repose before a landscape." But this world — a lyrical, novelistic one — is not and could not be a "motionless world." Neither a series of prints nor an album of photographs could represent it adequately. Not only do the actions of people stand out in their movement; even the setting is seen and the day heard in all its tumult, sometimes highly discordant. Oleza, the city

181

imagined by Miró, is not a dead place. Consider, in *Nuestro Padre San Daniel* (*Our Father Saint Daniel*), this enumeration of noises and reverberations, making a magnificent panorama of sound: "The mountain air crackled. The sounds of the town and the surrounding region wafted upward, shedding as they rose: the beat of a grist-mill, a peacock's scream, the pounding of a forge, the jingling of harness-bells on a stagecoach, a peasant's song, the broken moaning of wagon-wheel rims, a child's howls, the talking and laughter of two squires exchanging greetings between garden and balcony, and bells, broad, slow, tiny, rapid bells. Over the afternoon slid the cool rushing of the foaming sluices of the river. And amidst everything the vibrant canticle of a cock rang out sharply, and Don Magín sat up and said: 'That's mine!' "

In this paragraph there are few verbs, but there are some. (This is not always so in Miró's descriptions.) "Crackled," "wafted," "shedding," "rose," "exchanging," "slid," "rang out," and finally, "sat up and said." The nouns too indicate action, the more or less vigorous action of everything making sounds on that particular afternoon. The result is not an uproar, because the murmurs and songs are not intermingled, being connected only by the successive, not the simultaneous, attention of the person composing this piece of music. There is a center of observation in the person of Don Magín. It is he who, with his remark, closes the brief symphony. Don Magín, an imaginary lookout, gives novelistic unity to the moment. The one who actually achieves this unity is the novelist. He outlines the composition with great care. It is a composition, not an impression due to the chance happenings that beset a wayfarer, a traveler. The poet-novelist himself imposes this extreme tension of sound moving and stirring the air of the city: "beat," "scream," "pounding," "jingling," "song," "moaning," "howls," "talking and laughter," "rushing," "canticle."

182

ADEQUATE LANGUAGE

This is not the chaotic enumeration studied by Spitzer, because this heterogeneous collection of elements does not entail confusion, and everything fits harmoniously into a definite order: the order of sound. Things, animals, and people together sum up the city of Oleza. The grist-mill, the forge, the stagecoach, the wagon, the bells, the sluices; and the peacock, the cock; and the child, the peasant, the two squires, Don Magín. At the beginning, the air, where "sounds . . . wafted upward"; at the end, the river; crowning the afternoon, and the composition, the sharp, vibrant crowing of the cock. It is curious that the bells should be mentioned without the addition of the proper term: pealing. The object itself becomes something as changeable as its sound waves: "broad, slow, tiny, rapid bells," the adjectives referring to the strokes of the bell, slow and therefore broad, or rapid and therefore tiny. These metaphors of size to designate sounds demonstrate Miró's constant spatial vision, even though it is hearing we have here and not vision. The result is always an intense note of liveness, frequently dynamic. How well the air of Oleza "crackles"! The vocabulary extends from the colloquial "howls" to the supreme "canticle." Archaic adornment is not lacking: "the two squires." The description is thus "ennobled."

Description? Lyric creation, rather, for this is much more than the simple expression of an experience. If the origin of expression, an experience that was lived, furnishes the basis of the work — in which the author strives to capture reality with all exactness — complete expression rises to the height of creation, more opulent than its source. That is what makes it creation. T. S. Eliot makes it clear: "When the poem has been made, something new has happened, something that cannot be wholly explained by anything that went before. That, I believe, is what we mean by 'creation.'" Creation establishes a totality that was not in the experience, the raw materials of which have been transformed, surpassed. Let Miró's capital phrase be better understood: "Perhaps through the word I may be granted fullness of contemplation." Creative contemplation.

VII

The contemplator, the poet-novelist, confronts the broadest of horizons. Miró is indeed, as he wished to be, "the perceptive center of an immense ring of creation," and "the contact with naked creation drenched his skin and his blood." There is contact, but there is no attempt at the more or less pantheistic fusion that one of his characters dreams of: "He longed to be immense and light, he too, to change into blue sky, woodland, silence, everything, nothing." Sigüenza is not Saint Anthony, nor does Miró aspire like the Hindu to final dissolution. The world does indeed gleam with splendor, in "those happy experiences of simplicity and purity through which we seem to return to the sanctity of the first moments of life." Privileged moments. "A grace, an innocent felicity of light that . . . made one afraid it would break." It is like a vision of Paradise. "Has not Sigüenza just opened his eyes with the same emotion of innocence as the first man?" Fugitive moments. "The happiness and the innocence have been destroyed," our momentary Adam declares. Perhaps it is better thus. "Did not Sigüenza have an advantage over Father Adam in knowing himself to be mortal?" — which is to say, in knowing himself to be human. No, Miró's world is not filled with "the virgin flora, lush and enchanting, of Paradise." His is a world which, if it does not suffer from original sin, does suffer from the manifold sins of History. That is why he relates so many passions, evils, acts of violence. The narrator is tender. But the narration includes acts diametrically opposed to his own tenderness. Miró often takes pleasure in depicting cruelty.

184

ADEQUATE LANGUAGE

The victims are almost always animals, tormented by other animals or by men. A complete list of these tortures would be tedious. Many are the animals subjected to pain and death, especially to pain. "It was a morning of cruelty. We wanted to give in to pity, but we realized that a struggle of hatred was just beginning." Here is an example of the polarity that joins cruelty and compassion: "That gentle, pious man who in his own home preached of the yearning for life and love was deliriously embarking on a path of cruelty." Victims of that path were a cock-devil, some bees, a pigeon, a mastiff. Another man understood his guide to say that a serpent had killed an old woman, and asked about her. " 'What old woman?' replied the guide, horrified. 'The dead woman!' 'What dead woman? There isn't any dead woman! It's a sheep, a sheep! . . .' What becomes of our sense of pity! He confessed it to himself: he would rather the one poisoned had been the *old woman!* Lord, do we always have slumbering within us the base dregs of cruelty?" Cruelty to a bat, to dogs, the cruelty of a hawk to a pigeon; hunting scenes; a lizard, trap-shooting, a rat, a lamb, an eagle, frogs and storks, more rats, a cat, a crow, a wasp, eaglets, another rat, a turtle, a new-born kitten, a swallow, a fish. Even ice-cold water can be ferocious. "Then Felix looked with fear and rage at that ferocious water, so still and transparent." A little girl, Lucita, dies an atrocious death. Tales are told of the tortures inflicted on the Christian martyrs, and afterward of the tortures devised by the Huguenots; there are only allusions to "the outrages and tortures done to many Christian virgins." Father Bellod reads "avidly" the passage in which Prudentius relates the death of the Virgin Grace (Santa Engracia). We are told the "varieties of procedure in tortures" practised by a King of Assyria. Let us not oversimplify, then, the world of Miró, a man essentially full of pity, but a novelist to whom nothing is alien. Nature's cruelty

185

comes even before humanity's. A Jesuit is speaking: "All is filled with the grace and beauty of the Creator, and in all places we should receive the divine teaching of the Book of the Creation." But the priest could not continue his peroration, because "a furious uproar broke out." It was the hens, pecking viciously at some pigeons; they were fighting over a dead worm. Here is a lesson in cruelty that men have found easy to learn. "I am not given to pity! I am not given to pity!" exclaims the painter in *La novela de mi amigo*. Our novelist was given to pity, but his imagination — tortured, torturing — knew no pity. Gerardo Diego has explained it thus: "his tender compassion toward animals — obvious in his loving observation of them, no less than in his tacit, unspoken protest at the cruelties and martyrdom of which they are the victims."

Along with cruelty, pain. Miró sees it in both its physical and spiritual aggressions. *Del vivir* (*On Living*) is the title of the first really personal book published by Miró. The living in question is confined to Parcent, a village of lepers: terrible figures, at once ancient and contemporary. The book carries as its epigraph some lines from the Book of Job. If the young writer had not visited Parcent, in the province of Alicante, he would not have written this "report," so direct and vigorous. Nevertheless, what he saw there is set down by way of the Bible. No reader of Miró can be unaware of the influence on him of both the Old and the New Testament. His native region is identified, partially, with Palestine, and the landscapes of these lands at opposite ends of the Mediterranean are treated as if they were the same. The lepers of Parcent appear — or hide themselves — in the shadow of Biblical drama: they are creatures whom the God of Israel is putting to the test. There is no avoidance of the picture of suffering flesh and

186

its process of putrefaction. The same eyes that see matter as very beautiful can uncover the most horrible bodies. The horror goes beyond illness, and is embodied in monsters like *Cararajada*, Split-face, the pathetic character in *Nuestro Padre San Daniel*. (Split-face is one of Miró's most successful creations from the novelistic point of view.) The religious background of the author's world is obvious. And let us not forget the importance he attaches to the Evangelical figures surrounding Christ: *Figuras de la Pasión del Señor* (*Figures of the Passion of Our Lord*).

But Miró, as his readers well know, does not limit himself to the Bible. No Spanish writer of this century has set forth as much Catholic life, as much Catholic Church as has Miró in his lay tales, which teem with devout men and women, priests, friars, and nuns, and gleam with the splendors of the liturgy. It is true that in any Spanish city the ecclesiastical estate enjoys a privileged position, and Miró does no more than reflect a reality of Spanish life. For him, this reality reaches its culmination in Holy Week. That is when all the elements dearest to him are gathered together: province, remembered childhood, ceremonies, Scripture. He re-creates it all with warm understanding, but not with the acceptance of the strict believer. The fact is that the two contemporary Spanish writers most conversant with the Bible and with the Spanish Catholic and Apostolic Church are Unamuno and Miró, both of them free in their thinking, both critical. Every Spaniard understands these cases of people who combine, in a way very difficult to define, both faith and lack of faith. Miró's clerical sketches have implicit in them both admiration and satire. What he admires in the Church is its beauty: beauty of language, of cult, of architecture. Through this inclination, aesthetic in character, Miró belongs to that period that delighted

187

in combining the sacred and the profane, the erotic and the liturgical, through their common denominator of beauty.

"Beauty," while it is a term used by Miró, is not a primary aim of his writings. And his affinities with such writers as Rubén Darío and Valle-Inclán are secondary; they correspond largely to the youthful writings of this author, who was in general very little affected by the "aesthetic" or "decadent" style, except perhaps in the *Figuras de la Pasión*. We do, however, find traces of it: "and her head drooped little by little, like a pallid water-lily" (*La Novela de mi amigo*). Shortly afterward appears "an immense, glorious cloud of foam, like a flock of enchanted swans." Shades of *Prosas profanas!* — and so many other books of the same kind. Even worse: "And Felix took her pale hands, and kissed her fingers and her rings, and on one smooth amethyst he placed a long, slow kiss which clouded the stone. 'You are my bishop, Godmother mine!'" Are these sentences from *Las cerezas del cementerio,* or from *Sonata de Otoño?* Professor Meregalli speaks rightly in this connection of "the indubitable derivation from Valle-Inclán." This is a far cry from the mature Miró, who was to eliminate all the frippery and coloring of 1900.

In its essence, the immediate life of the man of the Levante does keep a vestige of History, and the religious background implies also a historical background — with its great, constant accompaniment, the Mediterranean, the ancient sea par excellence renewed with every morning sun: "and in the air everywhere Mediterranean brightness palpitates. And that air with the grace of ancient horizons . . ." It would be a noxious grace if it led to academic convention. But it does not: "Some imaginative souls saw in Benidorm a town with porticos, altars, and gods of white marble. Sigüenza saw in Benidorm nothing but Benidorm, without marbles, without anything classical." It is life today that constitutes the primary theme of Miró.

188

ADEQUATE LANGUAGE

Life today means social life: in moments of crisis, drama; in its daily manifestations, comedy. It is essential to stress its ironical aspect, possibly as important, or almost as important, as the lyrical. To the human landscape Miró reacts with another approach: his irony. An irony which does not diminish his tenderness. This man who was so complex amused himself by observing our society with a malicious joy that did not prevent his continued insistence on the delights of material things. Here we see his alter ego in a barber shop in Barcelona: "No sooner had he entered than Sigüenza felt constricted, intimidated . . . Those polished, perfumed, agile youths looked at him excessively. The place gleamed with the elegance and luxury of a lady's dressing table, and with the cold severity of a surgeon's instrument cabinet." Are we not aware already of the mocking confrontation of the humble resident of the provinces, in his truly Christian humility, with the refinements of elegance and of science? Sigüenza, the man from the country, contrasts with the flashiness of civilization. "They sat him in an armchair that was all articulated, docile and enormous, and our man was guilty of some uncouthness: such as showing his fright when the back apparently dropped away, letting him down into an abyss; nor could he conceal his pleasure when, immediately, he felt himself blandly and knowingly sheltered by the vertebrae and the arms and sides of that piece of furniture that was so human." It is not possible to humanize a piece of furniture with a more affectionate smile. The bewilderment and awkwardness of the provincial gentleman maintain the situation on a gently comic level. From here to the end we see the other aspect, the accumulation of sensations of touch: "They fastened around his neck the soft collar of cotton batting; they swathed him in a robe, a shoulder-cloth like an amice, a magnificent bib, imposing as a clergyman's pelisse,

189

and a smooth, handsome towel. And he looked at himself and thought: 'Lord! What obligations am I in for, wrapped in these ample, candid vestments?'" Observe the softness and smoothness of these nouns—collar of cotton batting, robe, shoulder-cloth, bib, towel—enhanced by the adjectives "soft," "magnificent," "smooth." Moreover, the sensation of touch is given an ironical cast, especially by the antiquated references, largely clerical: shoulder-cloth, amice, a clergyman's pelisse. Rhetoric serves here to form a smiling contrast. "Lord!" says Sigüenza (like the old people in Azorín), in a sentence whose tone is both old-fashioned and ecclesiastical: "What obligations am I in for, wrapped in these candid vestments?" And the word "candid" evokes the etymological ideas of whiteness and innocence. "The subtle, winged hands of the youth plunged delicately into the thicket of his hair. Sigüenza began to feel a childish drowsiness, a delightful resignation, a complete forgetfulness of self; all of Sigüenza was a scalp that shrank and stretched under that extremely gentle anointment." This is almost a "trance," in indulgent caricature. And always there is the sense of touch, here "that extremely gentle anointment." "And he half closed his eyes and thought: 'Let us sleep, my soul.'" (A parody echoing Segismundo's sublime imperative, "Let us dream, my soul.") "But from time to time there would come to his ear a placid buzzing, as of a bee." This "buzzing, as of a bee" insinuates the background of Nature so habitual with Miró. "It came from the hairdresser, who was consulting him reverently, and he, without understanding him, would answer weakly, 'Yes, of course.' And again he would doze off, and again the slight humming would bring him out of his lethargy, and he would say, 'Yes, all right.' And finally he murmured: 'Do whatever you like, it doesn't make any difference to me!' And they put soaps and creams on him; he was lost under a lather smelling of orange

190

blossoms; they poured on flacons of toilet water; next to his temples and the nape of his neck they burned little lamps with blue flames; they passed him magazines, books, leaflets, guides to the city, lighted cigarettes, and all of them dropped from his helpless hands. Suddenly the youth's fingers, his index and middle fingers, grasped his temples and chin, and in a tone of grave respect he said: 'Come.' 'Where?' asked Sigüenza, startled, seeing his lathered cheeks. The youth smiled a small, courtly, correct smile. That 'Come' was by way of invitation to tip and turn his head so he could go on shaving." The chiaroscuro and the gentle fun have been maintained thanks to the person, so pusillanimous that civilization intimidates him, and the language, relatively commonplace, but with noble adornments.

Miró admits, at the same time that he distinguishes between, the two opposite poles of the human spectacle, excellence and deficiency, and his interpretation of them is inevitably both incisive and good-natured. "Next door Sigüenza found a religious book-store. And he dozed off gently as to the cooing of doves as he read such dulcet titles as *Little Spark of Love, Celestial Dew, Little Garland of All that is Most Pleasing to God, Virginia or The Christian Maiden, Gallery of Deceptions.* When by chance there was some lay work among them, it was always an extremely innocent one, without the slightest suggestion of doubt or uneasiness about it, such as *The Canary: Its Origin, Strains, Raising, Breeding and Illnesses,* or *The Chess Player's Manual.*" A wonderful example of the window displays of religious book-stores in Spain! Linking with opposition: "the cooing of doves," referring to all that mellifluous sanctimoniousness, which so fascinated Miró. And along with these unctuously devout titles, the modest and concrete titles that attracted him also, raised to the ironical category of "innocent." Another example. This time it is a newlywed with patent-leather shoes. " 'All that patent-leather!' thought Sigüenza, gazing tenderly at his feet as if they were two little birds, two humble creatures." "Tenderly" is ironically excessive, but tenderness or sympathy were surely present in Sigüenza's eyes. This is the same taste we find in Cervantes for contrast between two orders or levels of being, one superior, the other inferior. A mad seminarian says: "Mine eyes are the eyes of eagles, and I come from the province of Gerona." This drop in level is found at every step. "Charles V had a haircut in Barcelona." Miró has read his Cervantes thoroughly, and often quotes him, or alludes to episodes and characters. Let us picture Miró between his two favorite books, the Bible and *Don Quixote*. His concept of reality was formed by them. Cervantes fortified in him what must have been an innate capacity for setting up in friendly contrast two opposing zones, which are at the same time exalted and belittled with affection and criticism. It is thus that the value can persist of a thing in which one does not completely believe. The novelist turns out to be the accomplice, in the long run, of the error, the weakness, the absurdity that he has satirized. Witness this brief exchange about a sailboat: "Oh white, fantastic apparitions bringing us the emotion of mysterious lands!" exclaims a quixoticized Sigüenza. " 'But, Sigüenza, all they are bringing is salt-fish, mostly codfish.' 'Martínez!' — and he detested him." Martínez here is a pseudonym for Sancho. Felix says to Beatriz in *Las cerezas del cementerio* (*The Cherries in the Cemetery*): "You are a princess disguised as a cook so that you can feed a poor, weak creature." A poor, weak creature in the presence of Dulcinea-Aldonza. This Cervantine game of opposites is most profound when it seems least so. Someone recalls the story of Daniel in the lions' den: "and Señor Egea folded his arms valiantly, imagining himself surrounded by fierce lions, emaciated with hunger, prostrating themselves before him and lick-

192

ing him from the baggy knees of his trousers to his mauve velvet slippers, embroidered by Doña Corazón Motos, the gentleman's cousin, the owner of a chocolate and candle shop on Veronica Street." The whole paragraph plunges downward from the Biblical den to a nondescript street of the present day — just as Don Quixote's first monologue on his first sally descends from "Scarce had the rubicund Apollo" to "the famous old battlefield of Montiel." Certainly the two great books come together here. And the Book of Daniel is to Miró's character, Don Daniel Egea, what the book of *Amadís* was to Don Quixote. This is the way we must interpret this flashing rhetoric, which has been denounced more than once; for the flash accompanies the essential attainment of a language that is truly expressive. "And that crass, gluttonous, crude creature who boasted chevrons and did not suffer any temptation or purify himself in asceticism, was *acceptable* in the eyes of the Lord!" And the word "acceptable" is in deceptive italics. Obviously, Miró loves these resounding words — and uses them with the hint of a wink. Cervantes derived this same sort of pleasure from chivalrous and pastoral prose; it is not always clear how much of his imitation is parody and how much is poetic re-creation. "And the sly little gleam in their eye . . ." These particular eyes belong to some sparrows that were looking at Sigüenza; but the words are much more applicable to Miró himself. A sly little gleam lurks in his eye, accustomed to seeing things completely in caricature. "His cheeks quivered, and his plump voice too, like still another cheek." And describing "the ladies and maidens of Oleza" in their gowns that were slightly out-of-date, Miró speaks of the "bosoms thrust back into the canebrake of their whalebones." Our poet-novelist's range is wide and varied. But irony, even when it is a governing force, must keep within bounds, and not everything, as the writer himself affirms, should be sub-

193

mitted to this treatment: "Irony as a rule of conduct, of art, and of dialogue is almost a farce."

IX

It was natural that Miró should choose the novel as the form best suited to his multiple endowments. In the novel there is room for everything. And Miró, so well aware of his lyrical gifts, poured all his ambition into narrative writing. The effort was successful. His capacity for describing landscapes is so exceptional that it seems to overshadow his vigor as a novelist. It pained Miró that his tales should be read as if they were no more than a collection of descriptive and lyric pieces. Let us not commit this error. There is an abundance of lives and of passions in the Levante created by Miró on the basis of his real Levante. *La novela de mi amigo* (*The Story of my Friend*, 1908) is the best of his youthful efforts. *Nuestro Padre San Daniel* (*Our Father Saint Daniel*, 1921) and *El obispo leproso* (*The Leprous Bishop*, 1926) mark the summit of his maturity. Pity, cruelty, sensuality, devoutness, love, ha-tred — motivate and agitate, raise up and destroy this multi-tude of gentlemen, churchmen, and villagers under a universal sun and moon — especially under the sun. Miró is a solar poet. His style, terse, compact, pithy, becomes an admirable screen reflecting everything, although for some readers it may con-stitute an obstruction that does not let the content show through. Even for some supposedly cultured readers, a well-written page is merely a decorative page, and all form to them smacks of formalism. In point of fact, there is no creation with-out its adequate expression, and Miró's world could not exist apart from this overflowing mass of vocabulary.

Even so, it is just possible that the shorter narratives are superior to the longer ones. They are closer to the author's personal experience, memories of his childhood or recollections of a less distant past; they are a treasure-house of the most intimate and direct experience of Miró: *Del vivir* (*On Living*, 1904), *Libro de Sigüenza* (*The Book of Sigüenza*, 1917), *El humo dormido* (*Slumbering Smoke*, 1919), *Años y Leguas* (*Years and Leagues*, 1928). He gives the name "sketches" to what are really short stories and fantasies in *El Angel, el Molino, el Caracol del Faro* (*The Angel, the Mill, the Lighthouse Conch-Shell*, 1921). In a separate category, a preeminent place is given to Palestine, the center of his world: *Figuras de la Pasión del Señor* (*Figures of the Passion of Our Lord*, 1916–1917). Some readers prefer the vast museum canvases of the latter, canvases with a great wealth of life and of moral value. Others are fascinated by the charms of the slumbering smoke and the wanderings of Sigüenza. Sigüenza . . . is he fiction or self-portrait? Yes and no, on both counts; up to a certain point. Sigüenza was to Miró what Juan de Mairena was to Antonio Machado and Xenius and Octavi de Romeu were to Eugenio d'Ors, what Rubín de Cendoya might have been to Ortega, what Azorín is to Martínez Ruiz. Sigüenza — with no first name — a sort of lay Franciscan, a poor unassuming creature from the Levantine coast of Spain, humble, very kind, gentle, idle, and curious, not without humor in his contemplative and exploratory bent, first appears in Parcent, the Biblical village, and his creator guides him along multitudinous roads. At the end of *Años y leguas*, which is perhaps Miró's masterpiece, there is a kind of farewell: "And here I shall leave Sigüenza, perhaps forever. It is better to leave him before youth takes leave of him. Because, without a touch of youth, there can be no Sigüenza." Yet this partial incarnation of the author's youth lived on beyond this final paragraph, because Miró the man identified himself more and more closely with the creature of his imagination. Many of his letters are signed only "Sigüenza," which is more the equivalent of a private "Gabriel" than of a

195

public "Miró." Even in conversations he would refer to himself as "Sigüenza." Nevertheless, his alter ego reveals only one part of Miró, who was infinitely more complex than his harried pilgrim. Novelists never limit their projection of themselves to a single character. Sigüenza is only one character; Miró is a true novelist. The inequality between the two proves it.

Gabriel Miró was a man without peer: handsome, blond, blue-eyed, tender, mocking, gesticulating with his whole body, with his hands, with the thousand changing expressions of his face and voice; brilliant, witty, an artist conscious of his artist's role; at home only in the domestic circle or a quiet corner, yet ambitious for fame; cheerful, sorrowful, passionate, with a vehemence shot through with the most exquisite sensibility; and sensitive, sensitive, sensitive to everything, and expressive, as much so as anyone, more so than anyone else. The spoken word was no less powerful in him than the written. His written style seems labored; as a matter of fact, it is close to what his conversation was, for in Gabriel Miró there was always functioning his double aptitude for feeling and expression. Miró represents with extraordinary intensity the type of man destined to the concrete world: Miró, or Concrete Man. From that superb specimen of the human animal, spirit emanated as a luminous irradiation from matter. And that combination of matter and spirit was marvelously organized for examining, suffering, feeling the world. In him sensations, emotions, passions developed continuously in constant gradation. Miró walks along the street, and the street is a new world to him, discovered for the very first time. He appears before us as a barbarian, bringing new materials. Quite the opposite of an intellectual, and even less of a rhetorician, even though rhetoric may appear in a subordinate position. For this man — an unusual barbarian, possessing great knowledge — everything turns into landscape: the earth and its inhabitants, space and

196

time; for Miró sees landscape with his eyes and with his memory. Hence the importance of recollection. Miró, in his attitude toward Nature, is sensitive and enthusiastic; in his attitude toward society, he is sensitive and mocking. Hence the importance of irony. This, then, is Gabriel Miró: sensitivity channeled through recollection and irony — and expression.

So opulent is the expression that, for some readers, it relegates content to second place. But the expression would not be opulent if it did not set forth a wealth of content. Professor Meregalli has emphasized "the organic originality of the moral world" presented in Miró's works. Alfred W. Becker has understood the "continuity of thought linking and harmonizing" the works. Becker divides Miró's characters into two groups: "those who seek an affirmative life" with full physical and spiritual development, and those who place obstacles in the path of this personal development, or give it up entirely. Miró the "humanist" concludes: "What I ask is man without a Guardian Angel on his right hand nor a Devil on his left. Man face to face with himself; let sin grieve him because he has offended himself; let all nature resound within his inmost being; astonished and complex; more a man than a person." That is to say, a man who accepts himself as complex in order to become . . . a man. María Alfaro has expressed it well: "It requires limitless perspicacity and fortitude to seek after clarity in all the corners of the world." Clarity which deserves an admirably expressive being. And Gabriel Miró admirably represents the type of writer who believes in the value of language: the typical Southerner, the Mediterranean man par excellence, whose most avid insistence coincides with his supreme gift: the word. "Perhaps through the word I may be granted fullness of contemplation." And of creation. And of life. Glory be to the word!

197

6

THE LANGUAGE
OF THE POEM
One Generation

The Language
of the Poem

One Generation

I

Some of the writer's friends have asked him to explain his own poetry, relating it more or less to the theme of this book: language and poetry. But discretion advises against yielding to these requests, and recommends instead a compromise. To avoid the first person protagonist, *le moi haïssable,* let us rather consider *us,* that group of poets who, with the attributes of a literary generation, lived and wrote in Spain between 1920 and 1936. This is the generation of Federico García Lorca, its best-known representative. Picasso and Lorca — who, with Manuel de Falla and Juan Ramón Jiménez, are the greatest modern Andalusians — are the two contemporary Spaniards most clearly visible on the horizon of European culture. They are without doubt the two who possess the greatest genius. Picasso had to go to Paris to find the cultural climate and the market his painting required. Lorca had no need to leave his country. In the Spain of his time literature was flourishing, and among his contemporaries were writers of major importance.

The first third of the twentieth century in Spain, fertile in great writers of prose, was also very rich in poets. In the steps of the older writers — Unamuno, Antonio Machado, Juan Ramón Jiménez, all much in evidence along with Gabriel Miró

201

and Ramón Gómez de la Serna — there appeared a number of young lyric writers who soon formed a coherent group. Coherent as a group, although composed of very different personalities. The concept of generations was already in the air. At that time the word meant a reality which was known empirically, not by induction a posteriori; and it is so used here. Seldom has a historical harmony revealed itself so clearly as it did during the twenties in the tastes and purposes of those young men, whose intellectual life was centered in Madrid. Of course nobody was consciously obeying a system established by logic — and therefore deadly — by one of those philosophers who trace on paper the symmetrical march of generations at strictly regular intervals. It is indeed paradoxical that this determinism *malgré lui* should be proclaimed under the auspices of the idea of life, of existence. Here we are dealing only with knowledge based on experience, with history that was lived, not studied. About the year 1925 certain Spanish poets found themselves in more or less intimate contact. If, as Ortega suggests, each generation gathers individuals born during a period of fifteen years, this generation would have as its key date the year 1898. In that year were born Federico García Lorca, Dámaso Alonso, and Vicente Aleixandre. Somewhat older were Pedro Salinas, Jorge Guillén, and Gerardo Diego, born in 1891, 1893, and 1896 respectively. A year after Lorca comes Emilio Prados, born in 1899. Then in this century come Luis Cernuda (1902), Rafael Alberti (1903), and the youngest, Manuel Altolaguirre (1905). From Salinas to Altolaguirre stretch the required fifteen years — required, that is, by theory. It would be superfluous to add more dates. A number of other writers fulfill their chronological duty: Antonio Espina, Pedro Garfias, Adriano del Valle, Juan Larrea, Juan Chabás, Juan José Domenchina, José María Hinojosa, Ernestina de Champourcín, José María Quiroga Pla, the writers of the *Meseta*, a

202

review published in Valladolid, those of the *Mediodía* of Seville . . . This enumeration is incomplete, unjustly so, and includes only lyric writers in verse, not lyric writers of narrative and essay. "Literature" at that time came to mean "lyricism." Most of these poets are Andalusians. Castile and Andalusia have always been the principal sources of Spanish poetry. In the past Castile predominated; today, and conspicuously so, it is Andalusia. All of them, Castilians and Andalusians, without any conscious effort on their part, were in every way contemporaries of their contemporaries in Europe and America. These poets found themselves attuned to the general atmosphere of the twenties, even though certain traits of their poetry belong to a tradition that is purely Spanish.

This basic characteristic of the group has been pointed out before. Even a generation of "innovators" such as this felt no need of repudiating its ancestors, remote or immediate, in order to establish itself. "The first thing to be noted," observes Dámaso Alonso, who is both member and chronicler of the group, "is that this generation does not rise up against anything." Quite the contrary: it has sunk its poetic roots deeper and deeper into the past. The writers of the Generation of 1898 had already reawakened interest in certain works and authors whom they considered "primitive": the *Poema del Cid*, Gonzalo de Berceo, the Archpriest of Hita. Now all the lyricists of the Golden Age were brought out into the light; not only Góngora. Between Garcilaso and Quevedo the admirable secondary figures took their place once more: Figueroa, Aldana, Medina, Medinilla, Medrano, Espinosa, Villamediana, Soto de Rojas. While the great Góngora was being restored to his rightful place others too were reëvaluated, and granted higher esteem than before: Gil Vicente, San Juan de la Cruz, Lope, Quevedo. This demonstration of good memory does not imply primarily the discrimination of the erudite, although the delights of erudition were not foreign to these poets, even to those who were not professors. (The poet-professors are Pedro Salinas, Jorge Guillén, Dámaso Alonso, and Gerardo Diego.) But Lorca too wrote on Góngora, and it was he who brought Soto de Rojas, a poet of Granada, to our attention. Even Rafael Alberti, the least academic of all, has continually demonstrated his enormous capacity for assimilation and cultural reminiscence. These frequent excursions into the poetry of the past were the work of poets acting as poets. And since all of them strove for the most exact expression, they admired both ancient and modern texts whenever these contributed to the authenticity of poetry. For this reason also they defended and studied Bécquer, who is so free from complications of form and such a pure phenomenon of inspiration. A place apart was reserved for Juan Ramón Jiménez — although Antonio Machado shared the same level of eminence — because Juan Ramón was a living example of fervent dedication to poetry. And finally, the foreign poets most read and loved were the French, from Baudelaire to the Surrealists.

II

Along all these paths, and without any dogmatic restrictions set by a school — there were neither school nor dogmas — these young men sought after a poetry that would be both art with all the severity of art and creation with all its genuine *élan*. An art of poetry, and therefore no mere effusion, neither in the manner of the last century nor as a violent, formless surge from the subconscious. There is no babble quite so empty as that of the subconscious left to its triviality. In Spain no one was ever satisfied with the surrealist "document." An art of poetry, but no empty formalism. Of course the semi-ignorant of our time, with all the air of prosecuting attorneys, cry "formalism" at the sight of any well-wrought form, that is to

204

say, a form carefully fitted to its content. Many and varied were the meters, strophes, modulations, and rhythms used by that group. One must needs employ the term *maestría*, artistic mastery. Some people substitute the word "virtuosity." In "virtuosity" there is "virtue," but a virtue worn and debased. Nevertheless "virtue" stands up under the denunciation. The mastery was attained in some cases with precocious speed. Thus Rafael Alberti was a master-poet almost, one might say, from birth. One cannot contrast the domination of form of some of these poets with the spontaneity of others, for these others — Lorca, for instance — were fully as "learned" as their professorial companions. Poetry as an art of poetry: the form of an incarnation. We could write this word with a capital I: the mystery of the Incarnation. The spirit becomes form incarnate mysteriously, with something which cannot be reduced to the intelligence, in this marriage of idea and music.

"Idea" here means reality in a state of feeling. Reality is depicted in the poem, but not described in its external *likeness*. Reality, not realism. And feeling, without which there is no poetry, has no need of gesticulation. Sentiment, not sentimentalism, which was damned by that group as the lowest of obscenities. This restraint in the displaying of emotions retains their vehemence, and indeed doubles their intensity. But for ears that hear not, harmonies such as these are almost confused with silence. That is why some of these poets were tried and found wanting for their coldness, even though they were dedicated to declaring their enthusiasm for the world, their fervor for life, their love for love. A change in the means of expression blinded certain readers — who have, however, after years of apprenticeship, come to understand and feel a love poem of erotic vehemence as a love poem. The same readers added to the accusation of coldness that of abstractness. They were so intellectual, these poets! In truth, many abstractions were interwoven with the more plastic components of some of these poems. This has always occurred; language cannot exist without the combination of the intellectual with the concrete. In any case, no one ever dreamed of writing poetry purely of the intelligence. Antonio Machado was right in maintaining that "the intellect does not sing." The incriminated poets never claimed that they could dispense with the springs from which lyric poetry flows by eliminating the heart. On this occasion the clear-thinking Machado's comment fell wide of the mark. These poets had left out nothing — nothing essential: they were poets. (On the other hand, Antonio Machado himself was very close to the edge of lyricism in those aphorisms in verse that are so closely related to the dissertations of Professor Juan de Mairena.)

In short, said the critics, the poets of the twenties were, if not cold nor purely abstract, at least difficult, hermetic, obscure. Difficult they were, like many another poet. Hermetic? This word, used ordinarily to designate their Italian contemporaries, never became current in Spain. Obscure? The term is obsolete. Little by little over the years almost all this so-called obscurity has drifted away — an "obscurity" more tolerated in poets of delirium and free form, like Vicente Aleixandre, than in those of greater logical concision, like Jorge Guillén. It would be impossible, moreover, to divide these poets into two groups, the easy and the difficult, a division which irritated Lorca. Certainly *Poeta en Nueva York* seems no more simple than *La voz a ti debida* or *Cántico*. Is not language that makes a point of being rational — the language of politics, for instance — in itself a seedbed of confusion? How much more fecund of confusion must be the language of a person who, in order to refer to the very depths of his life, has recourse to the ambiguity of images. These poets talked through images. And at this point — the preponderance of metaphor — all our threads come together. The American term "Imagists" could be applied to all writers of any imagination who were writing here or there in the twenties. Góngora, Rimbaud, Mallarmé, and the later ones — Hopkins, Eluard — every stimulus led them to refine and multiply their images. In this way, in the words of the *Romancero gitano*, *"la imaginación se quema"* — "imagination burns." This cultivation of the image is the most common among the very diverse characteristics that both joined and separated the poets of those years — and not only Spanish poets. *Imagen* was the title of an early work by Gerardo Diego. The cultivation of the image became a kind of superstitious cult: the extremists reduced poetry to a sequence of images from which all transitions of normal discourse had been removed. Only separate phrases remained: the ultimate condensation of literary activity. Logical or grammatical connections of any sort were suspected of poetic inertia. Nor did the images themselves submit to recognized relationships. Reality, surviving in spite of everything, was not duplicated by mere copying but was recreated in the freest manner possible. This freedom expressed the inner world of man — "the subconscious," it was frequently called — rather than the external realities known through reason. Of course, the degree of equivalence between the real and the imaginative varied a great deal. Some writers endeavored to elevate themselves to a second reality, independent of the primary common reality: the autonomy of the image.

III

The poet feels the word "poetry" in its full etymological meaning. (But this "creation" will always be secondary to that of the first Creator, of the book of Genesis. All poets are in this sense *poètes du dimanche,* — of the Sunday following the Saturday on which Jehovah rested.) To evoke the poetic atmosphere of the twenties, we must stress this determination to treat poetry as creation, a poem as a world in quintessence. Whether grave or gay, the works of that period aim at one essential goal, and they are anything but the frivolous sport that some critics saw in that swarm of images. Besides, nothing is more earnest than playing in earnest, and there can be no doubt that in 1925, in 1930, and in 1935 one played at writing the best poetry achievable with all possible ingenuity. These poets did not feel obliged to practice a poetic priesthood, nor did any religious, political, or social pomp mechanize their gestures. Neither were there any theatrical gestures. Their purpose was uncompromising poetry considered as creation. And what were the possibilities of achieving a poem that would be completely poetic? This ambition floated vaguely in the air in those days. Poetry and poem must be identified as fully as possible. It would be misleading to think that any organized doctrine existed. What did exist, in abundance, were conversations — and monologues — on the general aspects of the poetic craft. There were only two "isms" after the preliminary *Ultraísmo: Creacionismo*, whose Allah was Vicente Huidobro, an admirable Chilean poet, and whose Spanish prophets were Juan Larrea and Gerardo Diego; and Surrealism, which never crystallized as a movement, and served rather as an invitation to freedom of the imagination. Each in his own way aspired to the poem which, word by word and image by image, would be intensely poetic.

Poésie pure, then, "pure poetry"? This platonic idea could never take form in a concrete body. None among us dreamed of such absolute purity, none desired it, not even the author of *Cántico*, a book which can be defined negatively as the antithesis of Valéry's *Charmes*. Valéry, read and reread with great devotion by the Castilian poet, was a model of exemplary elevation of subject matter and of exemplary rigor of style —

with the light of a poetic consciousness. In the tradition of Edgar Allan Poe, Valéry believed scarcely or not at all in inspiration, — on which these Spanish poets were always dependent: *Muse* to some, *ángel* to others, *duende* (a familiar demon) to Lorca. These names, diurnal or nocturnal, quasi-celestial or quasi-infernal, designated for Lorca the power that acts in poets — without necessity of mystic ecstasy. A power alien to reason and will, providing those deep, unforeseen elements that constitute the *gracia* of the poem. Grace, enchantment, witchery, a *je ne sais quoi*, — and not manufactured *charme*. Valéry took a rather perverse pleasure in discoursing on the "manufacture of poetry." This phrase would have sounded in the ears of that group of Spaniards like just what it is: blasphemy. "To create," a proud term, "to compose," a sober, professional term, do not imply manufacture. Valéry was above all an inspired poet. Anyone who is always has things to say. T. S. Eliot, already a great critic in the twenties, later put it very clearly with his usual good sense: "Poets have other interests besides poetry — otherwise their poetry would be very empty: they are poets because their dominant interest has been in turning their experience and their thought . . . into poetry." Empty or near-empty formalism is a monster invented by incompetent readers, or is to be applied only to incompetent writers.

If there is to be poetry, it will have to be human. How could it be otherwise? Inhuman or superhuman poetry has perhaps existed. But a "dehumanized" poem is a physical and metaphysical impossibility, and the phrase "dehumanization of art," coined by our great philosopher Ortega y Gasset, rang false from the very beginning. "Dehumanization" is a completely inadmissible concept, and the poets of the twenties could have brought suit before the courts of law for the damages and prejudices caused by the use and abuse — in this case

209

identical — of that novel phrase as a supposed key for the interpretation of their poetry. A key that did not unlock a single poem. Ortega, who had analyzed and mirrored our times with such profundity, went astray on this occasion, despite the fact that he was himself so much a part of the artistic, literary, and philosophical atmosphere of the time. We should not forget — to forget would be ingratitude — the generous support that Ortega lent many young writers as editor of the *Revista de Occidente*. In one of the collections put out by this review, *Nova Novorum*, four books were published: *Romancero gitano, Cántico, Seguro Azar, Cal y Canto*. We remember today with both pride and melancholy that in those years the *Revista de Occidente*, according to our friend Henri Peyre, constituted, with the *Nouvelle Revue Française* and *The Criterion*, the supreme trinity of European reviews. And it was the same great Ortega who thought up that ugly word! It was not justified even for the abstract constructions of the Cubists. Who but men of great human refinement — Juan Gris, Picasso, Braque — could have done those still-life paintings that were so far from "still"? One can conceive of painting that is not representational. But the word is at once a sign and a communication: the sign of an idea, the communication of a state, as Vicente Aleixandre often says. It would have been quite another thing to speak of antisentimentalism, of antirealism.

IV

The major themes of human existence — love, nature, life, death — filled the lyric and dramatic works of this generation. (Only one major theme is seldom found: religion.) Of course these raw materials were presented re-created in creation, transformed into form, incarnated in verbal flesh. Of course this metamorphosis avoided grandiloquence and took pleasure in sobriety and restraint. The Spanish language has the word *efectismo,* "striving after effect." Well, *efectismo* was what these poets forbade themselves to use. *Efectista* is not the word for the generation whose chief figure was a tragic poet, Spain's only great tragic poet since Calderón. Lorca's *duende* was far removed from gesticulation and vociferation. In spite of all that, some of today's young Spaniards — and with what nostalgia do I say "young"! — have been naïve enough to believe that they have discovered human poetry. Let the old Spanish exclamation come to my aid here: May Saint Lucy protect their perspicacity! There stands the poetry of that decade; let them read or reread it from today's point of view, and see whether "dehumanization" or "asepsis" helps in the understanding of those pages. It is true that the word "asepsis" sometimes turned up in those days in casual conversation. But it was used in a purely superficial way, and exerted no pressure during the creative stage.

Our only purpose here is to evoke that common air that was breathed by a group of friends even when they were alone, and not just in cafés and *tertulias.* There was no program, there was no manifesto attacking or defending fixed positions. There were dialogues, letters, dinners, walks, and friendship under the bright light of Madrid, a delightful city, still the Court though with foreshadowings of a Republic, where so much wit was squandered and so many hours wasted, or apparently wasted, by those hard-working intellectuals, writers, and artists, who were working for their country's culture. Culture in a liberal sense. These poets, sons of a far from idle bourgeois class, were not militant in politics, yet were not ignorant of it, always oriented toward a future Spain of greater breadth and freedom. Some dull-witted souls have called the generation of Salinas and his friends "The Generation of the Dictatorship," when not one of them participated in any way in the regime of Primo de Rivera, a dictatorship so old-fashioned that

211

it required no concessions in the conduct or the writings of that generation. Writers of Dictatorship appeared at a later date. Between 1920 and 1936 there was free time to spare, free time for the fulfillment of each individual destiny.

These poets, who got along so well together, were very different one from the other. Each one had his own voice. Antonio Machado used to pause to distinguish the voices from the echoes. Among these poets only voices were to be heard, a fact that was recognized by the great Don Antonio, who respected these poets, even though he perhaps did not see some of their works clearly. They were fortunate poets: they received immediate recognition. The obvious definiteness of outline of each figure contributed to this quick recognition, due to Heaven knows what circumstances. The public — a limited public — was never hostile. These were poets of the so-called "vanguard": another word of the times. This military metaphor was hardly suited to poets who did not fight with anyone on any front. Nor did they set themselves any explosive goal. Their goal, always difficult, was that exact expression which fitted what they were trying to say. Each one sought after the word most authentic for him, and thus they proved to be modern, in harmony with their period. There is always some reader or onlooker who suspects slyness, trickery, insincerity, desire for fame, in painters or writers who are truly new — not realizing that they are staking their lives on every brush stroke, on every word.

v

How did this generation express itself? What was the nature of its poetic word? Is it impossible to reduce to a single formula the language — or languages — of writers so diverse? Joaquín González Muela has endeavored to formulate their

212

styles in an exact synthesis. What did Salinas and Altolaguirre, Prados and Cernuda have in common? As friends sitting around a table they understood one another, they spoke the same language: that of their generation. But at the "hour of truth," facing a blank sheet of paper, each was to express himself in a different style. These styles varied from the artifices of traditional versification to the irregularities of free verse. There was no break with tradition, and the new forms and rhythms introduced by Rubén Darío and his followers were to be enriched by these poets who, if they played down innovations, did not limit themselves to the forms used by either remote or immediate masters. The break with the past was much more complete in contemporary generations in other countries. The Spanish heritage was not renounced, and this heritage did not hinder originality of spirit. What French or Italian poet, particularly what Italian poet in those days would have dared to write a sonnet without blushing? These Spaniards could write sonnets with complete freedom, whenever they "felt like it" poetically. Even a Salinas, an Aleixandre composed an occasional sonnet, and not just to show off his virtuosity: it suited his creative impulse. That is why the repertory of forms of this generation was so rich and varied: they refused to take the vow of poverty demanded by the contemporary spirit of so many of its followers. There is one criticism that has never been made of these poets: that they wrote badly. They have, to be sure, been reproached for writing too well. This objection is really praise — accompanied by a kick in the shins. In short, not even in the case of Lorca did genius permit brilliantly formless writing, a surrender to the powers of darkness. The slightest song was composed with all artistic delicacy, and the long line of *La destrucción o el amor,* and later of *Hijos de la ira,* was "breathed" with the greatest ex-

213

actness. Within a single writer the most divergent styles might succeed one another, as in Gerardo Diego, and even be set against one another in the same composition, as in his *Fábula de Equis y Zeda*.

Any name seeking to give unity to a historical period is the invention of posterity. If we can guess how surprised Poliziano would have been at being called a "Renaissance man," we know that Verlaine disliked being classified as a "symbolist." To be sure, since the end of the nineteenth century there has been a swarm of theories and *isms*. But not in Spain. *Ultraísmo* was an exception; *Creacionismo*, like *Modernismo*, originated in Spanish America. Cubism, partly Spanish in origin because of Picasso and Juan Gris, grew up in France. How then shall we designate those restless and fertile years between the two World Wars? No label is convincing, especially to those who took part in those adventures. A "period look" does not signify a "group style," the style of a specific group. A generation possesses this or the other set of tastes, but does not develop a school line, a language line. These poets flung themselves into the use of their language without distrusting its efficacy. Wladimir Weidle says: "In Spain, poets are not obliged to distrust everyday language unduly, since that language has been divested of its poetic qualities much less than in France or in England." Castilian is, moreover, a copious and flexible language, more so than ever in the writings of the generation preceding this one. What happened afterward?

Poetry does not require any special poetic language. No word is excluded in advance; any expression can give shape to the phrase. Everything depends on the context. The one thing that matters is the placing of each component within the whole, and this functional value is the one that is decisive. The word "rose" is no more poetic than the word "politics." "Rose," of course, smells better than "politics," but this is

214

merely a difference of qualities perceptible to the sense of
smell. (As Shakespeare said, or rather as Juliet said to Romeo,
". . . a rose / By any other name would smell as sweet.")
Beauty is not poetry, although it is often her ally. For this
reason there are more lines of verse in which "rose" is at home
than "politics." A priori, off the written page, no poetic quality
can be ascribed to any noun, adjective, or participle. It is probable that the word "administration" has not yet been graced
with lyric resonance. But tomorrow, tomorrow morning, it
might be proffered poetically — with reverence, with tenderness, with anger, with scorn — "Administration!" All that
would be needed would be its poetic use, for only use is poetic,
that is to say, the effective action of the word within the poem,
which is the only real organism. There is only the language of
the poem: words situated in a whole. Each poet has his pref-
erences, his aversions, and sets his own limits — according
to a chosen level. The level of the poem varies, as the distance
varies between ordinary language and this new language, between colloquial speech and this more or less singing phrase.
On one level eloquence is justified. Nothing is more natural,
on another level, than prosaic expression, now no longer prosaic. In short, a poetic text is written in a certain key, just as
a musical text is. It would be absurd to try to transfer notes
from *La Realidad y el deseo* to *Soledades juntas* or *Jardín cerrado*. A poetic language does not exist. What does exist is the
language of the poem, modulated in gradations of intensity
and never pure. That kind of purity would be a mere phantom
conceived by abstraction. Poetry exists by piercing, by illuminating all sorts of raw materials. And these materials must be
given different names on different levels of re-creation. Only
in this need for re-creation does the language of these poets —
inspired, free, exacting poets — coincide.

VI

We shall never know how long that community of friends might have remained intact, had not a catastrophe given it the sudden ending of a drama or a tragedy. Tragedy beyond question was the assassination of Federico García Lorca, a child of genius beyond question. It was a tragedy with its traitors, its blood guilt, and its chorus: all of Spain, the whole world. We have also lost the eldest of our generation, Pedro Salinas, who died prematurely at the peak of his creative maturity. The final dedication of *Cántico* calls him *perfecto amigo* — "perfect friend." And so he was always, with a constant, endless generosity. Manuel Altolaguirre lost his life in a tragic accident; it is a moving loss, more premature than that of Salinas. Our generation worked as a group between 1920 and 1936. The gatherings in Madrid ended in that fatal year of the Civil War, ominous prelude to the Second World War. But this could not be called a "lost generation"; in spite of so many vicissitudes, these poets have gone on with their work. Pedro Salinas developed considerably in America, and his production was never so fertile as during the forties. Gerardo Diego, Vicente Aleixandre, Dámaso Alonso have broadened and deepened their youthful work. The rest, in forced or voluntary exile, have remained faithful to their vocation. Some day it will be possible to evaluate correctly the influence of exile on these men of *la España peregrina* — "wandering," and so "pilgrim," Spain. Meanwhile Spain, greater than all these crises, remains standing, and will continue to do so. Professor Fritz Schalk recalls that *Cántico* affirms this faith against wind and tide:

> Que los muertos entierren a sus muertos,
> Jamás a la esperanza.

> *Let the dead bury their dead,*
> *Never their hope.*

216

SPANISH TEXTS

Spanish quotations are from the *Obras* of San Juan de la Cruz, ed. P. Silverio de Santa Teresa, Barefoot Carmelite (3rd ed.; Burgos, 1953). The following abbreviations have been used:

S. *Subida del Monte Carmelo*
N.O. *Noche oscura del alma*
C.E. *Cántico espiritual*
Ll. *Llama de amor viva*
A.y S. *Avisos y sentencias espirituales.*

Quotations in English prose are from *The Complete Works of Saint John of the Cross*, trans. and ed. E. Allison Peers (3 vols.; London: Burns, Oates and Washbourne Ltd., 1934–1935), by permission of Burns & Oates, Limited, and the American publisher, The Newman Press (Westminster, Maryland). Quotations in English verse are from Roy Campbell, *The Poems of St. John of the Cross* (New York: Pantheon Books, 1951) by permission of Pantheon Books Inc., and the English publisher, Harvill Press (London). In a few instances a more literal translation has been necessary for the study of the poems; both versions are noted below.

For the convenience of the reader, the complete text of the three poems studied follows. The Spanish text is that of P. Silverio de Santa Teresa (*Obras*). The version of the *Cántico espiritual* used is that of the San Lúcar de Barrameda manuscript (*Obras*, III, 7–13).

NOCHE OSCURA DEL ALMA

En una noche oscura,	*Upon a gloomy night,*
Con ansias en amores inflamada,	*With all my cares to loving*
¡Oh dichosa ventura!	*ardours flushed,*
Salí sin ser notada,	*(O venture of delight!)*
Estando ya mi casa sosegada.	*With nobody in sight*
	I went abroad when all my house
	was hushed.
A escuras, y segura,	*In safety, in disguise,*
Por la secreta escala disfrazada,	*In darkness up the secret stair*
¡Oh dichosa ventura!	*I crept,*
	(O happy enterprise!)

219

A escuras, y en celada,
Estando ya mi casa sosegada.

Concealed from other eyes
When all my house at length in
silence slept.

En la noche dichosa,
En secreto, que nadie me veía,
Ni yo miraba cosa,
Sin otra luz y guía,
Sino la que en el corazón ardía.

Upon that lucky night
In secrecy, inscrutable to sight,
I went without discerning
And with no other light
Except for that which in my heart
was burning.

Aquesta me guiaba
Mas cierto que la luz del medio-
día,
A donde me esperaba
Quien yo bien me sabía,
En parte donde nadie parecía.

It lit and led me through
More certain than the light of
noonday clear
To where One waited near
Whose presence well I knew,
There where no other presence
might appear.

¡Oh noche, que guiaste,
Oh noche amable más que el
alborada:
Oh noche, que juntaste
Amado con Amada,
Amada en el Amado transfor-
mada!

Oh night that was my guide!
Oh darkness dearer than the
morning's pride,
Oh night that joined the lover
To the beloved bride,
Transfiguring them each into the
other.

En mi pecho florido,
Que entero para él sólo se guar-
daba,
Allí quedó dormido,
Y yo le regalaba,
Y el ventalle de cedros aire daba.

Within my flowering breast
Which only for himself entire I
save
He sank into his rest
And all my gifts I gave
Lulled by the airs with which the
cedars wave.

El aire de la almena,
Cuando yo sus cabellos esparcía,
Con su mano serena
En mi cuello hería,
Y todos mis sentidos suspendía.

Over the ramparts fanned
While the fresh wind was flutter-
ing his tresses,
With his serenest hand
My neck he wounded, and
Suspended every sense with its
caresses.

220

SAN JUAN DE LA CRUZ

Quedéme, y olvidéme,
El rostro recliné sobre el Amado,
Cesó todo, y dejéme,
Dejando mi cuidado
Entre las azucenas olvidado.

Lost to myself I stayed
My face upon my lover having
    laid
From all endeavor ceasing:
And all my cares releasing
Threw them amongst the lilies
    there to fade.

CÁNTICO ESPIRITUAL

ESPOSA

¿A dónde te escondiste,
Amado, y me dejaste con gemido?
Como el ciervo huiste,
Habiéndome herido;
Salí tras tí clamando, y eras ido.

BRIDE

Where can your hiding be,
Beloved, that you left me thus to
    moan
While like the stag you flee
Leaving the wound with me?
I followed calling loud, but you
    had flown.

Pastores, los que fuerdes
Allá por las majadas al otero,
Si por ventura vierdes
Aquel que yo más quiero,
Decilde que adolezco, peno y
    muero.

O shepherds, you that, yonder,
Go through the sheepfolds of the
    slope on high,
If you, as there you wander,
Should chance my love to spy,
Then tell him that I suffer, grieve,
    and die.

Buscando mis amores,
Iré por esos montes y riberas,
Ni cogeré las flores,
Ni temeré las fieras,
Y pasaré los fuertes y fronteras.

To fetch my loves more near,
Amongst these mountains and
    ravines I'll stray,
Nor pluck flowers, nor for fear
Of prowling beasts delay,
But pass through forts and fron-
    tiers on my way.

PREGUNTA A LAS CRIATURAS

Oh bosques y espesuras,
Plantadas por la mano del Amado,
Oh prado de verduras,
De flores esmaltado,
Decid si por vosotros ha pasado.

QUESTION TO ALL CREATURES

O thickets, densely-trammelled,
Which my love's hand has sown
    along the height:
O field of green, enamelled
With blossoms, tell me right
If he has passed across you in his
    flight.

221

SPANISH TEXTS

RESPUESTA DE LAS CRIATURAS

Mil gracias derramando,
Pasó por estos sotos con presura,
Y yéndolos mirando,
Con sola su figura
Vestidos los dejó de hermosura.

REPLY OF THE CREATURES

Diffusing showers of grace,
In haste among these groves his
path he took,
And only with his face,
Glancing around the place,
Has clothed them in his beauty
with a look.

ESPOSA

¡Ay, quién podrá sanarme!
Acaba de entregarte ya de vero.
No quieras enviarme
De hoy más ya mensajero,
Que no saben decirme lo que
quiero.

BRIDE

Oh who my grief can mend!
Come, make the last surrender
that I yearn for,
And let there be an end
Of messengers you send
Who bring me other tidings than
I burn for.

Y todos cuantos vagan,
De ti me van mil gracias refiriendo
Y todos más me llagan,
Y déjame muriendo
Un no sé qué que quedan bal-
buciendo.

All those that haunt the spot
Recount your charm, and wound
me worst of all
Babbling I know not what
Strange rapture, they recall,
Which leaves me stretched and
dying where I fall.

Mas, ¿cómo perseveras,
Oh vida, no viviendo donde vives,
Y haciendo porque mueras,
Las flechas que recibes,
De lo que del Amado en ti con-
cibes?

How can you thus continue
To live, my life, where your own
life is not?
With all the arrows in you
And, like a target, shot
By that which in your breast he
has begot.

¿Por qué, pues has llagado
A aqueste corazón, no le sanaste?
Y pues me le has robado,
¿Por qué así le dejaste,
Y no tomas el robo que robaste?

Why then did you so pierce
My heart, nor heal it with your
touch sublime?
Why, like a robber fierce,
Desert me every time
And not enjoy the plunder of
your crime?

222

SAN JUAN DE LA CRUZ

Apaga mis enojos,
Pues que ninguno basta a desha-
cellos,
Y véante mis ojos,
Pues eres lumbre dellos,
Y sólo para ti quiero tenellos.

Come, end my sufferings quite
Since no one else suffices for
physician:
And let mine eyes have sight
Of you, who are their light,
Except for whom I scorn the gift
of vision.

Descubre tu presencia,
Y máteme tu vista y hermosura;
Mira que la dolencia
De amor, que no se cura
Sino con la presencia y la figura.

Reveal your presence clearly
And kill me with the beauty you
discover,
For pains acquired so dearly
From Love, cannot recover
Save only through the presence of
the lover.

¡Oh cristalina fuente,
Si en esos tus semblantes platea-
dos,
Formases de repente
Los ojos deseados,
Que tengo en mis entrañas dibu-
jados!

O brook of crystal sheen,
Could you but cause, upon your
silver fine,
Suddenly to be seen
The eyes for which I pine
Which in my inmost heart my
thoughts design!

Apártalos, Amado,
Que voy de vuelo.

Withhold their gaze, my Love,
For I take wing.

ESPOSO

      Vuélvete, paloma,
Que el ciervo vulnerado
Por el otero asoma,
Al aire de tu vuelo, y fresco toma.

THE BRIDEGROOM

      Turn, Ringdove, and alight,
The wounded stag above
The slope is now in sight
Fanned by the wind and fresh-
ness of your flight.

ESPOSA

Mi Amado, las montañas,
Los valles solitarios nemorosos,
Las ínsulas extrañas,
Los ríos sonorosos,
El silbo de los aires amorosos.

THE BRIDE

My Love's the mountain range,
The valleys each with solitary
grove,
The islands far and strange,
The streams with sounds that
change,
The whistling of the lovesick
winds that rove.

223

La noche sosegada
En par de los levantes de la aurora,
La música callada,
La soledad sonora,
La cena, que recrea y enamora.

Before the dawn comes round
Here is the night, dead-hushed
with all its glamours,
The music without sound,
The solitude that clamours,
The supper that revives us and
enamours.

Nuestro lecho florido,
De cuevas de leones enlazado,
En púrpura tendido,
De paz edificado,
De mil escudos de oro coronado.

Now flowers the marriage bed
With dens of lions fortified
around it,
With tent of purple spread,
In peace securely founded,
And by a thousand shields of gold
surmounted.

A zaga de tu huella
Las jóvenes discurren al camino
Al toque de centella,
Al adobado vino,
Emisiones de bálsamo Divino.

Tracking your sandal-mark
The maidens search the roadway
for your sign,
Yearning to catch the spark
And taste the scented wine
Which emanates a balm that is
divine.

En la interior bodega
De mi amado bebí, y cuando salía
Por toda aquesta vega,
Ya cosa no sabía,
Y el ganado perdí, que antes
seguía.

Deep-cellared is the cavern
Of my love's heart, I drank of
him alive:
Now, stumbling from the tavern,
No thoughts of mine survive,
And I have lost the flock I used
to drive.

Allí me dió su pecho,
Allí me enseñó ciencia muy sa-
brosa,
Y yo le dí de hecho
A mí, sin dejar cosa;
Allí le prometí de ser su esposa.

He gave his breast; seraphic
In savour was the science that
he taught;
And there I made my traffic
Of all, withholding naught,
And promised to become the bride
he sought.

Mi alma se ha empleado,
Y todo mi caudal en su servicio:
Ya no guardo ganado,

My spirit I prepare
To serve him with her riches and
her beauty.
No flocks are now my care,

224

SAN JUAN DE LA CRUZ

Ni ya tengo otro oficio;	No other toil I share,
Que ya sólo en amar es mi ejercicio.	And only now in loving is my duty.
Pues ya si en el ejido	So now if from this day
De hoy más no fuere vista ni hallada,	I am not found among the haunts of men,
Diréis que me he perdido,	Say that I went astray
Que andando enamorada,	Love-stricken from my way,
Me hice perdidiza, y fuí ganada.	That I was lost, but have been found again.
De flores y esmeraldas	Of flowers and emerald sheen,
En las frescas mañanas escogidas,	Collected when the dews of dawning shine,
Haremos las guirnaldas,	A wreath of garlands green
En tu amor florecidas,	(That flower for you) we'll twine
Y en un cabello mío entretejidas.	Together with one golden hair of mine.
En solo aquel cabello,	One hair (upon my nape
Que en mi cuello volar consideraste,	You loved to watch it flutter, fall, and rise)
Mirástele en mi cuello,	Preventing your escape,
Y en él preso quedaste,	Has snared you for a prize
Y en uno de mis ojos te llagaste.	And held you, to be wounded from my eyes.
Cuando tú me mirabas,	When you at first surmised me
Tu gracia en mí tus ojos imprimían:	Your gaze was on my eyes imprinted so,
Por eso me adamabas,	That it effeminized me,
Y en eso merecían	And my eyes were not slow
Los míos adorar lo que en tí vían.	To worship that which set your own aglow.
No quieras despreciarme,	Scorn not my humble ways,
Que si color moreno en mí hallaste,	And if my hue is tawny do not loathe me.
Ya bien puedes mirarme,	On me you well may gaze
Después que me miraste,	Since, after that, the rays
Que gracia y hermosura en mí dejaste.	Of every grace and loveliness will clothe me.

Cogednos las raposas,
Que está ya florecida nuestra viña,
En tanto que de rosas
Hacemos una piña,
Y no parezca nadie en la montiña.

Chase all the foxes hence
Because our vine already flowers
apace:
And while with roses dense
Our posy we enlace,
Let no one on the hillside show
his face.

Detente, Cierzo muerto;
Ven, Austro, que recuerdas los amores,
Aspira por mi huerto,
Y corran sus olores,
Y pacerá el Amado entre las flores.

Cease, then, you arctic gale,
And come, recalling love, wind
of the South:
Within my garden-pale
The scent of flowers exhale
Which my Beloved browses with
his mouth.

ESPOSO

Entrádose ha la Esposa
En el ameno huerto deseado;
Y a su sabor reposa,
El cuello reclinado
Sobre los dulces brazos del Amado.

BRIDEGROOM

Now, as she long aspired,
Into the garden comes the bride,
a guest:
And in its shade retired
Has leant her neck to rest
Against the gentle arm of the
Desired.

Debajo del manzano,
Allí conmigo fuiste desposada,
Allí te dí la mano,
Y fuiste reparada
Donde tu madre fuera violada.

Beneath the apple-tree,
You came to swear your troth
and to be mated,
Gave there your hand to me,
And have been new-created
There where your mother first
was violated.

A las aves ligeras,
Leones, ciervos, gamos saltadores,
Montes, valles, riberas,
Aguas, aires, ardores,
Y miedos de las noches veladores:

You birds with airy wings,
Lions, and stags, and roebucks
leaping light,
Hills, valleys, creeks, and springs,
Waves, winds, and ardours bright,
And things that rule the watches
of the night:

Por las amenas liras
Y canto de serenas os conjuro

By the sweet lyre and call
Of sirens, now I conjure you to
cease

SAN JUAN DE LA CRUZ

Que cesen vuestras iras,
Y no toquéis al muro,
Porque la Esposa duerma más
  seguro.

Your tumults one and all,
Nor echo on the wall
That she may sleep securely and
  at peace.

ESPOSA

BRIDE

Oh ninfas de Judea,
En tanto que en las flores y rosales
El ámbar perfumea,
Mora en los arrabales,
Y no queráis tocar nuestros um-
  brales.

Oh daughters of Judea,
While yet our flowers and roses
  in their flesh hold
Ambrosia, come not here,
But keep the outskirts clear,
And do not dare to pass across our
  threshold.

Escóndete, Carillo,
Y mira con tu haz a las montañas,
Y no quieras decillo:
Mas mira las compañas
De la que va por ínsulas extrañas.

Look to the mountain peak,
My darling, and stay hidden from
  the view,
And do not dare to speak
But watch her retinue
Who sails away to islands strange
  and new.

ESPOSO

BRIDEGROOM

La blanca palomica
Al Arca con el ramo se ha tornado,
Y ya la tortolica
Al socio deseado
En las riberas verdes ha hallado.

The dove so snowy-white,
Returning to the Ark, her frond
  bestows;
And seeking to unite
The mate of her delight
Has found him where the shady
  river flows.

En soledad vivía,
Y en soledad ha puesto ya su nido,
Y en soledad la guía
A solas su querido,
También en soledad de amor heri-
  do.

In solitude she bided,
And in the solitude her nest she
  made:
In solitude he guided
His loved-one through the shade
Whose solitude the wound of love
  has made.

ESPOSA

BRIDE

Gocémonos, Amado,
Y vámonos a ver en tu hermosura

Rejoice, my love, with me
And in your beauty see us both
  reflected:

227

Al monte y al collado,
Do mana el agua pura;
Entremos más adentro en la es-
  pesura.

By mountain-slope and lea,
Where purest rills run free,
We'll pass into the forest un
  detected:

Y luego a las subidas
Cavernas de la piedra nos iremos,
Que están bien escondidas,
Y allí nos entraremos,
Y el mosto de granadas gustare-
  mos.

Then climb to lofty places
Among the caves and boulder
  of the granite,
Where every track effaces,
And, entering, leave no traces,
And revel in the wine of th
  pomegranate.

Allí me mostrarías
Aquello que mi alma pretendía,
Y luego me darías
Allí tú, vida mía,
Aquello que me diste el otro día.

Up there, to me you'll show
What my own soul has longed f
  all the way:
And there, my love, bestow
The secret which you know
And only spoke about the oth
  day.

El aspirar del aire,
El canto de la dulce Filomena,
El soto y su donaire,
En la noche serena
Con llama que consume y no da
  pena.

The breathing air so keen;
The song of Philomel: the wavir
  charm
Of groves in beauty seen:
The evening so serene,
With fire that can consume y
  do no harm.

Que nadie lo miraba,
Aminadab tampoco parecía,
Y el cerco sosegaba,
Y la caballería
A vista de las aguas descendía.

With none our peace offendin
Aminadab has vanished with l
  slaughters:
And now the siege had ending,
The cavalcades descending
Were seen within the precinct
  the waters.

LLAMA DE AMOR VIVA

¡Oh llama de amor viva,
Que tiernamente hieres
De mi alma en el más profundo
  centro!
Pues ya no eres esquiva,

Oh flame of love so living,
How tenderly you force
To my soul's inmost core yc
  fiery probe!
Since now you've no misgivir

SAN JUAN DE LA CRUZ

Acaba ya si quieres,	End it, pursue your course
Rompe la tela deste dulce encuen-	And for our sweet encounter tear
tro.	the robe!
¡Oh cauterio suave!	Oh cautery most tender!
¡Oh regalada llaga!	Oh gash that is my guerdon!
¡Oh mano blanda! ¡Oh toque	Oh gentle hand! Oh touch how
delicado,	softly thrilling!
Que a vida eterna sabe,	Eternal life you render,
Y toda deuda paga!	Raise of all debts the burden
Matando, muerte en vida la has	And change my death to life, even
trocado.	while killing!
¡Oh lámparas de fuego,	Oh lamps of fiery blaze
En cuyos resplandores	To whose refulgent fuel
Las profundas cavernas del sen-	The deepest caverns of my soul
tido,	grow bright,
Que estaba obscuro y ciego,	Late blind with gloom and haze,
Con extraños primores	But in this strange renewal
Calor y luz dan junto a su querido!	Giving to the belov'd both heat
	and light.
¡Cuán manso y amoroso	What peace, with love enwreath-
Recuerdas en mi seno,	ing,
Donde secretamente solo moras:	You conjure to my breast
Y en tu aspirar sabroso	Which only you your dwelling
De bien y gloria lleno	place may call:
Cuán delicadamente me ena-	While with delicious breathings
moras!	In glory, grace, and rest,
	So daintily in love you make me
	fall!

Page 82

¡Oh dichosa ventura! "O venture of delight!" Roy Campbell, for the sake of the rhyme, translates this line in the second stanza: "O happy enterprise!"

Page 83

Estando ya mi casa sosegada. "I went abroad when all my house was hushed." Roy Campbell translates the second time as: "When all my house at length in silent slept."

dichoso escondrijo del corazón, que tiene tanto valor, que lo sujeta todo . . . A la M. María de Jesús, 1589.

229

Oh noche amable más que el alborada: "Oh night that is more kindly than the dawn!" Roy Campbell: "Oh darkness dearer than the morning's pride."

Allí quedó dormido, "There he lay asleep." Roy Campbell: "He sank into his rest."

Page 85

De donde David . . . dice así: Si durmiéredes entre los dos coros, las plumas de la paloma serán plateadas . . . C.E., XII, 4.

Page 88

El alma que anda en amor, ni cansa ni se cansa. A.y S., *Puntos de Amor*, 18.

Y adonde no hay amor, ponga amor y sacará amor . . . A la M. *María de la Encarnación*, 1591.

Page 89

que es como el aire, que en queriendo cerrar el puño, se sale. N.O., I, IX, 6.

Pages 90–91

antes sería ignorancia pensar que los dichos de amor en inteligencia mística, cuales son los de las presentes canciones, con alguna manera de palabras se puedan bien explicar; porque el Espíritu del Señor que ayuda nuestra flaqueza, como dice San Pablo, morando en nosotros, pide por nosotros con gemidos inefables lo que nosotros no podemos bien entender ni comprender para lo manifestar. Porque, ¿quién podrá escribir lo que a las almas amorosas, donde él mora, hace entender? Y ¿quién podrá manifestar con palabras lo que las hace sentir? Y ¿quién finalmente, lo que las hace desear? Cierto, nadie lo puede; cierto, ni ellas mismas por quien pasa lo pueden; porque ésta es la causa por qué con figuras, comparaciones y semejanzas, antes rebosan algo de lo que sienten, y de la abundancia del espíritu vierten secretos y misterios que con razones lo declaran. Las cuales semejanzas, no leídas con la sencillez del espíritu de amor e inteligencia que ellas llevan, antes parecen dislates que dichos puestos en razón, según es de ver en los divinos Cantares de Salomón y en otros libros de la Escritura Divina, donde no pudiendo el Espíritu Santo dar a entender la abundancia de su sentido por términos vulgares y usados, habla misterios en extrañas figuras y semejanzas. De donde se sigue, que los santos doctores, aunque mucho dicen y más digan, nunca pueden acabar de declararlo por palabras, así como tampoco por palabras se pudo ello decir; y así, lo que de ello se declara, ordinariamente es lo menos que contiene en sí.

Por haberse, pues, estas canciones compuesto en amor de abundante inteligencia mística, no se podrán declarar al justo, ni mi intento será tal, sino sólo dar alguna luz general (pues V. R. así lo ha querido); y esto tengo por mejor, porque los dichos de amor es mejor declararlos en su anchura para que cada uno de ellos se aproveche según su modo y caudal de espíritu, que abreviarlos a un sentido a que no se acomode todo paladar. Y así, aunque en alguna manera se declaran, no hay para qué atarse a la declaración; porque la sabiduría mística (la cual es por amor, de que las presentes canciones tratan), no ha menester distintamente entenderse para hacer efecto de amor y afición en el alma; porque es a modo de la fe, en la cual amamos a Dios sin entenderle. C.E., *Prólogo*

Page 92

porque sólo el que por ello pasa, lo sabrá sentir, mas no decir. S., *Prólogo*

Bien así como el que viese una cosa nunca vista, cuyo semejante tampoco jamás vió, que aunque la entendiese y gustase, no la sabría poner nombre ni decir lo que es, aunque más hiciese, y esto con ser cosa que la percibió con los sentidos; cuánto menos, pues, se podrá manifestar lo que no entró por ellos. Porque esto tiene el lenguaje de Dios, que por ser él muy íntimo al alma y espiritual, que excede todo sentido, luego hace cesar y enmudecer toda la armonía y habilidad de los sentidos exteriores e interiores. N.O. 2, XVII, 3

De donde por cuanto la sabiduría de esta contemplación es lenguaje de Dios al alma de puro espíritu a espíritu puro, todo lo que es menos que espíritu, como son los sentidos, no lo perciben, y así les es secreto y no lo saben ni pueden decir, ni tienen gana porque no le ven. N.O., 2, XVII,4

mas no hay decir lo que el alma tiene ni la sacarán más que términos generales semejantes a éstos. Otra cosa es cuando las cosas que el alma tiene son particulares, como visiones, sentimientos, etc., las cuales como ordinariamente se reciben debajo de alguna especie en que participa el sentido, que entonces debajo de aquella especie se puede, o debajo de otra semejanza, decir. N.O., 2, XVII, 5

sino también echa de ver cuán bajos y cortos y en alguna manera impropios son todos los términos y vocablos con que en esta vida se trata de las cosas divinas, y cómo es imposible por vía y modo natural, aunque más alta y sabiamente se hable en ellas, poder conocer y sentir de ellas como ellas son, sino con la iluminación de esta mística teología. Y así, viendo el alma en la iluminación de ella esta verdad, de que no se puede alcanzar ni menos declarar con términos humanos ni vulgares, con razón la llama secreta. N.O., 2, XVII, 6

porque así como no se entiende, así tampoco se sabe decir, aunque, como he dicho, se sabe sentir. C.E. VII, 10

Pages 92–93

Alguna repugnancia he tenido, muy noble y devota señora, en declarar estas cuatro canciones que Vuestra Merced me ha pedido, por ser de cosas tan interiores y espirituales, para las cuales comúnmente falta lenguaje; porque lo espiritual excede al sentido, y con dificultad se dice algo de la sustancia del espíritu . . . Y con este presupuesto, arrimándome a la Escritura Divina, y como se lleve entendido que todo lo que se dijere es tanto menos de lo que allí hay, como lo es lo pintado de lo vivo, me atreveré a decir lo que supiere. Ll., *Prólogo*.

Page 93

Todo lo que se puede en esta canción decir es menos de lo que hay, porque la transformación del alma en Dios es indecible. Ll. III, 8

Porque la cortedad del manifestarlo y hablarlo exteriormente mostró Jeremías, cuando habiendo Dios hablado con él no supo qué decir, sino a a a. Y la cortedad interior, esto es, del sentido interior de la imaginación, y juntamente la del exterior acerca de esto, también la manifestó Moisés delante de Dios en la zarza, cuando no solamente dijo a Dios que después que hablaba con él no sabía ni acertaba a hablar . . . N.O., 2, XVII, 4

Digamos lo que dijo de ello Cristo a San Juan en el Apocalipsis por muchos términos y comparaciones, en siete veces, por no ser comprendido aquello en un vocablo, ni en una vez, porque aún en todas aquéllas se quedó por decir. C.E., XXXIII, 7

Page 94

porque a ninguna criatura le es lícito salir fuera de los términos que Dios la tiene naturalmente ordenados para su gobierno. Al hombre le puso términos naturales y racionales para su gobierno; luego querer salir de ellos no es lícito, y querer averiguar y alcanzar cosas por vía sobrenatural, es salir de los términos naturales. Luego es cosa no lícita; luego Dios no gusta de ello, pues de todo lo ilícito se ofende. Bien sabía esto el rey Acab, pues que, aunque de parte de Dios le dijo Isaías que pidiese alguna señal, no quiso hacerlo diciendo: *Non petam, et non tentabo Dominum.* Esto es: No pediré tal cosa, ni tentaré a Dios. Porque el tentar a Dios es querer tratarle por vías extraordinarias, cuales son las sobrenaturales. S., 2, XXI, 1

Que eso es lo que quiso decir Salomón, cuando dijo: ¿Qué necesidad tiene el hombre de querer y buscar las cosas que son sobre su capacidad natural? Como si dijéramos: Ninguna necesidad tiene para ser perfecto de querer cosas sobrenaturales por vía sobrenatural, que es sobre su capacidad. S., 2, XXVII, 6

Page 95

todo lo que la imaginación puede imaginar y el entendimiento recibir y entender en esta vida, no es ni puede ser medio próximo para la unión de Dios. S., 2, VIII, 4

Quiero decir, que nunca te quieras satisfacer en lo que entendieres de Dios, sino en lo que no entendieres de él . . . C.E., I, 12

no se comunica Dios al alma mediante algún disfraz de visión imaginaria, o semejanza o figura, ni la ha de haber; sino que boca a boca, esto es, en esencia pura y desnuda de Dios, que es la boca de Dios en amor con esencia pura y desnuda del alma, que es la boca del alma en amor de Dios. S., 2, XVI, 9

las formas y fantasías de las cosas que por los sentidos corporales se reciben. S., 2, XVI, 9

dándoles a entender cómo es más preciosa delante de Dios una obra o acto de voluntad hecho en caridad, que cuantas visiones y comunicaciones pueden tener del cielo, pues éstas ni son mérito ni demérito. S., 2, XXII, 19

todas las visiones, revelaciones y sentimientos del cielo, y cuanto más ellos quisieren pensar, no valen tanto como el menor acto de humildad . . . S., 3, IX, 4

esto puede estorbar mucho para ir a la divina unión, porque aparta mucho al alma, si hace caso de ello, del abismo de la fe, en que el entendimiento ha de estar oscuro, y oscuro ha de ir por amor en fe y no por mucha razón. S., 2, XXIX, 5

233

Page 96

Pues con no hacer caso de ellas, negándolas, se excusa todo eso y se hace lo que se debe. S., 2, XVIII, 7

Por tanto, aunque todas las cosas se le rían al hombre y todas sucedan prósperamente, antes se debe recelar que gozarse . . . El corazón del necio, dice el Sabio, está donde está la alegría; mas el del Sabio donde está la tristeza. S., 3, XVIII, 5

no hay mejor remedio que padecer y hacer y callar, y cerrar los sentidos con uso e inclinación de soledad y olvido de toda criatura y de todos los acaecimientos, aunque se hunda el mundo. *A las Carmelitas Descalzas de Beas*, 1587

La primera purgación o noche es amarga y terrible para el sentido, como ahora diremos. La segunda no tiene comparación, porque es horrenda y espantable para el espíritu, como luego diremos . . . N.O., 1, VIII, 2

como el que tienen aprisionado en una oscura mazmorra atado de pies y manos, sin poderse mover ni ver, ni sentir algún favor de arriba ni de abajo, hasta que aquí se humille, ablande y purifique el espíritu, y se ponga tan sutil y sencillo y delgado, que pueda hacerse uno con el espíritu de Dios . . . N.O., 2, VII, 3

las tinieblas que aquí padece son profundas y horribles y muy penosas, porque como se sienten en la profunda sustancia del espíritu, parecen tinieblas sustanciales. N.O., 2, IX, 3

En el horror de la visión nocturna, cuando el sueño suele ocupar a los hombres . . . C.E., XV, 17

Pages 96–97

Este cáliz es morir a su naturaleza, desnudándola y aniquilándola, para que pueda caminar por esta angosta senda . . . S., 2, VII, 7

Page 97

una cosa sola necesaria, que es saberse negar de veras, según lo exterior e interior dándose al padecer por Cristo y aniquilarse en todo. S., 2, VII, 8

Dirá alguno, que bueno parece esto; pero que de aquí se sigue la destrucción del uso natural y curso de las potencias, y que quede el hombre como bestia, olvidado, y aun peor, sin discurrir ni acordarse de las necesidades y operaciones naturales; y que Dios no destruye la naturaleza, antes la perfecciona, y de aquí necesariamente se sigue su destrucción, pues se olvida de lo moral y racional para obrarlo, y de lo natural para ejercitarlo; porque de nada de esto se puede acordar, pues se priva de las noticias y formas, que son el medio de la reminiscencia. S., 3, II, 7

Un solo pensamiento del hombre vale más que todo el mundo; por tanto, sólo Dios es digno de él. A.y S., 32

Porque como esta alma había de salir a hacer un hecho tan heroico y tan raro, que era unirse con su Amado divino . . . N.O., 2, XIV, 1

el estado de esta divina unión consiste en tener el alma según la voluntad con total transformación en la voluntad de Dios, de manera que no haya en ella cosa contraria a la voluntad de Dios, sino que en todo y por todo su movimiento sea voluntad solamente de Dios. S., 1, XI, 2

el alma se hace deiforme y Dios por participación. C.E., XXXIX, 4
Y el alma más parece Dios que alma, y aun es Dios por participación. S., 2, V, 7; N.O., 2, XX, 5; Ll., II, 34; III, 8, 78

Pages 97–98

según dice San Pablo trayendo esta misma comparación, diciendo: El que se junta al Señor, un espíritu se hace con él; bien así como cuando la luz de la estrella o de la candela se junta y une con la del sol, que ya el que luce ni es la estrella ni la candela, sino el sol, teniendo en sí difundidas las otras luces. C.E., XXII, 3

Page 98

Mira que, pues Dios es inaccesible, no repares en cuanto tus potencias pueden comprender y tu sentido sentir, porque no te satisfagas con menos y pierda tu alma la ligereza conveniente para ir a él. A.y S., 52

En lo cual eres maravillosamente letificada según toda la armonía de tu alma, y aun la de tu cuerpo, hecha todo un paraíso de regadío divino . . . Ll., III, 7

Comunícala principalmente dulces misterios de su Encarnación, y los modos y maneras de la redención humana . . . C.E., XXIII, 1

Porque allí ve el alma que verdaderamente Dios es suyo, y que ella le posee con posesión hereditaria, con propiedad de derecho, como hijo de Dios adoptivo . . . Ll., III, 78

estos embestimientos divinos y gloriosos, a manera de encuentros . . .
con que siempre penetra, endiosando la sustancia del alma, haciéndola
divina, en lo cual absorbe al alma sobre todo ser el ser de Dios. Ll., 1,
35

le parece al alma que no tiene él otra en el mundo a quien regalar,
ni otra cosa en que se emplear, sino que todo es para ella sola; y
sintiéndolo así lo confiesa como la esposa en los Cantares, diciendo:
Dilectus meus mihi et ego illi. Ll., II, 36

Page 99

Un no sé qué que quedan balbuciendo. "A nameless 'something'
they keep stammering." Roy Campbell translates: "Babbling I know
not what / Strange rapture."

es tal un no sé qué que se siente quedar por decir, y una cosa que se
conoce quedar por decir, y un subido rastro que se descubre al alma
de Dios quedándose por rastrear, y un altísimo entender de Dios
que no se sabe decir, que por eso lo llama no sé qué . . . que eso
quiere decir balbucir, que es el hablar de los niños, que es no acertar
a decir y dar a entender qué hay que decir. C.E., VII, 9, 10

Que queriéndolo ella decir no lo dice, sino quédase con la estimación
en el corazón y con el encarecimiento en la boca por este término
oh, diciendo: ¡Oh cauterio suave! Ll., II, 5

Page 101

Y como está entonces suspensa la imaginativa, aunque entonces la
hagan cosas que causen dolor, no lo siente; porque sin imaginación no
hay sentimiento . . . S., 3, II, 6

Page 103

Judea llama a la parte inferior del alma, que es la sensitiva. Y llámala
Judea, porque es flaca y carnal y de suyo ciega, como lo es la gente
judaica. Y llama ninfas a todas las imaginaciones, fantasías y movimientos y aficiones de esta porción inferior. C.E., XVIII, 4

ahogados los gitanos en la mar de la contemplación, donde el gitano
del sentido, no hallando pie ni arrimo, se ahoga y deja libre al hijo
de Dios. Ll., III, 38

Page 105

Pero el acomodado sentido de este verso, es decir que el alma . . .
C. E., XXVIII, 10

236

SAN JUAN DE LA CRUZ

Pages 105–106

En los cuales versos pone los tres enemigos del alma, que son: mundo, demonio y carne, que son los que hacen guerra y dificultan el camino. Por las fieras entiende el mundo, por los fuertes el demonio, y por las fronteras la carne.

Llama fieras al mundo, porque el alma que comienza el camino de Dios, parécele que se le representa en la imaginación el mundo como a manera de fieras . . . A los demonios, que es el segundo enemigo, llama fuertes, porque ellos con grande fuerza procuran tomar el paso de este camino . . . Dice también el alma que pasará las fronteras, por las cuales se entiende, como habemos dicho, las repugnancias y rebeliones que naturalmente la carne tiene contra el espíritu . . . C.E., III, 6, 7, 9, 10

Page 106

Y pacerá el Amado entre las flores. A. Peers translates this: "And the Beloved shall pasture among the flowers"; Roy Campbell translates it: "Which my Beloved browses with his mouth."

no dice el alma aquí, que pacerá el Amado las flores, sino entre las flores; porque como quiera que la comunicación suya, es a saber, del Esposo, sea en la misma alma mediante el arreo ya dicho de las virtudes, síguese que lo que pace es la misma alma transformada en sí, estando ya ella guisada, salada y sazonada con las dichas flores de virtudes y dones y perfecciones, que son la salsa con que y entre que la pace; las cuales por medio del aposentador ya dicho, están dando al Hijo de Dios sabor y suavidad en el alma, para que por este medio se apaciente más en el amor de ella; porque ésta es la condición del Esposo, unirse con el alma entre la fragancia de estas flores. La cual condición nota muy bien la Esposa en los Cantares, como quien tan bien la sabe, por estas palabras diciendo: Mi Amado descendió a su huerto a la erica y aire de las especias odoríferas, para apacentarse en los huertos y coger lirios. Y otra vez dice: Yo para mi Amado, y mi Amado para mí, que se apacienta entre los lirios; es a saber que se apacienta y deleita en mi alma, que es el huerto suyo, entre los lirios de mis virtudes y perfecciones y gracias. C.E., XVII, 10

Page 107

Y miedos de las noches veladores: "And fears that rule the watches of the night." Roy Campbell translates: "And things that rule the watches of the night."

237

Primeramente, conjura el Esposo y manda a las inútiles digresiones de la fantasía e imaginativa que de aquí adelante cesen, y también pone en razón a las dos potencias naturales irascible y concupiscible, que antes algún tanto afligían al alma; y pone en perfección de sus objetos a las tres potencias del alma, memoria, entendimiento y voluntad, según se puede en esta vida. Demás de esto conjura y manda a las cuatro pasiones del alma, que son: gozo, esperanza, dolor y temor, que ya de aquí adelante estén mitigadas y puestas en razón . . . Llama aves ligeras a las digresiones de la imaginativa, que son ligeras y sutiles en volar a una parte y a otra . . . Por los leones entiende las acrimonias e ímpetus de la potencia irascible, porque esta potencia es osada y atrevida en sus actos como los leones. Y por los ciervos y gamos saltadores entiende la otra potencia del alma que es la concupiscible, que es la potencia de apetecer, la cual tiene dos efectos: el uno de cobardía, y el otro de osadía . . . Montes, valles, riberas. Por estos tres nombres se denotan los actos viciosos y desordenados de las tres potencias del alma, que son memoria, entendimiento y voluntad . . . Aguas, aires, ardores,/Y miedos de las noches veladores. También por estas cuatro cosas entiende las aficiones de las cuatro pasiones, que, como dijimos, son dolor, esperanza, gozo y temor. C.E., XX, 4, 5, 6, 8, 9

Page 109

allende de otras muchas diferencias de visitas que Dios hace al alma, con que la llaga y levanta en amor, suele hacer unos escondidos toques de amor que a manera de saeta de fuego hieren y traspasan el alma y la dejan toda cauterizada con fuego de amor, y éstas propiamente se llaman heridas de amor, de las cuales habla aquí el alma. C.E., I, 17

Pages 109–110

La piedra que aquí dice, según San Pablo, es Cristo: Las subidas cavernas de esta piedra son los subidos y altos y profundos misterios de sabiduría de Dios que hay en Cristo . . . Allí, conviene a saber, en aquellas noticias y misterios divinos nos entraremos . . . Las granadas significan aquí los misterios de Cristo y los juicios de la sabiduría de Dios y las virtudes y atributos de Dios, que del conocimiento de estos misterios y juicios se conocen en Dios, que son innumerables. Porque así como las granadas tienen muchos granicos, nacidos y sustentados en aquel seno circular, así cada uno de los atributos y misterios y juicios y virtudes de Dios contiene en sí gran multitud de ordenaciones maravillosas y admirables efectos de Dios,

238

contenidos y sustentados en el seno esférico de virtud y misterio, etc.,
que pertenecen a aquellos tales efectos. Y notamos aquí la figura
circular o esférica de la granada, porque cada granada entendemos
aquí por cualquiera virtud y atributo de Dios, el cual atributo o
virtud de Dios es el mismo Dios, el cual es significado por la figura
circular o esférica, porque no tiene principio ni fin. C.E., XXXVII,
3, 6, 7

Page 113

Declara el Esposo al alma en esta canción la admirable manera y
traza que tuvo en redimirla y desposarla consigo, por aquellos mismos
términos que la naturaleza humana fué estragada y perdida, diciendo
que así como por medio del árbol vedado en el Paraíso fué perdida
y estragada en la naturaleza humana por Adán, así en el árbol de la
cruz fué redimida y reparada, dándole allí la mano de su favor y
misericordia por medio de su muerte y pasión, alzando las treguas
que del pecado original había entre el hombre y Dios. Y así dice:
Debajo del manzano. Esto es debajo del favor del árbol de la cruz,
que aquí es entendido por el manzano, donde el Hijo de Dios redimió,
y por consiguiente desposó consigo la naturaleza humana, y con-
siguientemente a cada alma, dándole él gracia y prendas para ello en
la cruz . . . Y fuiste reparada, / Donde tu madre fuera violada.
Porque tu madre la naturaleza humana fué violada en tus primeros
padres debajo del árbol, y tú allí también debajo del árbol de la cruz
fuiste reparada; de manera que si tu madre debajo del árbol te dió la
muerte, yo debajo del árbol de la cruz te di la vida. C.E., XXIII, 2,
3, 5

El consumar significa aquí acabar y perfeccionar. C.E., XXXIX, 14

En la interior bodega / De mi Amado bebí . . . A. Peers translates
this: "In the inner cellar / of my Beloved have I drunk . . ." and
Roy Campbell translates it: "Deep-cellared is the cavern / Of my
love's heart, I drank of him alive."

Pages 113–114

Porque así como la bebida se difunde y derrama por todos los miem-
bros y venas del cuerpo, así se difunde esta comunicación de Dios
sustancialmente en toda el alma, o por mejor decir, el alma se
transforma en Dios, según la cual transformación bebe el alma de su
Dios según la sustancia de ella y según sus potencias espirituales.
C.E., XXVI, 5

239

Page 114

la noche en par de los levantes, ni del todo es noche ni del todo es
día, sino como dicen, entre dos luces . . . C.E., XV, 23

Pages 114–115

en esta última canción, en la cual dice cinco cosas. La primera, que
ya su alma está desasida y ajena de todas las cosas. La segunda, que
ya está vencido y ahuyentado el demonio. La tercera, que ya están
sujetadas las pasiones y mortificados los apetitos naturales. La cuarta
y la quinta, que ya está la parte sensitiva e inferior reformada y
purificada, y que está conformada con la parte espiritual; de manera
que no sólo no estorbará para recibir aquellos bienes espirituales, mas
antes se acomodará a ellos, porque aun de los que ahora tiene participa según su capacidad. C.E., XL, 1

Page 115

Decir, pues, el alma: "A oscuras y en celada", es decir que por cuanto
iba a oscuras de la manera dicha, iba encubierta y escondida del
demonio, y de sus cautelas y asechanzas. N.O., 2, XXIII, 2

Pages 115–116

Entendiendo por el muro el cerco de la paz y vallado de virtudes y
perfecciones con que la misma alma está cercada y guardada . . .
C.E., XXI, 18

Page 116

El cauterio es el Espíritu Santo; la mano es el Padre, y el toque el
Hijo. Ll., II, 1

el olor de las azucenas de los ríos sonorosos, que decíamos era la
grandeza de Dios . . . C.E., XXIV, 6

Page 118

En lo cual se ha de entender que todo lo que aquí se declara, está
en Dios eminentemente en infinita manera, o, por mejor decir, cada
una de estas grandezas que se dicen es Dios, y todas ellas juntas son
Dios . . . Estas montañas es mi Amado para mí. C.E., XIV, 5, 6

si el alma busca a Dios, mucho más la busca su Amado a ella; y si
ella le envía a él sus amorosos deseos, que le son a él tan olo-
rosos como la virgulica del humo que sale de las especias aromáticas
de la mirra y del incienso . . . Ll., III, 28

240

BÉCQUER

BÉCQUER

Quotations from Bécquer are from *Obras Completas*, edited by Dionisio Gamallo Fierros (6th ed.; Madrid: Aguilar, 1949). Another edition consulted is *Páginas Desconocidas* (3 vols., Madrid, 1923). Page numbers follow the Spanish text.

P.D. *Páginas Desconocidas.*

Page 128

Cuando la materia duerme, el espíritu vela. En tanto que el cuerpo del caudillo permanece inmóvil y sumergido en un letargo profundo, su alma se reviste de una forma imaginaria y huye de los lazos que la aprisionan para lanzarse al éter; allí la esperan las creaciones del Sueño, que le fingen un mundo poblado de seres animados con la vida de la idea, visión magnífica, profética y real en su fondo, vana sólo en la forma. 86

Page 129

Sevilla, con su Giralda de encajes, que copia temblando el Guadalquivir, y sus calles morunas, tortuosas y estrechas, en las que aún se cree escuchar el extraño crujido de los pasos del rey Justiciero; Sevilla, con sus rejas y sus cantares, sus cancelas y sus pendencias y sus músicas, sus noches tranquilas y sus siestas de fuego, sus alboradas color de rosa y sus crepúsculos azules; Sevilla con todas las tradiciones que veinte centurias han amontonado sobre su frente, con toda la pompa y la gala de su Naturaleza meridional, con toda la poesía que la imaginación presta a un recuerdo querido, apareció como por encanto a mis ojos, y penetré en su recinto, y crucé sus calles, y respiré su atmósfera, y oí los cantos que entonan a media voz las muchachas que cosen detrás de las celosías, medio ocultas entre las hojas de las campanillas azules; y aspiré con voluptuosidad la fragancia de las madreselvas que corren por un hilo de balcón a balcón, formando toldos de flores; y torné, en fin, con mi espíritu a vivir en la ciudad donde he nacido, y de la que tan viva guardaré siempre la memoria. 674

Madrid, envuelto en una ligera neblina, por entre cuyos rotos jirones levantaban sus crestas oscuras las chimeneas, las buhardillas, los campanarios y las desnudas ramas de los árboles.

Madrid, sucio, negro, feo como un esqueleto descarnado tiritando bajo su inmenso sudario de nieve. 671

Yo nada sé, nada he estudiado; he leído un poco, he sentido bastante y he pensado mucho, aunque no acertaré a decir si bien o mal. 655

El tenía veinte años: la cabeza llena de sueños y el corazón de esperanzas. Era poeta y tenía fe en la poesía. 1095

Page 130

mientras vela, gesticula y habla solo, discurriendo por entre el laberinto de hojas y flores, alguno de esos filósofos derrotados y silvestres: tipo original del que no faltan ejemplares en la corte. 1095

Podrá no haber poetas, pero siempre / habrá poesía. 379

Page 131

Pero "la época no era de poesías, era de armas", dice uno de sus biógrafos al llegar a este punto de su vida. En efecto, la época no era de la poesía escrita, de esa poesía que nace en el silencio del gabinete al calor de la inteligencia, como una hermosa y delicada flor del ingenio; era época de grandes pasiones que excitaban los espíritus; época de trastornos, de peligros y de combates; época de poesía en acción; época, en fin, la más adecuada para desarrollar en la mente de los nombres destinados a romper más tarde las enojosas trabas de la poesía de academia, los gérmenes de la grande, de la verdadera, de la tradicional poesía española. 1228

El agua lame la tierra y vive en el cieno. Yo discurro por las regiones etéreas y vuelo en el espacio sin límites. Sigue los movimientos de tu corazón, deja que tu alma suba como la llama y las azules espirales del humo. ¡Desdichado el que, teniendo alas, desciende a las profundidades para buscar el oro, pudiendo remontarse a la altura para encontrar amor y sentimiento! 312

Yo sólo te podré decir que él (el amor) es la suprema ley del universo; ley misteriosa por la que todo se gobierna y rige, desde el átomo inanimado hasta la criatura racional; que de él parte y a él convergen como a un centro de irresistible atracción todas nuestras ideas y acciones; que está, aunque oculto, en el fondo de toda cosa y — efecto de una primera causa: Dios — es, a su vez, origen de esos mil pensamientos desconocidos, que todos ellos son poesía, verdadera y espontánea que la mujer no sabe formular, pero que siente y comprende mejor que nosotros. 664

El amor es poesía; la religión es amor. 666

242

BÉCQUER

Sí; el amor es el manantial perenne de toda poesía, el origen fecundo de todo lo grande, el principio eterno de todo lo bello; y digo el amor porque la religión, nuestra religión sobre todo, es un amor también, es el amor más puro, mas hermoso, el único infinito que se conoce, y sólo a estos dos astros de la inteligencia puede volverse el hombre cuando desea luz que alumbre en su camino, inspiración que fecundice su vena estéril y fatigada. 661

Entonces reparé en que todas aquellas figuras, cuyas largas sombras se proyectaban en los muros y en el pavimento, cuyas flotantes ropas parecían moverse, en cuyas demacradas facciones brillaba una expresión indescriptible, santo y sereno gozo, tenían sus pupilas sin luz vueltas al cielo, como si el escultor quisiera asemejar que sus miradas se perdían en el infinito buscando a Dios. 670

A Dios, foco eterno y ardiente de hermosura, al que se vuelve con los ojos, como a un polo de amor, el sentimiento de la tierra. 671

es digna de ser observada una influencia que las creencias religiosas ejercen sobre la imaginación de los pueblos que crean un nuevo estilo. 332

Pages 131–132

Ni Roma ni Bizancio tuvieron una arquitectura absolutamente original y completa; sus obras fueron modificaciones, no creaciones, porque como dejamos dicho, sólo una nueva religión puede crear una nueva sociedad, y sólo en ésta hay poder de imaginación suficiente a concebir un nuevo arte. 334

Page 132

Una de las más grandes misiones del arte ha sido en todas las épocas levantar el espíritu por medio de sus obras a regiones elevadas, predisponiéndole a la concepción de cierto género de ideas. El catolicismo se ha valido de él como de un poderoso intérprete para llegar hasta el fondo del alma por medio de los sentidos. P, II, 143

"¿Qué es poesía?", dices mientras clavas
en mi pupila tu pupila azul.
"¿Qué es poesía? ¿Y tú me lo preguntas?
Poesía . . . eres tú." 392

La poesía eres tú, porque esa vaga aspiración a lo bello que la caracteriza, y que es una facultad de la inteligencia en el hombre, en ti pudiera decirse que es un instinto.

La poesía eres tú, porque el sentimiento, que en nosotros es un fenómeno accidental y pasa como una ráfaga de aire, se halla tan íntimamente unido a tu organización especial, que constituye una parte de ti misma.
Ultimamente la poesía eres tú, porque tú eres el foco de donde parten sus rayos. 656

El genio verdadero tiene algunos atributos extraordinarios, que Balzac llama femeninos y que, efectivamente, lo son. En la escala de la inteligencia de poeta hay notas que pertenecen a la de la mujer, y éstas son las que expresan la ternura, la pasión y el sentimiento. Yo no sé por qué los poetas y las mujeres no se entienden mejor entre sí. Su manera de sentir tiene tantos puntos de contacto . . . Quizá por eso . . . 657

La poesía es en el hombre una cualidad puramente del espíritu; reside en su alma, vive con la vida incorpórea de la idea, y para revelarla necesita darle una forma. Por eso la escribe.
En la mujer, sin embargo, la poesía está como encarnada en su ser; su aspiración, sus presentimientos, sus pasiones y su Destino son poesía: vive, respira, se muere en una indefinible atmósfera de idealismo que se desprende de ella, como un flúido luminoso y magnético; es, en una palabra, el verbo poético hecho carne. 657

Y todo este tesoro inagotable de sentimiento, todo este animado poema de esperanzas y de abnegaciones, de sueños y de tristezas, de alegrías y de lágrimas, donde cada sensación es una estrofa y cada pasión un canto, todo está contenido en vuestro corazón de mujer. 665–666

Mientras exista una mujer hermosa / Habrá poesía. 379

Además, el espectáculo de lo bello, en cualquier forma que se presente, levanta la mente a nobles aspiraciones. Yo, que profeso esta teoría, creo de todas veras que una mujer hermosa civiliza tanto como un libro. Sin querer, al contemplarla se buscan sus afinidades y se encuentra al cabo que la virtud es, en el orden moral, lo que en el físico la hermosura. 1247

Y si consideramos la cuestión desde otro aspecto, la silueta de una mujer que se destaca ligera y graciosa sobre la sábana de espuma del mar y el dilatado horizonte del cielo, ¿qué sentimientos no despierta?, ¿cuánta poesía no tiene? 706

244

BÉCQUER

Inútil fuera el querer hoy dar formas a los mil y mil pensamientos que asaltaron nuestra mente al contemplar los mudos despojos de esa civilización titánica que, después de haber sometido al mundo, dejó en cada uno de sus extremos las asombrosas huellas de su paso; eran tan rápidas las ideas, que se atropellaban entre sí en la imaginación, como las leves olas de un mar que pica el viento; tan confusas, que deshaciéndose las unas en las otras, sin dar espacio a completarse, huían como esos vagos recuerdos de un sueño que no se puede coordinar; como esos fantasmas ligerísimos, fenómenos inexplicables de la inspiración, que al querer materializarlos pierden su hermosura, o se escapan como la mariposa que huye dejando entre las manos que la quieren detener el polvo de oro con que sus alas se embellecen. 750

el sol doraba apenas las más altas agujas de la ciudad; la brisa del crepúsculo comenzaba a acariciar mi frente, cuando, absorto al contemplar aquellos silenciosos restos de otras edades más poéticas que la material en que vivimos y nos ahogamos en pura prosa, dejé caer de mis manos el lápiz y abandoné el dibujo, recostándome en la pared que tenía a mis espaldas y entregándome por completo a los sueños de la imaginación. ¿Qué pensaba? No sé si sabré decirlo . . .

Todas estas cosas veía yo, y muchas más de esas que después de pensadas no pueden recordarse; de esas tan inmateriales que es imposible encerrar en el círculo estrecho de la palabra . . . 165

Un mundo de ideas se agolpó a mi imaginación en aquel instante. Ideas ligerísimas sin forma determinada, que unían entre sí como un invisible hilo de luz, la profunda soledad de aquellos lugares, el alto silencio de la naciente noche y la vaga melancolía de mi espíritu. 132

Por el fondo de la iglesia atravesaba en aquel momento uno de los religiosos con su luenga capa oscura, ornada con la histórica cruz verde. Sea prestigio de la imaginación, sea efecto del fantástico cuadro en que la vi destacarse, aquella figura me trajo a la memoria no sé qué recuerdos confusos de siglos y de gentes que han pasado; generaciones de las que sólo he visto un trasunto en las severas estatuas que duermen inmóviles sobre las losas de sus tumbas, pero que entonces me pareció verlas levantarse, como evocadas por un conjuro, para poblar aquellas ruinas.
La atmósfera de la tradición, que aún se respira allí en átomos impalpables, comenzaba a embriagar mi alma, cada vez más dispuesta a sentir sin razonar, a creer sin discutir. 697–698

si tú supieras cuán imperceptible es el hilo de luz que ata entre sí
los pensamientos más absurdos que nadan en su caos . . . 154

Un hilo de luz, ese hilo de luz que se extiende rápido como la idea y
brilla en la oscuridad y la confusión de la mente, y reúne los puntos
más distantes y los relaciona entre sí de un modo maravilloso, ató
mis vagos recuerdos, y todo lo comprendí o creí comprenderlo . . . 175

Page 134

Después que hube abarcado con una mirada el conjunto de aquel
cuadro, imposible de reproducir con frases siempre descoloridas y
pobres, me senté en un pedrusco, lleno de esa emoción sin ideas que
experimentamos siempre que una cosa cualquiera nos impresiona
profundamente y parece que nos sobrecoge por su novedad o su hermosura. En esos instantes rapidísimos, en que la sensación fecunda
a la inteligencia y allá en el fondo del cerebro tiene lugar la misteriosa concepción de los pensamientos que han de surgir algún día
evocados por la memoria, nada se piensa, nada se razona, los sentidos
todos parecen ocupados en recibir y guardar la impresión que anali-
zarán más tarde.

Sintiendo aún las vibraciones de esta primera sacudida del alma,
que la sumerge en un agradable sopor, estuve, pues, un largo espacio
de tiempo, hasta que gradualmente comenzaron a extinguirse, y poco
a poco fueron levantándose las ideas relativas. 504–505

Page 137

puedo asegurarte que cuando siento no escribo. 658

Pages 137–138

Guardo, sí, en mi cerebro escritas, como en un libro misterioso, las
impresiones que han dejado en él su huella al pasar; estas ligeras y
ardientes hijas de la sensación duermen allí agrupadas en el fondo de
mi memoria hasta el instante en que, puro, tranquilo, sereno y
revestido, por decirlo así, de un poder sobrenatural, mi espíritu las
evoca, y tienden sus alas transparentes, que bullen con un zumbido
extraño, y cruzan otra vez a mis ojos como en una visión luminosa
y magnífica.

Entonces no siento ya con los nervios que se agitan, con el pecho
que se oprime, con la parte orgánica y material que se conmueve al
rudo choque de las sensaciones producidas por la pasión y los
afectos . . . 658

246

BÉCQUER

Page 138

Sólo a algunos seres les es dado el guardar como un tesoro la memoria viva de lo que han sentido. Yo creo que éstos son los poetas. Es más: creo que únicamente por esto lo son. 658-659

Yo no sé si ese mundo de visiones vive fuera o va dentro de nosotros . . . 427

Pages 138-139

Si tú supieras cómo las ideas más grandes se empequeñecen al encerrarse en el círculo de hierro de la palabra; si tú supieras qué diáfanas, qué ligeras, qué impalpables, son las gasas de oro que flotan en la imaginación al envolver esas misteriosas figuras que crea y de las que sólo acertamos a reproducir el descarnado esqueleto . . . 660

Page 139

Ser rey, señor de señores; ver cruzar ante los ojos, como las visiones de un sueño, las perlas, el oro, los placeres y la alegría . . . 66

las imágenes de las andas se dibujan confusas y asemejan gentes vivas que miran y ven con sus ojos de vidrio, causando la impresión de algo que, semejante a la visión del sueño, flota entre el mundo real y el imaginario . . . 1552

todo semejaba cosa de ilusión o ensueño. 563

La arquitectura árabe parece la hija del sueño de un creyente dormido después de una batalla a la sombra de una palmera . . . 334

Siguió la ceremonia; el músico, que la presenciaba absorto y aterrado, creía estar fuera del mundo real, vivir en esa región fantástica del sueño, en que todas las cosas se revisten de formas extrañas y fenomenales. 324

Y esa mujer, que es hermosa como el más hermoso de mis sueños de adolescente . . . 127

Me recuerda los días de mi infancia, aquellas horas sin nombre que precedían a mis sueños de niño, aquellas horas en que los genios, volando alrededor de mi cuna, me narraban consejas maravillosas, que, embelesando mi espíritu, formaban la base de mis delirios de oro. 79

Pages 139–140

La inteligencia del hombre, embotada por su contacto con la materia, no concibe lo puramente espiritual . . . 604

Page 140

Hay momentos en que el alma se desborda como un vaso de mirra que ya no basta a contener el perfume; instantes en que flotan los objetos que hieren nuestros ojos, y con ellos flota la imaginación. El espíritu se desata de la materia y huye, huye a través del vacío a sumergirse en las ondas de luz, entre las que vacilan los lejanos horizontes.

La mente no se halla en la tierra ni en el cielo. Recorre un espacio sin límites ni fondo, océano de voluptuosidad indefinible, en el que empapa sus alas para remontarse a las regiones donde habita el amor. 78

— ¿Qué me quieres, realidad de mi símbolo, padre que me diste el ser para que sirviera de eslabón invisible entre lo finito y lo infinito, entre el mundo de los hombres y el de las almas, sirviendo para bajar las potencias del Cielo y elevar las de la Tierra hasta que se toquen en el vacío, que es el lugar de mi soberanía? 84

Cuando la materia duerme, el espíritu vela. En tanto que el cuerpo del caudillo permanece inmóvil y sumergido en un letargo profundo, su alma se reviste de una forma imaginaria y huye de los lazos que la aprisionan para lanzarse al éter; allí la esperan las creaciones del Sueño, que le fingen un mundo poblado de seres animados con la vida de la idea, visión magnífica, profética y real en su fondo, vano sólo en la forma. 76

Los sueños son el espíritu de la realidad con las formas de la mentira: los dioses descienden en él hasta los mortales, y sus visiones son páginas del porvenir o recuerdos del pasado. 86

¿Será verdad que cuando toca el sueño
con sus dedos de rosa nuestros ojos,
de la cárcel que habita huye el espíritu
    en vuelo presuroso?

¿Será verdad que huésped de las nieblas,
de la brisa nocturna al tenue soplo
alado sube a la región vacía
    a encontrarse con otros?

248

BÉCQUER

¿Y allí, desnudo de la humana forma,
allí los lazos terrenales rotos,
breves horas habita de la idea
    el mundo silencioso?

¿Y ríe y llora, y aborrece y ama,
y guarda un rastro del dolor y el gozo,
semejante al que deja cuando cruza
    el cielo un meteoro?

¡Yo no sé si ese mundo de visiones
vive fuera o va dentro de nosotros;
pero sé que conozco a muchas gentes
    a quienes no conozco! 426

y todos confundidos, seremos la fuerza motora, el rayo vital de la
creación, que circula como un flúido por sus arterias subterráneas. 312

Pages 140–141

En las plateadas hojas de los álamos, en los huecos de las peñas, en las
ondas del agua, parece que nos hablan los invisibles espíritus de la
Naturaleza, que reconocen un hermano en el inmortal espíritu del
hombre. 46

Page 141

Yo me creía transportado no sé dónde, pues todo lo que veía me
recordaba un paisaje cuyos contornos eran los mismos de siempre,
pero cuyos colores se habían borrado, por decirlo así, no quedando
de ellos sino una media tinta dudosa. La impresión que experimentaba
sólo puede compararse a la que sentimos en esos sueños en que,
por un fenómeno inexplicable, las cosas son y no son a la vez, y los
sitios en que creemos hallarnos se transforman en parte de una
manera estrambótica e imposible. 637–638

El insomnio y la fantasía siguen y siguen procreando en monstruoso
maridaje. ¡Sus creaciones, apretadas ya como las raquíticas plantas de
un vivero, pugnan por dilatar su fantástica existencia, disputándose
los átomos de la memoria como el escaso jugo de una tierra estéril! 4

Acaso es un jirón de la niebla que se desgarra en los dentellados muros
del castillo; tal vez un último rayo de luz que se desliza fugitivo
sobre los calcinados sillares. Pero ¿quién nos impide soñar que es
una mujer enamorada, que aún vuelve a oír el eco de un cantar grato
a su oído? 722

Page 142

esas historias, cuyo vago desenlace flota, por último, indeciso, en ese punto que separa la vigilia del sueño . . . 153

Después de mecerse un instante en ese vago espacio que media entre la vigilia y el sueño . . . 205–206

No dormía; vagaba en ese limbo
en que cambian de forma los objetos,
misteriosos espacios que separan
la vigilia del sueño. 420

En esos ligeros y cortados sueños de la mañana, ricos en imágenes risueñas y voluptuosas, sueños diáfanos y celestes como la luz que entonces comienza a transparentarse a través de las blancas cortinas del lecho . . . 209

cuando de repente entreabrió los ojos sobresaltado e incorporóse a medias, lleno aún de ese estupor del que vuelve en sí de improviso después de un sueño profundo. 206

— Sin duda soñaba con las majaderías que nos refirió el zagal — exclamó Garcés, restregándose los ojos con mucha calma y en la firme persuasión de que cuanto había creído oír no era más que esa vaga huella del ensueño que queda, al despertar, en la imaginación, como queda en el oído la última cadencia de una melodía después que ha expirado temblando la última nota. 206

No sé lo que he soñado
en la noche pasada . . . 418

Estas palabras sin ilación ni sentido, que flotan en el espacio acompañadas de suspiros apenas perceptibles y de largos sollozos, comienzan a reunirse unas con otras, como se reúnen al despertar las vagas ideas de un sueño, y ya reunidas forman un inmenso y doloroso poema, en el que cada campana canta su estrofa, y todas juntas interpretan, por medio de sonidos simbólicos, el pensamiento que hierve callado en el cerebro de los que oyen sumidos en honda meditación. 736

Después de una noche de insomnio y de terrores ¡es tan hermosa la luz clara y blanca del día! 284

El sentido común, que es la barrera de los sueños, comienza a flaquear, y las gentes de diversos campos se mezclan y confunden. Me cuesta trabajo saber qué cosas he soñado y cuáles me han sucedido.

250

BÉCQUER

Mis afectos se reparten entre fantasmas de la imaginación y personajes reales. Mi memoria clasifica revueltos nombres y fechas de mujeres y días que han muerto o han pasado, con los días y mujeres que no han existido sino en mi mente. 5

Yo creo que he visto unos ojos como los que he pintado en esta leyenda. No sé si en sueños, pero yo los he visto. 41

El resplandor de todas las luces la iluminó de pronto, y pude verle el rostro. Al mirarlo tuve que ahogar un grito. Yo conocía a aquella mujer: no la había visto nunca, pero la conocía de haberla contemplado en sueños; era uno de esos seres que adivina el alma o los recuerde acaso de otro mundo mejor, del que, al descender a éste, algunos no pierden del todo la memoria. 174

Page 143

Poco a poco logré darme cuenta de lo que me rodeaba, y entonces vi a una mujer arrodillada al pie del sepulcro. Yo no he soñado esa mujer . . . ¿Había visto, en efecto, el sepulcro de Garcilaso? ¿O era todo una historia forjada en mi mente sobre el tema de un sepulcro cualquiera? Tenía un medio de salir de dudas: consultar la guía del forastero en Toledo. Pero temía equivocarme. Después de todo, yo no trataba de hacer un estudio serio de la población, ni de pertrecharme de datos eruditos. Tanto me importaba creer que lo había visto, como verlo. 1195, 1197, 1198

¿No has soñado nunca? Al despertar, ¿te ha sido alguna vez posible referir, con toda su inexplicable vaguedad y poesía, lo que has soñado? 660

Necesario es abrir paso a las aguas profundas, que acabarán por romper el dique, diariamente aumentadas por un manantial vivo. 4

No quiero que en mis noches sin sueño volváis a pasar por delante de mis ojos en extravagante procesión, pidiéndome con gestos y contorsiones que os saque a la vida de la realidad del limbo en que vivís, semejantes a fantasmas sin consistencia. 5

Pages 143–144

¿Cómo la palabra, cómo un idioma grosero y mezquino, insuficiente a veces para expresar las necesidades de la materia, podrá servir de digno intérprete entre dos almas?
Imposible. 660

SPANISH TEXTS

Page 144

como la estela nebulosa que señala el paso de un desconocido cometa,
como los átomos dispersos de un mundo en embrión . . . 5

Yo quisiera poder cincelar la forma que ha de conteneros, como se
cincela el vaso de oro que ha de guardar un preciado perfume. Mas es
imposible. 4–5

Pero ¡ay, que entre el mundo de la idea y el de la forma existe un
abismo que sólo puede salvar la palabra; y la palabra, tímida y
perezosa, se niega a secundar sus esfuerzos! 4

porque Manrique era poeta; ¡tanto, que nunca le habían satisfecho las
formas en que pudiera encerrar sus pensamientos, y nunca los había
encerrado al escribirlos! 118

Page 145

Cantos celestes como los que acarician los oídos en los momentos
de éxtasis; cantos que percibe el espíritu y no los puede repetir el
labio . . . ignota música del cielo que solo la imaginación comprende . . . 34

Todo esto era la música, y algo más que no puede explicarse ni apenas
concebirse. 324

Y yo pensé entonces algo que no puedo recordar, y que, aunque lo
recordase, no encontraría palabras para decirlo. 360

A donde no alcanza, pues, ni la paleta del pintor con sus infinitos
recursos, ¿cómo podrá llegar mi pluma sin más medios que la palabra,
tan pobre, tan insuficiente para dar idea de lo que es todo un efecto
de líneas, de claroscuro, de combinación de colores, de detalles que
se ofrecen junto a la vista . . . ? 528

Pages 145–146

La hora en que se ve, la luz que recibe o el horizonte sobre que se
dibuja, modifican hasta tal punto las apariencias de un mismo objeto,
que sería difícil fijar su verdadero carácter aislándolo del fondo que lo
rodea o contemplándolo desde otro punto de vista del que le conviene.
1206

Page 146

En las plateadas hojas de los álamos, en los huecos de las peñas,
en las ondas del agua, parece que nos hablan los invisibles espíritus de

252

la Naturaleza, que reconocen un hermano en el inmortal espíritu del hombre. 46

En las nubes, en el aire, en el fondo de los bosques, en las grietas de las peñas, imaginaba percibir formas o escuchar sonidos misteriosos, formas de seres sobrenaturales, palabras ininteligibles que no podía comprender. 119

Esas fantasías ligeras y, por decirlo así, impalpables, son, en cierto modo, como las mariposas, que no pueden cogerse en las manos sin que se quede entre los dedos el polvo de oro de sus alas. 153

Sacudimiento extraño
que agita las ideas, . . .

   murmullo que en el alma
se eleva y va creciendo, . . .

   actividad nerviosa
que no halla en qué emplearse,
sin rienda que lo guíe
caballo volador;

   locura que el espíritu
exalta y enardece;
embriaguez divina
del genio creador . . .
   ¡Tal es la inspiración!

Gigante voz que el caos
ordena en el cerebro, . . .

   brillante rienda de oro
que poderosa enfrena . . .

   atmósfera en que giran
con orden las ideas,
cuál átomos que agrupa
recóndita atracción; . . .

   ¡Tal es nuestra razón!
Con ambas siempre lucha
y de ambas vencedor,
tan sólo el genio puede
a un yugo atar las dos. 378

Page 148

fenómenos incomprensibles de nuestra naturaleza misteriosa, que el hombre no puede ni aún concebir. 52

Hay otros (momentos) en que se desliga de la carne, pierde su personalidad y se confunde con los elementos de la naturaleza, se relaciona con su modo de ser, y traduce su incomprensible lenguaje. 355

   Yo sé un himno gigante y extraño
que anuncia en la noche del alma una aurora,
y estas páginas son de ese himno,
cadencias que el aire dilata en las sombras.

   Yo quisiera escribirlo, del hombre
domando el rebelde, mezquino idïoma,
con palabras que fuesen a un tiempo
suspiros y risas, colores y notas.

   Pero en vano es luchar; que no hay cifra
capaz de encerrarlo, y apenas, ¡oh hermosa!,

si, teniendo en mis manos las tuyas,
pudiera al oído cantártelo a solas. 375

Pages 148–149

Hay una poesía magnífica y sonora; una poesía hija de la meditación
y el arte, que se engalana con todas las pompas de la lengua, que se
mueve con una cadenciosa majestad, habla a la imaginación, completa
sus cuadros y la conduce a su antojo por un sendero desconocido,
seduciéndola con su armonía y su hermosura.

Hay otra natural, breve, seca, que brota del alma como una chispa
eléctrica, que hiere el sentimiento con una palabra y huye, y desnuda
de artificio, desembarazada dento de una forma libre, despierta, con
una que las toca, las mil ideas que duermen en el océano sin fondo de
la fantasía.

La primera tiene un valor dado: es la poesía de todo el mundo.

La segunda carece de medida absoluta, adquiere las proporciones
de la imaginación que impresiona: puede llamarse la poesía de los
poetas. 675–676

Page 149

De seguro no los podré describir tal cuales ellos eran: luminosos,
transparentes como las gotas de la lluvia que se resbalan sobre las
hojas de los árboles después de una tempestad de verano. De todos
modos, cuento con la imaginación de mis lectores para hacerme
comprender en este que pudiéramos llamar boceto de un cuadro
que pintaré algún día. 41

Las obras de la imaginación tienen siempre algún punto de contacto
con la realidad. 369

Sucede con estos pueblecitos tan pintorescos, cuando se ven en lonta-
nanza tantas líneas caprichosas, tantas chimeneas arrojando pilares de
humo azul, tantos árboles y peñas y accidentes artísticos, lo que con
otras muchas cosas del mundo, en que todo es cuestión de la distancia
a que se miran, y la mayor parte de las veces, cuando se llega a ellos,
la poesía se convierte en prosa. 502

Page 150

Cierto que para abarcar grandes conjuntos con esa prolijidad de
detalles que ofrecen algunos monumentos, la fotografía lleva en
ocasiones inmensa ventaja al arte; pero, por lo común, su impresión
deja traslucir algo de la aridez y la prosa de un procedimiento
mecánico e ininteligente, faltando en sus producciones ese sello de

buen gusto, ese tacto para dejar o tomar aquello que más conviene al carácter de la cosa, ese misterioso espíritu, en fin, que domina en la obra del artista, la cual no siempre hace aparecer el objeto tal cual realmente es, sino como se presenta a la imaginación, con un relieve y acento particular en ciertas líneas y detalles que produce el efecto que, sin duda, se propuso su autor al concebirlo y trazarlo. 1188–1189

¿Y usted cree que cuando tiembla ligeramente la mano del artista poséido de una idea o un sentimiento, no deja el pincel un rastro propio, no acusan las líneas algo particular, algo impalpable, indefinible, pero que permanece palpitando allí como la estela del perfume y luz que deja tras sí una divinidad que ha desaparecido; algo que nos dice: "por aquí ha pasado la inspiración"? 705

Más reposada, más severa, más fría si se quiere (que "la moderna escuela dramática"), la tragedia de Ventura de la Vega, fruto de un trabajo concienzudo, retrato fiel de una época histórica, vestida con galas poéticas tan graves, tan sencillas como la toga y el manto de sus personajes, habla a un mismo tiempo a la inteligencia que al sentimiento, y de la dulce armonía que forman al combinarse las dos cuerdas que vibran a la vez en el corazón y en la cabeza de los espectadores, resulta ese placer profundo, tranquilo e indefinible que producen las verdaderas obras de arte en los que alcanzan a comprenderlas y están organizados para poder sentirlas. P.D., III, 123

Page 152

Cuando sopla el cierzo, cae la nieve o azota la lluvia los vidrios del balcón de mi celda, corro a buscar la claridad rojiza y alegre de la llama, y allí teniendo a mis pies el perro, que se enrosca junto a la lumbre, viendo brillar en el oscuro fondo de la cocina las mil chispas de oro con que se abrillantan las cacerolas y los trastos de la espetera al reflejo del fuego, ¡cuántas veces he interrumpido la lectura de una escena de La tempestad, de Shakespeare, o del Caín, de Byron, para oír el ruido del agua que hierve a borbotones, coronándose de espuma y levantando con sus penachos de vapor azul y ligero la tapadera de metal que golpea los bordes de la vasija! 470

Page 156

Yo soy sobre el abismo
el puente que atraviesa;
yo soy la ignota escala
que el cielo une a la tierra.

255

Yo soy el invisible
anillo que sujeta
el mundo de la forma
al mundo de la idea.
Yo, en fin, soy ese espíritu,
desconocida esencia,
perfume misterioso
de que es vaso el poeta. 382

GABRIEL MIRÓ

Quotations from Miró are from the *Obras Completas* (Madrid:
Biblioteca Nueva, 1943).

Page 159

. . . quizá por la palabra se me diese la plenitud de la contemplación.
1023

Page 160

La palabra era la más preciosa realidad humana. 843

. . . hay episodios y zonas de nuestra vida que no se ven del todo
hasta que los revivimos y contemplamos por el recuerdo; el recuerdo
les aplica la plenitud de la conciencia; como hay emociones que no
lo son del todo hasta que no reciben la fuerza lírica de la palabra,
su palabra plena y exacta. Una llanura de la que sólo se levantaba un
árbol, no la sentí mía hasta que no me dije "Tierra caliente y árbol
fresco". Cantaba un pájaro en una siesta lisa, inmóvil, y el cántico la
penetró, la poseyó toda, cuando alguien dijo: "Claridad". Y fué como
si el ave se transformase en un cristal luminoso que revibraba hasta en
la lejanía. 614

Pages 161–162

Es que la palabra, esa palabra, como la música, resucita las realidades,
las valora, exalta y acendra, subiendo a una pureza precisamente
inefable, lo que por no sentirse ni decirse en su matiz, en su exactitud,
dormía dentro de las exactitudes polvorientas de las mismas miradas
y del mismo vocablo y concepto de todos. 614

Page 162

En él (un niño) se abría la curiosidad y la conciencia de las cosas
bajo la palabra del capellán. 810

256

GABRIEL MIRÓ

. . . Pues en esos "días frutales" se ha oído a sí mismo pronunciar: "Seamos dichosos". Y al decirlo comenzaba a serlo; su vida se abría gozosamente para recibir los finos oreos y las largas contemplaciones de la dicha prometida. Porque en aquellas palabras había un principio de voluntad y de conciencia de la dicha . . . 572–573

Page 163

. . . es una voz pastosa, y todo lo que pronuncia tiene figura y un contorno de sonido tierno, tan gustoso que lo recogéis en todo vuestro cuerpo, y os quedáis paladeando sus mismas palabras como un dulce exquisito. 547

. . . pero las cosas que más participan de nuestra vida hay que decírnoslas también a nosotros mismos. 777

Ella también miraría el agua, los árboles, el cielo, y diría: río, árbol, cielo. Cuando saliesen los palomos de su terrado a volar por las huertas, ella los vería y pronunciaría: palomos, aire, sol . . . Así se afanaba Pablo en pensar y regalarse con las palabras que María Fulgencia tuviera en sus labios, como si le tomase una miel con los suyos. 921

. . . apreté dentro de palabras lo que yo más amaba, lo que creí más mío; y las pronuncié y se me deshacían, y para no perderlas las escribí en piedras con un esfuerzo recóndito como si las tallase; y no las arrojé, sino que las puse en la faz de las aguas, y al sumergirse sentí un ruido de ascua y de corazón . . . Pero entonces dejaban en todo el mar un fermento de humanismo, y el mar palpitaba gloriosamente con pobre vida mía. 671

Pasó un labriego con su azada de sol, y, mirando al forastero, le dijo:
— ¡A la sombra, a la sombra! — Y en la boca seca de ese hombre, enjuto y acortezado, la palabra sombra tuvo una frescura nueva, como si acabase de crearla. 948

Alegría de la revelación y de la pronunciación de la palabra "pueblo". 951

Page 164

— Ibi, Tibi, Famorca, Benisa, Jávea . . . Los nombres de los pueblos suyos son concretamente ellos en su profundidad; profundidad máxima, que es la del lenguaje . . . ¿Es la delicia de la palabra por ella misma? Pero es que la palabra no sería deliciosa si no significase una calidad. Y estos nombres rurales en boca de sus gentes dejan un sabor de fruta, que emite la de todo el árbol con sus raíces y su pellón de tierra, y el aire, y el sol y el agua que lo tocan y calan; fruta que aunque la lleven otros terrenos, no es como la del frutal propio. 1007

Entonces, Sigüenza, por un furor de burla contra el fracaso de sus memorias, se puso a buscar palabras atroces, que precisamente por serlo harían resaltar la pureza de las resonancias y de los lugares. Y las gritó de dos sílabas:

— ¡Cha-rol! ¡U-jier! ¡Cuen-ta! ¡Sport-man!

En seguida de tres sílabas:

— ¡Dic-ta-men! ¡Mé-to-do! ¡Viz-con-de! ¡De-fi-nir!

Luego de cuatro:

— ¡Pro-vi-sio-nal! ¡Di-pu-ta-do! ¡Dis-tin-gui-do!

Y hasta fórmulas de cortesía, como:

— ¡Muy-se-ñor-mío!

La voz de Sigüenza, desincorporada, cada vez más lejos, esparcía desde sus máscaras, con inocencia y exactitud: Viz-con-de . . . Pro-vi-sio-nal . . . Muy-se-ñor-mío . . . ; revelando y esparciendo los pobres conceptos en el aire inmóvil, diáfano, rasgado únicamente por las alas de los halcones. 1005

Pages 164–165

Alcalalí, sin pensar en etimologías, Alcalalí, pequeñito y agudo como un esquilón. Agres, umbrio y ermitaño. Ya junta la imagen con la palabra, cumpliéndose en sí mismo que sus nombres, como los de los dioses para Platón, aunque no los comprendamos, son sin duda "la exacta expresión de la verdad". 1008

Page 165

. . . un Mediterráneo de urna . . . 1046

Page 166

Sigüenza principia a sentirse receloso de la oratoria de su pensamiento. Demasiado ancho. Es menester el ahinco de la precisión para que este hombre se acepte a sí mismo. Se afanará por las exactitudes. 1026

Y amé loca, inmensamente la vida hasta en mi posteridad más lejana. Por eso desde entonces ando, camino, subo montañas, recorro los peñascales y arenas de la costa, atravieso los campos, oigo el estruendo de mi sangre como un torrente íntimo, y cuando no puedo más, me acuesto sobre la tierra mirando a la altura . . . 115

¡Oh vida, vida, vida mía! ¡Y así todas las mañanas! 115

— ¡Tenemos salud!, y hace un día grande y caliente . . . Vivamos hacia lo alto, ¿no es eso? 112

258

GABRIEL MIRÓ

Esta voluntaria o forzada degradación no me pesa. La tengo por virtud de asimiento a todo plano y especie de vida . . . 113

Page 167

"¡Mirad el aire; sólo os pido que miréis! . . . ¿No veis, no descubrís nada dentro? ¡Pues todo hierve de gérmenes ansiosos de vida!" 116

No olvide que yo estoy sano y que vivo por el impulso y virtud de quererlo . . . yo vivo sabiéndolo y queriéndolo, y a solas conmigo mismo, con mis tejidos, con mis huesos, con mi sangre . . . Estoy amenazado y me defiendo, porque amo la vida con toda mi alma y todo mi cuerpo. No es querer la vida por . . . es un asimiento con lo creado. Se me figura que tengo raíces y que penetran en todo. ¡Qué alegría la de los árboles enormes y centenarios: sentirse palpitar y estremecerse y vivir por la raigambre alejada! 124

. . . su mismo sacrificio irremediable, irremediable porque, más que de un concepto de rigidez, se originaba de su voluntad que le encorvaba bajo la gloria de la vida como si temiese tropezar en una cueva. 781–782

Las venas duras de San Antonio — del San Antonio de Flaubert — se le engordan y atirantan casi a punto de romperse . . . Quiere tener alas, corteza, concha, garfa, trompa . . . descender hasta el fondo de la materia; ser la materia . . . Pero Sigüenza no es San Antonio. 980–981

La adivinación sensitiva de que están imantadas las vidas primorosas la hizo volverse a lo profundo de los olivares. 731

Sin saberlo, estaba poseída de lo hondo y magnífico de la sensación de las cosas. 731

"¡Ay, sensualidad, y cómo nos trapasas de anhelos de infinito!" 943

Page 168

Dicen que es un agua dormida. ¡Cómo ha de estar dormida el agua que acoge sensitivamente todo lo que se le acerca, para mostrarlo, aunque no haya nadie que la mira!
. . Y los follajes, los troncos, la peña, la nube, el azul, el ave, todo se ve dentro, y, muchas veces, se sabe que es hermoso, porque el agua lo dice. Entonces, todo adquiere el misterio y la vida de la emoción suya. Es ya la belleza contemplada; es el concepto y la fórmula de una belleza que se produce en esa soledad como en el alma del hombre, y el agua es como una frente que ha pensado este

paisaje. Paisaje junto al agua clara, desnuda; paisaje sumergido y alto, ¡cómo te tiembla y se te dobla el corazón en la faz y en las entrañas del agua! 666–667

todo eso, que le exalta y le recoge con una felicidad tan vieja y tan virgen, y que *es como es* por nuestro concepto, por nuestro recuerdo, por nuestra lírica, ha de seguir sin nuestra emoción, sin nuestros ojos, sin nosotros. 1060

Necesidad biológica y estética de haber sido y ser siempre de allí, con un sentimiento étnico y exclusivista de sangre de Israel. 1032

Pages 168–169

Muchas veces ha proclamado Sigüenza, con Somoza, que el paisaje natal, el nuestro, es el que nos mantiene la emoción y la comprensión de todo paisaje. Pero un paisaje para un lírico es el paisaje, la evocación de todos, con lo que puede poblarlo nuestra vida y con las regiones solitarias de nuestra vida. Un paisaje, y, entre todos, el nuestro, abre la mirada desde lo lineal, desde el rasgo más sutil, hasta la esencia del campo sin confines . . . 1027

Page 169

Afirmó que el mes de junio era el más hermoso del año. Olía a felicidad. Monera dijo que sí. Pero don Daniel modificó su concepto.
— Es la felicidad la que tiene su olor, olor de mes de junio. 727

Casi siempre huelen las flores a un instante de felicidad que ya no nos pertenece. 769

Los jazmines, las rosas, los naranjos; los campos, el aire, la atmósfera de los tiempos de las viejas promesas; olor de felicidad no realizada . . . 937

Don Arcadio miraba un rato los "leales afectos." Después volvía a plegar la carta reverentemente, y aspiraba conmovido el olor de oblea marchita. 469

Pages 169–170

¿Se ha fijado en las chimeneas? Huelo los humos de sus cocinas; hasta me parece oler los dormitorios, las alacenas y cómodas de las casas, y creo vivir y participar de todas las familias. 128–129

Page 170

¡Las leguas y los años que se ven allí! 1031

260

GABRIEL MIRÓ

Se le acerca su pasado a Sigüenza respirando en la exactitud de su conciencia de ahora. Otra vez. 1056

Pages 170–171

Se recordaba sin recuerdos. Era una contradicción de su lírica sustancial. Le faltaba coincidir consigo mismo. No asistir, no pertenecer al propio pasado, es una ausencia, un síncope de alma, imperdonable en Sigüenza, que vive a costa de la continuidad de su modelación íntima. 1015

Page 171

Penetró más en la soledad del collado. Soledad cincelada en un paisaje de cumbres. Y desde que se asomó Sigüenza, todo comenzó a respirar dentro de la órbita del tiempo, tiempo de las soledades contado ya por el pulso de Sigüenza. 1059

. . . y cuando desaparecen se fija en los montes el tiempo, sin nadie, como si se reanudara una emoción de eternidad. 1039

Con una mirada corre Sigüenza muchas horas de ese sendero; de modo que puede mirar el porvenir de la mujercita hasta que llegue, muy de noche, a su casa. 1031

Conservan sus aposentos oscuridad antigua, oscuridad reposada, remansada, oscuridad de años anteriores . . . 111

Las horas doradas de los campos en las vísperas de las fiestas la internaban en una evidencia de sí misma a través de una luminosidad de muchos tiempos. 731

Los días también rodaban encima de Oleza. 721

Las ciudades grandes, ruidosas y duras, todavía tienen alguna parcela con quietud suya, con tiempo suyo acostado bajo unas tapias de jardines. 947

Page 172

Eso sería no ser ya niño: depender del pasado sentir, de su memoria, de sus acciones, de su conciencia, de los instantes desaparecidos . . . 930

Pages 172–174

'Acabo de descubrir un lugar delicioso dormido entre los años . . .' Todo eso casi lo pronunciaba Sigüenza asomándose de puntillas a un

261

jardín de escombros. Nadie. El silencio con el aliento de todo. Cuando llegó, se escaparon los ruiseñores, las golondrinas, los mirlos. Se sentía caer los jazmines, crujir los finos nervios de las plantas, esconderse los grandes lagartos de piel deslumbradora y glacial como una seda húmeda y bordada.

Poco a poco volvieron los pájaros; se asomaron las salamandras al sol verdoso de las piedras; se recalentaron las cigarras; las golondrinas se pusieron a espulgarse en un ciprés seco, y en cada jazmín sonó una abeja . . . Todo, todo lo mismo que cuando vino el forastero. El cual miraba el huerto como si fuese suyo, no por dineros, sino por antigua posesión de linaje y de pensamientos. Lo habría heredado desde mucha distancia de años, desde que todo aquello comenzó a caerse; y ahora visitaba su herencia doliéndose y agradándole el abandono en que dejó lo suyo.

Siete cipreses en hilera, pero nada más quedaban dos con follaje macizo; los otros estaban descarnados en su leña. Era menester arrancarlos, y de sus troncos se labraría Sigüenza una mesa, un ropero y un arcón.

Frente al portal, dos adelfos que arriba se juntaban en un techado de hojas duras y de flores rojas. Dentro de la sombra da un poco de angustia; nuestra piel se comunica de la amargura que hincha las cortezas del baladre.

Un jazminero cegaba las rejas y la mitad del muro. Lo plantarían cuando edificaran la casa, hace setenta, noventa, cien años . . . Hace mucho tiempo también que se derrumbó del peso de sus sarmientos y biznagas, y sigue verde y tierno. Es una masa torrencial, inmóvil, de olores virginales. Toda la tierra del contorno está mullida de nieve de la flor. El aire se cuaja de un perfume de novia, muy bueno, pero tanto que la novia se multiplica en un palomar de doncellas que nos ahoga de suavidad. Las sienes y los párpados de Sigüenza se le traspasaban de olor. Se le precipitó la disnea de beber ese olor sensual de castidad.

Otro viejo elemento de hermosura de aquel recinto era el laurel.

Sigüenza se recostó en el tronco liso del laurel. Le parecía tocarlo íntimamente en cada frutilla, en cada arista de hoja, brote por brote. Todo su conjunto le latía en su vida, fresco, tierno, definitivo y eterno. Laurel con todos sus méritos de belleza para que un dios lo haga suyo, pero laurel del todo vegetal, sin predestinaciones a temas mitológicos y alegóricos. Arbol con todas las virtudes antes de servir para nada y sin cuidado de que aproveche a nadie. Se ha criado libre, puro y bello, sin que se espere de él más que eso: que viva grande, hermoso y recogido. Y este laurel no es sólo su tronco y su copa que tienden un paño húmedo y azulado de umbría, sino que es también

262

GABRIEL MIRÓ

su retoñar a borbollones que hienden la tierra y sale por la escombra y revienta por el tapial, multiplicándose barrocamente la planta sin perder su unidad clásica. Está en sí mismo y traspasando las losas y trasfundiendo su tono de serenidad en la convivencia de los cipreses, de los adelfos, del jazminero, y en un bancal escalonado de naranjos con lindes de parras y rosales. Todo había de acoger en medio, como fondo suyo, una casa lisa y blanca. 1009-1010

Page 175

De los bancales segados, de las tierras maduras, de la quietud de las distancias, sube un humo azul que se para y se duerme. Aparece un árbol, el contorno de un casal; pasa un camino, un fresco resplandor de agua viva. Todo en una trémula desnudez.

Así se nos ofrece el paisaje cansado o lleno de los días que se quedaron detrás de nosotros. Concretamente no es el pasado nuestro; pero nos pertenece, y de él nos valemos para revivir y acreditar episodios que rasgan su humo dormido. Tiene esa lejanía un hondo silencio que se queda escuchándonos. La abeja de una palabra recordada lo va abriendo y lo estremece todo.

No han de tenerse estas páginas fragmentarias por un propósito de memorias; pero leyéndolas pueden oírse, de cuando en cuando, las campanas de la ciudad de Is, cuya conseja evocó Renan, la ciudad más o menos poblada y ruda que todos llevamos sumergida dentro de nosotros mismos. 589

Page 176

Un día vimos a un desconocido . . . Decimos: ¡Ya no volvimos a verle!, recordando al que se extravió para nosotros dentro de la vida o se hundió dentro de la muerte; y entonces es cuando le vemos prorrumpir del humo dormido, más claro, más acendrado, como no le veíamos teniéndole cerca, que sólo sería repetir la mirada sin ahondarla, sin agrandarla, quedándose en la misma huella óptica que se va acortezando por el ocio. 591

. . . porque hay episodios y zonas de nuestra vida que no se ven del todo hasta que los revivimos y contemplamos por el recuerdo; el recuerdo les aplica la plenitud de la conciencia . . . 614

Pages 176-177

Agua de pueblo, de este pueblo, que Sigüenza bebió hace veinte años. Tiene un dulzor de dejo amargo, pero de verdad química, que todavía es más verdad lírica. Bebiéndola se le aparece en la lengua

263

el mismo sabor preciso del agua y de su sed de entonces. En aquella
sed estaban contenidas todas las promesas de las claridades de un
agua lejana para todas sus avideces. Desde aquella sed, junto a la pila
de esta fuente, ¡cuánto mundo, Señor, cuánto mundo se le deparaba
entre el arco de sus sienes! Y, ahora, todos esos años, los veinte
años, venían dóciles como corderos y se paraban a beber y mirarse
en la pila viejecita, donde cabía temblando el firmamento. 997

Page 177

Ahora se acuesta y se distiende en la huella del recuerdo espacial,
tibia de sí mismo. 1049

Las frondas reciben y se envían la circulación de los aires de ruidos
marineros de espumas, y huelen a pueblo, a reposo de hace veinte
años. 1056

Sentirse claramente a sí mismo, ¿era sentirse a lo lejos, o en su
actualidad? Pero sentirse en su actualidad, ¿no era sentirse a costa
de entonces, de entonces, que iba cegado por el instante? Y al
inferirse y extraerse de él, saciándose de su imagen desaparecida,
¿no alcanzaba una predisposición a la felicidad que no fué entonces,
cuando pudo ser, ni es ahora, porque ya pasó, y sin realidades, y
por no tenerlas, encontraba una fórmula de plenitud? 1056

Page 178

Se ha de ser lo preciso el antecesor de sí mismo. 1049

Veo así como dicen que Dios contempla lo pasado, lo presente y lo
futuro, en un *presente continuado*. 122

Los recuerdos, para mí, no habitan sólo en la memoria, sino dentro
de toda mi carne . . . 106

¡Soy carne de recuerdos! 111

Y porque nos oprime la verdad del tiempo devanado tuvo más fuerza
alucinante la emoción de esta hora que se había quedado inmóvil
para Sigüenza desde entonces. Y hasta hizo un ademán suave de
tocarla, de empujarla. 949

Asiste Sigüenza a una pura emoción de eternidad del campo. Como
esta tarde pudo ser otra tarde de siglos lejanos. Sigüenza se cree
retrocedido en el tiempo, se cree prolongado en esta naturaleza de
piedras y de rosas pálidas y moradas, de mar descolorida, de aire

GABRIEL MIRÓ

inmóvil. Lo mismo, lo mismo esta tarde que una tarde de septiembre de 1800, de 1700, de 1600. 1031

Page 179

Hallábame también en ese estado de reiteración de "sí mismo", de creer que ya se ha vivido "ese" instante, y que todo en la casa de Ordóñez estaba y sucedía según una promesa infalible. 607

Pages 179–180

Y llegamos a su casa. Casa antigua y señorial, de sillares morenos y dinteles esculpidos. Todo estaba en una grata sombra de celosías verdes, que semejaban exprimir todo el fresco y olor del verano. Porque sentíase que fuera se espesaban los elementos crudos del verano como en corteza, y dentro sólo la deleitosa y apurada intimidad. En el vestíbulo, en las salas, en el comedor, había muchos jarrones, cuencos, canastillas, juncieras desbordando de magnolias, gardenias, frutas y jazmines; y por las entornadas rejas interiores se ofrecía una rápida aparición de la tarde de jardín umbroso y familiar. Ya sé que muchas casas tienen en julio magnolias, jazmines, frutas, gardenias; pero es eso nada más: flores, flores porque se cogen y caen demasiadas en el huerto; y frutas: melocotones, ciruelas, peras, manzanas . . . y, sin querer, sabemos en seguida la que morderíamos. Y allí, no; allí flores y frutas integrando una tónica de señorío y de belleza, una emoción de vida estival y de mujer. No "eran" melocotones, ciruelas, peras, manzanas . . . clasificadamente, sino fruta por emoción de fruta, además de su evocación de deliciosos motivos barrocos; y "aquella" fruta, el tacto de su piel con sólo mirarla, y su color aristocrático de esmalte, y flores que sí que habían de ser precisamente magnolias, gardenias y jazmines por su blancura y por su fragancia, fragancia de una felicidad recordada, inconcreta, de la que casi semeja que participe el oído, porque la emoción de alguna música expande como un perfume íntimo de magnolias, de gardenias, de jazmines que no tienen una exactitud de perfume como el clavel. 607

Page 182

Crujía el aire serrano. Subían deshojándose en la altitud los rumores del pueblo y del contorno: la palpitación de un molino, el alarido de un pavo real, el repique de una fragua, un retozo de colleras de una diligencia, una tonada labradora, la rota quejumbre de las llantas de un carro, un berrinche de criatura, un hablar y reír de dos hidalgos que se saludaban desde un huerto a una galería, y campanas,

campanas anchas, lentas, menuditas, rápidas. Sobre la tarde iba resbalando el fresco retumbo de las presas espumosas del río. Y entre todo revibró inflamado y afiladísimo el cántico de un gallo, y don Magín incorporóse diciendo:
— ¡Ese es el mío! 736

Page 184

Ser el centro sensible de un ruedo inmenso de creación . . . 362

Un contacto de creación desnuda que calaba la piel y la sangre. 671

Y cuando con más encendimiento apetecía ser él también inmenso y leve, trocándose en azul, en boscaje, en silencio, en todo, en nada . . . 317

. . . estos venturosos tránsitos de sencillez y pureza por los que parece que volvemos a la santidad de los primeros instantes de la vida . . . 335

Una gracia, una felicidad inocente de claridades que, como la felicidad y la inocencia de los hombres, daba miedo de que se rompiesen. 977

¿No acaba de abrir los ojos Sigüenza con una emoción de inocencia de primer hombre? 1050

La felicidad y la inocencia se han roto. 978

¿No *aventajaba* Sigüenza al padre Adán en saberse mortal? 1052

y nos resucita y llena de flora virgen, fuerte y deliciosa del Paraíso. 347

Page 185

Y era mañana de crueldad. 116

Y mi amigo, el hombre manso, piadoso, que predicaba en su hogar anhelos de vida y amor, se entraba delirantemente por caminos de crueldad . . . 117

¡Una sierpe había matado a una vieja! . . .
— ¿Cuál vieja? dijo espantado el guía.
— ¡La muerta!
— ¿Qué muerta? ¡Si no hay ninguna vieja! ¡Es una ovella, una ovella! . . . ¡Adónde huye nuestra piedad! Le recorría heladamente la sangre. Se lastimaba de la cordera y odiaba la vieja. Se lo confesó: ¡hubiera preferido que la emponzoñada fuese la *vieja*! ¿Señor, es que

266

duerme siempre en nuestras entrañas una hez abyecta de crueldad? 366-367

Entonces, Félix miró con miedo y rabia esa ferocísima agua, tan mansa y diáfana. 361

—Están también los ultrajes y suplicios de muchas vírgenes cristianas, que de ningún modo debes ver. 915

En el tormento de la virgen Engracia leyó con avidez los versos de Prudencio . . . 915

Page 186

. . . todo está lleno de la gracia y hermosura del Creador, y en todos los lugares debiéramos recibir la divina enseñanza del libro de la Creación . . .

No pudo seguir porque en aquel momento se produjo un furioso estruendo entre el averío . . . Parece que todo este odio lo originó el hallazgo de un gusanico muerto . . . 561

No soy piadoso, ¡yo no soy piadoso! 107

Page 188

. . . y su cabeza se fué doblando como una flor pálida de lago. 135

. . . y del confín oriental se remontaba una nube magna, gloriosa, de espuma, como un bando de cisnes de encantamiento! 140

Y Félix le tomó las pálidas manos, y besó sus dedos y sus sortijas, y en una llana amatista puso un beso muy lento que empañó la joya.
— ¡Eres mi prelada, madrina mía! 345

. . . y en todo el aire palpita la claridad del Mediterráneo. Y ese aire de gracia de antiguos horizontes . . . 565

Algunos imaginativos veían en Benidorm un pueblo con pórticos, aras y dioses de mármoles blancos. Sigüenza no veía en Benidorm más que Benidorm, sin mármoles, sin nada clásico. 977

Pages 189–191

Apenas entró Sigüenza, sintióse apocado, encogido, como si fuese a pedir una carta de recomendación para oposiciones.

Aquellos mancebos pulidos, perfumados, ágiles, le miraban demasiadamente. Resplandecía la sala de lujo y primores de tocador de alta señora, y con fría severidad de vitrina de sabio cirujano. Le sentaron en un sillón todo articulado, dócil y enorme, y nuestro caballero cometió algunas torpezas: como manifestar su susto cuando el respaldo pareció que se derribaba atrayéndole a un abismo; tampoco pudo reprimir su complacencia cuando, en seguida, sintióse blanda y sabiamente amparado por las vértebras y los brazos y los costados de ese mueble tan humano.

Le ciñeron el suave collarín de algodones; le vistieron un peinador bata, un cendal como un amito, un babero rozagante, una fazaleja atusada y hermosa. Y él se miró y se dijo: ¡Señor, ¿a qué estaré obligado, envuelto con estas vestiduras tan amplias y cándidas?

Las manos del mancebo, sutiles, aladas, se internaron delicadamente en la frondosidad de su cabellera. Sigüenza comenzó a sentir un sueño infantil, una deliciosa renunciación, un cabal olvido de sí mismo; todo Sigüenza era piel que se encogía y descogía bajo el suavísimo adobo.

Y entornó los párpados y pensó: Durmamos, alma mía. Pero de tiempo en tiempo llegaba a su oído un plácido abejeo. Era que el oficial le consultaba con mucha reverencia, y él, sin entenderle, le respondía débilmente:

— Claro; sí.

Y de nuevo dormitaba, y otra vez el leve zumbidillo le quitaba de su letargo, y él decía:

— Bueno; sí.

Y, por último, murmuró:

— ¡Lo que usted quiera; a mí me es igual!

Y le pasaban jabones y pastas; perdióse bajo una espuma que olía a azahar; le derramaban pomos de fragancia; ardían junto a sus sienes, junto a su cerviz unas lamparitas de llamas azules; le daban revistas, libros, anuncios, guías de la ciudad, cigarritos ya encendidos, y todo se le iba cayendo blandamente de las manos.

De súbito, los dedos del mancebo, el índice y el cordal, se le fijaron en las sienes y en la barba, y haciendo una gentil mesura le dijo:

— ¿Vamos?

— ¿Dónde? — preguntó Sigüenza todo sobresaltado viendo sus mejillas jabonosas.

El mancebo hizo una sonrisa menuda, cortesana y seria.

Ese *vamos* era como un modo de invitación de que ladease, de que volviese la cabeza para seguir rasurando. 563–564

Page 191

Al lado, encuentra Sigüenza una librería religiosa. Y se adormece blandamente, como si oyera el canto de las tórtolas, leyendo los dulces títulos de *Chispitas de amor, Rocío Celestial, Ramillete de lo más agradable a Dios, Virginia o la doncella cristiana, Galería del desengaño.*

268

GABRIEL MIRÓ

Si por acaso hay alguna obra profana, siempre es de mucha inocencia, sin la más leve duda ni inquietud, como *El canario, su origen, razas, cría, cruzamientos y enfermedades*, o el *Manual del Ajedrecista*. 575

Page 192

¡Cuánto charol!, pensaba Sigüenza mirándole los pies con mucha ternura. 541

"Tengo los ojos de un águila, y soy de la provincia de Gerona." 879

. . . Carlos V se corta el pelo en Barcelona. 563

— ¡Oh blancas y fantásticas apariciones que nos traéis la emoción de tierras de misterio! — Pues, Sigüenza, no traen sino salazones; casi siempre de bacalao. — ¡Martínez! Y lo aborreció. 524

— ¡Eres una princesa vestida de cocinera para dar de comer a un pobrecito! 349

Pages 192–193

— ¡Es que es verdad! ¡Daniel! ¡Se llamaba como yo, Dios mío! — y el señor Egea cruzaba valerosamente sus brazos, viéndose rodeado de feroces leones, enflaquecidos de hambre, que se le postraban y le lamían desde las rodilleras hasta sus zapatillas de terciopelo malva, bordadas por doña Corazón Motos, prima del hidalgo, y dueña de un obrador de chocolates y cirios de la calle de la Verónica. 701

Page 193

¡Y esa criatura crasa, glotona, torpe, que lucía galones y no sufría ninguna tentación ni se apuraba en la ascética, era acepta a los ojos del Señor! 392

Y las lumbrecillas socarronas de sus ojos miran a Sigüenza, que se va acomodando en el correo de su tierra. 584

Le temblaban los carrillos y la voz rolliza, como otro carrillo. 819

. . . pechos retrocedidos entre el cañaveral de las ballenas. 863

Pages 193–194

La ironía pensada muy de antemano; la ironía como pragmática de conducta, de arte y de diálogo, es casi una farsa, una chocarrería contrahecha de ingeniosidad. 581

269

Page 197

Lo que pido es el hombre sin Angel de la Guarda a la derecha, ni Demonio a la izquierda. El hombre cara a cara de sí mismo: que le duela el pecado por haberse ofendido a sí mismo; que le resuene toda la naturaleza en su intimidad; atónito y complejo; más hombre que persona. 622

NOTES

Quotations from Berceo are from *Poesías* in Tomás Antonio Sánchez, *Colección de poesías castellanas anteriores al siglo* XV (Eugenio de Ochoa, ed., París: Baudry, 1842), pp. 70–226. Numerical references indicate the stanza. The following abbreviations have been used:

S.O.   *Vida de Santa Oria*
S.M.   *Vida de San Millán*
S.D.   *Vida de Santo Domingo*
M.L.   *Martirio de San Lorenzo*
M.   *Milagros de Nuestra Señora*
D.V.   *Duelo de la Virgen María*
S.   *Los Signos que aparecerán antes del Juicio*
E.S.M. *El sacrificio de la Misa.*

Other editions consulted are:

Vida de Santo Domingo, ed. John D. Fitz-Gerald (Paris: Bouillon, 1904).
El sacrificio de la Misa, ed. A. J. Solalinde (Madrid, 1913).
Milagros de Nuestra Señora, ed. A. J. Solalinde (Madrid: Clásicos castellanos, 1944).
C. Carrol Marden, *Cuatro poemas de Berceo* (Madrid, 1929).
C. Carrol Marden, *Veintitrés milagros* (Madrid: Revista de Filología Española, Anejo X, 1929).
C. Carrol Marden, *Berceo's Martirio de San Lorenzo* (Baltimore, 1930).

Page 4

Américo Castro, *La realidad histórica de España* (México: Porrúa, 1954), pp. 341–342.

Azorín, "Al margen de los clásicos," *Obras completas* (Madrid: Aguilar, 1947), III, 179.

Pages 7–8

Américo Castro, *La realidad histórica*, p. 261.

Page 8

William Hazlitt, *Lectures on the English Poets* (3rd ed., London, 1941), p. 45.

273

Page 9

Ovid, *Metamorphoseon*, XV, 749.

Page 10

Rafael Lapesa, *Diccionario de literatura española* (Madrid: Revista de Occidente, 1949), p. 76.

Pages 11–12

Azorín, "Los primitivos en Madrid," XLV, *Obras completas* (Madrid: Aguilar, 1948), VI, 289–290: "En un tablero de nogal, liso, desnudo, un vaso de buen vino . . . Y una nuez, nada más una nuez, acaso vana y tres chirivías . . . El bodegón es bonito. No lo ha pintado mejor Lucas Menéndez."

Page 13

M. Menéndez y Pelayo, *Antología de poetas líricos castellanos Edición nacional de las Obras Completas* (Santander: Consejo, 1944), I, 168–171.

Page 14

G. Guerrieri-Crocetti, *Gonzalo de Berceo* (Brescia: La Scuola Editrice, 1947), p. 60: "Perciò i suoi santi, le sue vergini, i suoi martiri, le figure sopranaturali del suo mondo si fanno contemporanei ed attuali: vivono come la sua povera gente, parlano il linguaggio del paese e della campagna, sono vicini a lui, perchè diventano uomini del suo tempo e della sua terra."

Page 16

Job, 13:28; 40:10.

Psalms, 40:2,3,4.

Page 17

Erich Auerbach, *Mimesis*, trans. W. Trask (New York: Doubleday, 1957), pp. 131–132.

Quintilianus, *De Institutione Oratoria*, XII.

Auerbach, *Mimesis*, p. 172. See chapter VII.

Page 18

George Lyman Kittredge, *Chaucer and his poetry* (Cambridge, Mass.: Harvard University Press, 1951), p. 47.

GÓNGORA

Gli scritti di San Francesco d'Assisi, ed. P. Vittorino Facchinetti, O.F.M. (Milano, 1921), pp. 193, 197–198.

Page 19

Fray Luis de León, "Salmo CIII," 36, *Obras Completas*, ed. P. Félix García (Madrid, 1951), p. 1663.

Rutebeuf, *Oeuvres Complètes* (Paris: Paul Daffis, 1874), II, 156.

Page 21

Voltaire, *La Pucelle* (Paris: Didot, 1801), p. 2.

Tomás Antonio Sánchez, *Poetas castellanos anteriores al siglo XV* (Madrid: Rivadeneyra, 1864), p. 145.

Page 24

María Rosa Lida de Malkiel, *Juan de Mena — Poeta del prerenacimiento español* (México, D.F.: El Colegio de México, 1959), pp. 251, 291.

Arthur Rimbaud, "Adieu," *Une saison en enfer*, in *Oeuvres Complètes* (Paris: Pléiade, 1946), p. 229.

GÓNGORA

Quotations from Góngora refer to the *Obras Completas*, eds. Juan Millé y Giménez and Isabel Millé y Giménez (4th ed., Madrid: Aguilar, 1956).

Page 29

Dámaso Alonso, *La lengua poética de Góngora* (Madrid: Revista de Filología Española, Anejo XX, 1935), pp. 17–18.

Page 30

Ibid., p. 40.

Page 32

Fernando de Herrera, *Obras de Garci Lasso de la Vega con anotaciones* (Sevilla: Alonso de la Barrera, 1580), pp. 574–575.

Page 33

Andrés Cuesta, *Notas al Polifemo*, MS. 3906 of the Biblioteca Nacional de Madrid, folio 330.

Juan Corominas, *Diccionario crítico etimológico de la lengua castellana* (Madrid: Gredos y Berna, 1956), III, 1069.

Dámaso Alonso, *La lengua poética*, pp. 45–46.

Page 34

Antonio Machado, "Sobre poesía. Fragmentos de lecciones," *Juan de Mairena*, in Manuel y Antonio Machado, *Obras Completas* (Madrid: Plenitud, 1951), p. 1013.

Page 42

García de Salcedo Coronel, *Fábula de Polifemo y Galatea* (Madrid, 1629), folio 103.

Page 43

Joseph Pellicer, *Lecciones solemnes a las obras de Don Luis de Góngora y Argote, Pindaro Andaluz, Príncipe de los Poetas líricos de España*. Escrivíalas Don Joseph Pellicer de Salas y Tovaz, Señor de la Casa de Pellicer, y Chronista de los Reinos de Castilla . . . M.D.C. XXX . . . En Madrid, en la Imprenta del Reino, folios 318–319.

Page 44

Antonio Vilanova, *Las Fuentes y los temas del Polifemo de Góngora* (Madrid: Revista de Filología Española, Anejo LXVI, 1957), p. 789.

Page 45

The Solitudes of Don Luis de Gongora, trans. Edward Meryon Wilson (Cambridge: The Minority Press, 1931), p. 34.

Luis de Góngora, *Las Soledades*, ed. Dámaso Alonso (3rd ed., Madrid: Sociedad de Estudios y Publicaciones, 1956), p. 147.

Page 47

Francisco de Aldana, *Obras Completas*, ed. Manuel Moragon Maestre (Madrid: Consejo, 1953), I, 152.

Page 49

Francisco García Lorca, "Análisis de dos versos de Garcilaso," *Hispanic Review* (April 1956), pp. 87–100.

276

GÓNGORA

Dámaso Alonso, *Estudios y ensayos gongorinos* (Madrid: Gredos, 1955), pp. 336–337.

Page 50

Vilanova, *Las Fuentes*, II, 327.

Page 53

Pellicer and Alfonso Reyes, quoted by J. and I. Millé, p. 1186.

Pellicer, *Lecciones solemnes*, folio 323: "Estaba indecisa la agua (eso es neutral) sobre a cuál había de cielo a Cíclope, si había de juzgar por cielo humano a Polifemo por verle con un sol en la frente o por Cíclope celestial al cielo, por tener un ojo."

Page 56

Dámaso Alonso, *Las Soledades*, p. 183.

Page 57

Wilson, *Solitudes*, p. 72, 31.

Dámaso Alonso, *Las Soledades*, p. 145.

Page 58

Pedro Díaz de Ribas, *Anotaciones al Polifemo*, MS. 3906 of the Biblioteca Nacional de Madrid, folio 136 v.: "Aunque la haya parece árbol inepto para navíos porque con el humor se corrompe y es poroso y lento con todo eso es cosa cierta que de él se hacen navíos porque éstos tienen en los costados dos órdenes de tablas y los que lava el agua son de robre (materia sólida) pero las tablas interiores son de haya y todo el demás aparato del navío como mástiles, aposentos de popa por ser materia ligera que no se agrava el navío y si la mayor de él consta de haya con mucha razón el poeta lo llamó así."

Salcedo Coronel, *Fábula*, folio 110 v.: "Pedro de Ribas le defiende, yo quisiera que todos los que le culpan quedasen satisfechos, pero no parece fácil."

Pellicer, *Lecciones solemnes*, folio 330: "Dos objecciones hace a Don Luis la calumnia. La primera: que en tiempo de Polifemo, los genoveses no manejaban los comercios, como agora. La segunda, que llamó haya a la nave, no fabricándose deste árbol los navíos por ser inhábil para la fabricación. Ambas dudas se absuelven con facilidad."

Page 59

Cuesta, *Notas al Polifemo*, folio 308; Pellicer, *Lecciones solemnes*, folio 65; Salcedo Coronel, *Fábula*, folio 18r. and v.: "La fiera que el poeta describe, según las señas de crueldad, ligereza y variedad de manchas en la piel, es la tigre; animal que no se cría en los montes de Sicilia, ni en toda Italia . . . Por estas razones, parece culpable olvido en D. Luis, pero como quiera que este error es de accidente, y no de ignorancia del arte, facilmente se puede satisfacer, porque los poetas siguen las cosas verosímiles y no se han de condenar cuando siguiesen las inciertas, si en algún modo son verosímiles."

Edward Churton, *Góngora, An Historical and Critical Essay on the Times of Philip III and IV of Spain* (London: John Murray, 1862), II, 200: "No beast in all her wilds Trinacria rear'd . . . / Panther or pard, whose roar the wood-gods fear'd."

Vilanova, *Las Fuentes*, I, 498–499.

Page 60

Pinheiro da Veiga, *La Fastiginia*, trans. Narciso Alonso Cortés (Valladolid, 1916), p. 25: "Y para el bautismo comenzaron a hacer ahora una galería . . . pasadizo para ir del palacio a la iglesia de San Pablo, que está enfrente . . . Y después de provista con la madera que pareció necesaria . . . se cubrió todo de paños de raso y oro riquísimos."

Cuesta, *Notas al Polifemo*, folio 341: "Ni puedo dejar de defender aquí a D. Luis de una calumnia que le pone su comentador Pellicer, que no contentándose con morder todos los escritores, digo traspalar los mordiscos que halla en el tesoro crítico, y con asir la ocasión por donde no tiene pelo, no repara en pellizcar a quien comenta, debiendo todo lo posible defendelle."

Page 61

Salcedo Coronel, *Fábula*, folio 47 v.–48 r.: "así entiendo yo este lugar, aunque Don Gabriel de Corral, cuyo ingenio y erudición honran felizmente a España, me dixo lo entendía de otra manera."

Page 62

Dámaso Alonso, *Las Soledades*, p. 178.

278

GÓNGORA

Page 66

Dámaso Alonso, *Las Soledades* (2nd ed., Madrid: *Cruz y Raya*, 1936), pp. 396, 427.

Page 67

Pedro Salinas, *Reality and the Poet in Spanish Poetry* (Baltimore: The Johns Hopkins Press, 1940), p. 146.

Page 68

Miguel de Cervantes Saavedra, *Journey to Parnassus*, trans. James Y. Gilson (London, 1883), p. 39.

Page 69

Cuesta, *Notas al Polifemo*, folio 314: "D. Luis, de quien se cuenta que se estaba en revisar un verso muchos días, imitando a Virgelio."

Page 70

Wilson, *Solitudes*, p. 46.

Page 71

Stéphane Mallarmé, *Correspondance*, 1862–1871, eds. Henri Mondor and Jean-Pierre Richard (Paris: Gallimard, 1959), p. 245.

Page 72

T. S. Eliot, *On Poetry and Poets* (New York: Farrar, Straus and Cudahy, 1957), p. 22.

Dámaso Alonso, *Poesía Española, Ensayo de métodos y límites estilísticos* (2nd ed., Madrid: Gredos, 1952), p. 388.

Page 73

Wilson, *Solitudes*, p. 41.

Lupercio and Bartolomé L. de Argensola, *Rimas*, ed. José Manuel Blecua (Zaragoza: Institución "Fernando el Católico," 1951), II, 669.

Pages 74–75

T. S. Eliot, *On Poetry and Poets*, p. 24.

NOTES

SAN JUAN DE LA CRUZ
Page 81

Paul Valéry, *Degas Danse Dessin* (4th ed., Paris: Gallimard, 1938), pp. 109–110.

Page 85

Dámaso Alonso, *La poesía de San Juan de la Cruz* (Madrid: Consejo, 1942), pp. 180–182, 188–190, 202–215.

Page 88

San Juan de la Cruz, *Poesías completas,* ed. Pedro Salinas (Santiago de Chile: Cruz del Sur, 1947), pp. 12–13.

Pages 99–100

L'autobiografia e gli scritti della Beata Angela da Foligno, ed. Mons. M. Faloci Pulignani, trans. Maria Castiglioni Humani . . . (Citta di Castello, 1932), pp. x, xii–xiii, xx, 40, 41, 205.

Page 100

Santa Caterina da Siena, *Libro della Divina Dottrina volgarmente detto della Divina Provvidenza,* ed. Matilde Fiorelli (Bari: Laterza, 1912), pp. 411–412.

Jacob Böhme, *Works* (English trans., London, 1764), I, XIV.

William Blake, *Letters,* ed. G. B. Russell (London: Methuen, 1906), pp. 115–116, 171.

Pages 103–104

Jean Baruzi, *Saint Jean de la Croix et le problème de l'expérience mystique* (Paris: Alcan, 1924), p. 335.

Page 110

Benedetto Croce, *La poesia di Dante* (7th ed., Bari: Latera, 1952), pp. 14–15. *Nuovi saggi di Estetica* (Bari, 1926), pp. 331–338: "dove si considera l'allegoria non si considera la poesia, e dove si considera la poesia non si considera l'allegoria."

Page 119

Dante, *Paradiso,* XXXIII, 115–123.

BÉCQUER

Jean Baruzi, "Angelus Silesius," *Création religieuse et pensée contemplative* (Paris: Aubier, 1951), pp. 134, 200.

Salinas, *Reality and the Poet,* pp. 127–128.

Page 121

Baudelaire, *Les Fleurs du Mal,* eds. Jacques Crépet et George Blin (Paris: José Cortí, 1942), p. 216.

BÉCQUER

Page 126

J. P. F. Richter (Jean Paul), *Sämtliche Werke* (Berlin: Reiner, 1860–1862), XIII, 227.

J. P. F. Richter (Jean Paul), *Sämtliche Werke,* ed. Berend (Weimar, (1931), Series II, vol. II, 436.

J. P. F. Richter (Jean Paul), *Campaner Thal and other writings* (U.S. Book Company), p. 373.

Novalis, *The Disciples at Sais and other fragments,* trans. F. V. M. T. and U. C. B. (London, 1903), p. 79.

Novalis, *Schriften,* ed. Kluckhohn (Leipzig, n.d.), III, 117, 291.

Hölderlin, *Werke* (Berlin: Tempel-Klassiker), II, 6.

Robert Wernaer, *Romanticism and the romantic school in Germany* (New York-London: Appleton, 1910), p. 111.

Page 127

Albert Béguin, *L'âme romantique et le rêve* (Marseille: Les Cahiers du Sud, 1937), II, 280–288.

Alfred de Vigny, *La maison du Berger.*

Charles Nodier, "Smarra, Préface nouvelle," *Contes fantastiques* (Paris: Fasquelle, 1904), p. 295.

Charles Nodier, "Le pays des rêves," *Contes de la Veillée* (Paris: Fasquelle), p. 199.

Page 128

Gérard de Nerval, "Aurélia," *Oeuvres,* eds. Albert Béguin and Jean Richter (Paris: Pléiade, 1952), p. 359.

281

NOTES

Coleridge, Samuel T., "On the Characteristics of Shakespeare's Dramas," *Complete Works* (New York: Harper, 1853), IV, 57.

Page 130

José María de Cossío, *Notas y estudios de crítica literaria, Poesía Española, Notas de asedio* (Madrid: Espasa-Calpe, 1936), p. 322.

Page 136

Marcel Proust, A *la recherche du temps perdu* (Paris, Pléiade, 1954), I, 48.

Page 137

Minor, *Friedrich Schlegels Jugend schriften*, II, 187.

Achim von Arnim, *Werke*, ed. Bing (Leipzig, 1908), II, 21.

Novalis, *Schriften*, I, 186.

Page 143

Narciso Campillo, "Biografía de Gustavo Adolfo Bécquer," *La Ilustración de Madrid*, I (1871) 12; also in *Páginas Desconocidas*, I, 13–27.

Page 146

Rafael Alberti, "Mundo y Vigilia de Gustavo Adolfo Bécquer," *El Sol* (Madrid, 1931).

Page 147

Joaquín Casalduero, "Las 'Rimas' de Bécquer," *Cruz y Raya* (Madrid, November 1935), pp. 99–100.

Page 148

Luis Cernuda, "Bécquer y el romanticismo español," *Cruz y Raya* (Madrid, May 1935), p. 47.

Page 149

Dámaso Alonso, *Ensayos sobre poesía española* (2nd ed., Buenos Aires: Revista de Occidente Argentina, 1946), p. 275.

Page 153

Edmund L. King, *Gustavo Adolfo Bécquer — From Painter to Poet* (Mexico: Editorial Roma, 1953), pp. 110, 153.

MIRÓ

Page 154

José Pedro Díaz, G. A. *Bécquer, Vida y Poesía* (Montevideo: La Galatea, 1953), p. 240.

King, *Gustavo Adolfo Bécquer*, p. 120.

Page 167

Flaubert, *La Tentation de Saint Antoine* in *Oeuvres* (Paris: Pléiade, 1946), I, 198: "J'ai envie de voler, de nager, d'aboyer, de beugler, de hurler. Je voudrais avoir des ailes, une carapace, une écorce, souffler de la fumée, porter une trompe, tordre mon corps, me diviser partout, être en tout, m'émaner avec les odeurs, me développer comme les plantes, couler comme l'eau, vibrer comme le son, briller comme la lumière, me blottir sur toutes les formes, pénétrer chaque atome, descendre jusqu'au fond de la matière!"

Page 168

José Somoza, *Una mirada en redondo* (Salamanca, 1843), in Leopoldo Augusto de Cueto, *Poetas líricos del siglo XVIII*, tomo III, B.A.E., LXVII, 554: "El campo ha sido y es mi amigo íntimo, y así no hay una sombra, un soplo de aire, un ruido de hojas o aguas que yo no sepa entender ni apreciar. Pero ¡cosa rara! el campo que no es de mi país, no es comprensible para mí, ni me da casi placer."

Page 169

Pedro Salinas, prologue to Miró, *Obras Completas*, VII, xvi.

Page 170

Joaquín Casalduero, "Gabriel Miró y el cubismo," *La Torre* (Puerto Rico, 1957), p. 80.

Page 171

Miguel de Unamuno, prologue to Miró, *Obras Completas*, II, xiii.

Page 175

Ernest Renan, *Souvenirs d'enfance et de jeunesse*, in *Oeuvres Complètes* (Paris: Calman-Lévy, 1948), II, 713: "Une des légendes les plus répandues en Bretagne est celle d'une prétendue ville d'Is, qui, à une époque inconnue, aurait été engloutie par la mer. On montre, à divers endroits de la côte, l'emplacement de cette cité fabuleuse, et les pêcheurs vous en font d'étranges récits. Les jours de tempête, assurent-ils, on voit, dans le creux des vagues, le sommet des flêches de ses églises; les jours de calme, on entend monter de l'abîme le son de ses cloches, modulant l'hymne du jour. Il me semble souvent que j'ai au fond du coeur une ville d'Is, qui sonne encore des cloches obstinées à convoquer aux offices sacrées des fidèles qui n'entendent plus. Parfois je m'arrête pour prêter l'oreille à ces tremblantes vibrations qui me paraissent venir de profondeurs infinies, comme des voix d'un autre monde. Aux approches de la vieillesse surtout, j'ai pris plaisir, pendant le repos de l'été, à recueillir ces bruits lointains d'une Atlantide disparue."

Page 176

Mariano Baquero Goyanes, *La prosa neomodernista de Gabriel Miró* (Murcia: La Real Sociedad Económica de Amigos del País, 1952), p. 8.

Proust, "Le temps retrouvé," *A la recherche du temps perdu*, III, 866–867.

Page 177

Proust, "Du côté de chez Swann," *A la recherche du temps perdu*, I, 48. "Tout Combray et ses environs, tout cela qui prend forme et solidité, est sorti, ville et jardins, de ma tasse de thé."

Page 178

Casalduero, "Gabriel Miró," p. 85, comments: "Las itálicas son de Miró, quien nos está dando la fluidez del tiempo no en su pasar sino en su presencia."

Page 181

Baquero Goyanes, *La prosa neomodernista*, pp. 11–16.

Page 183

Eliot, *On Poetry and Poets*, p. 124.

Page 186

Gerardo Diego, "Gabriel Miró," *Cuadernos de literatura contemporanea*, 5–6 (Madrid, 1942), 207.

Page 188

Franco Meregalli, *Gabriel Miró* (Varese Milano: Istituto Editoriale Cisalpino), p. 19.

284

ONE GENERATION

Page 197

Meregalli, *Gabriel Miró*, p. 68. "Ed è questo il più sicuro sintomo della grandezza ancora in parte sconosciuta, specie per quanto riguarda l'organica originalità del mondo morale che vi è espresso, dell' opera di Miró."

Alfred W. Becker, *El hombre y su circunstancia en las obras de Gabriel Miró* (Madrid: Revista de Occidente, 1958), pp. 134, 174.

María Alfaro, "Gabriel Miró en su obra y en mi recuerdo," *Cuadernos Americanos* (Mexico, November-December 1953), p. 282.

Page 203

Dámaso Alonso, *Poetas españoles contemporáneos* (Madrid: Gredos, 1952), p. 172.

Page 209

T. S. Eliot, *On Poetry and Poets*, pp. 129–130.

Page 212

Joaquín González Muela, *El lenguaje poetica de la generación Guillén-Lorca* (Madrid: Insula, 1954).

ONE GENERATION

BOOKS MENTIONED IN CHAPTER VI.

Poeta en Nueva York	Federico García Lorca
La voz a ti debida	Pedro Salinas
Cántico	Jorge Guillén
Romancero gitano	Federico García Lorca
Seguro Azar	Pedro Salinas
Cal y Canto	Rafael Alberti
La destrucción o el amor	Vicente Aleixandre
Hijos de la ira	Dámaso Alonso
La realidad y el deseo	Luis Cernuda
Soledades juntas	Manuel Altolaguirre
Jardín cerrado	Emilio Prados

INDEX

INDEX

289

INDEX

Herrera, Fernando de, 30, 32
Hijos de la ira, 213
Hinojosa, José María, 202
Hita, Archpriest of. *See* Ruiz, Juan
Hoffman, E. T. A., on dreams, 127
Hölderlin, Friedrich, quoted, 126
Hopkins, Gerard Manley, 207
House of Fame, The, 5
Huidobro, Vicente, 208
Humo dormido, El, 175, 179, 195
Hugo, Victor, 128

Ilustre y hermosísima Maria, 39
Imagen, 207
In Praise of don Gonzalo de Berceo, 21
Introducción sinfónica, 129, 130, 141
Introduction. *See Introducción sinfónica*

Jardín cerrado, 215
Jean Paul (J. P. F. Richter), quoted, 126
Jiménez, Juan Ramón, 201, 204
Job, Book of, 96–98, 186
Journey to Parnassus, 68

Keats, John, 73
King, Edmund: quoted, 153, 154; translation by, 155
Kittredge, George Lyman, quoted, 18

Lapesa, Rafael, 10
Larrea, Juan, 202, 208
Lascaux, deer of, 6
Leprous Bishop, The. *See Obispo leproso, El*
Lerma, Panegyric to the Duke of. *See Panegírico al Duque de Lerma*
Levante, The, 166–167. *See also* Miró
Libro della Divina Dottrina, volgarmente detto Dialogo della Divina Provvidenza, 100
Lida de Malkiel, María Rosa, on Berceo, 24
Life of Saint Oria, 14
Lis IX Joies Nostre Dame, quoted, 19–20

Literary letters to a Woman. *See Cartas literarias a una mujer*
"Little Seneca." *See* "Senequita"
Living Flame of Love. *See Llama de amor viva*
Llama de amor viva, 80, 87, 95, 102, 103–104, 115; prologue, 92–93
Lope de Vega. *See* Vega, Lope de
Lorca. *See* García Lorca, Federico

Machado, Antonio, 34, 195, 201, 204, 206, 212
Macrí, Oreste, 38
Madrid (1920-1936), 202, 211, 216
Magín, Don, 182, 183
Maids in Waiting, The. *See Meninas, Las*
Mairena, Juan de, 195, 206
Mallarmé, Stéphane, 71, 72, 81, 207
Manrique, 144
Marcilly, Professor, on Góngora, 48, 49–50
María de Jesús, Mother, letter to, 83
Marino, il Cavalier, 44, 50
Martínez Ruiz, Jose. *See* Azorín
Medina, Francisco de, 203
Medinilla, Baltasar Elisio de, 203
Mediodía (review published in Seville), 203
Medrano, Francisco de, 203
Memoriale, 99–100
Menéndez, Lucas, 12
Menéndez y Pelayo, Marcelino, 13
Meninas, Las, 4
Meregalli, Franco, 188; quoted, 197
Meseta (review published in Valladolid), 202–203
Millé y Giménez, Juan and Isabel, on Góngora, 38
Miracles of Our Lady, 20
Miró, Gabriel, 157–197, 201
Miserere, El, 139, 145
Modernismo, 214
Moncayo (mountain), 149, 152
Monte de las ánimas, El, 142

Nerval, Gérard de, quoted, 128

291

INDEX

293